The Negro Question

The Negro Question

*A Selection of Writings on
Civil Rights in the South*
by
George W. Cable

EDITED BY ARLIN TURNER

Doubleday Anchor Books
Doubleday & Company, Inc.
Garden City, New York
1958

TYPOGRAPHY BY EDWARD GOREY

Library of Congress Catalog Card Number 58–7796

A NOTE

Six of the selections in this volume, as indicated where
they occur in the text, are published here for the first
time. They are printed from manuscripts in the Cable
Collection at the Tulane University Library and are included with the permission of the librarian, Dr. Garland
F. Taylor, and of Cable's daughter, Mrs. L. L. C. Biklé.
For the essays which were published in *The Silent South*,
the text follows the revised edition of that work in 1889.
The essays from *The Negro Question* follow the text of
that volume rather than the earlier magazine versions. In
the preparation of the text, from both manuscript and
printed sources, capitalization, spelling, and punctuation
have been regularized, and slips of the pen or typographi-
cal errors have been silently mended.

CONTENTS

Introduction

George W. Cable remarked in 1885, "The greatest social problem before the American people today is, as it has been for
a hundred years, the presence among us of the Negro." This
was the Negro question or the Southern problem, in the
phrases current in the post-Reconstruction years. Not many
thoughtful Americans either North or South would have challenged his assertion; and during the three quarters of a century since that time the question has never stayed long out
of public attention, for instead of a solution it has reached no
more than an uneasy postponement. For ten years after making this remark, Cable lectured and wrote extensively on
Southern issues; he published during those years the fullest,
most consistently developed statement of the case for extending unrestricted civil rights to the Negroes that has appeared
in America.

To take up the cause of Negro rights, Cable had to turn
away, at least half away, from a successful literary career. He
had introduced Creole New Orleans to the pages of fiction, and
as a consequence that picturesque and romantic old city was
considered his particular literary province. By 1885 he had
published the stories which make up the volume *Old Creole
Days*, the two novels *The Grandissimes* and *Dr. Sevier*, the
novelette *Madame Delphine*, and the historical work *The
Creoles of Louisiana*. He was called on both sides of the Atlantic one of the greatest novelists who had yet written in
America, and it was not uncommon for him to be compared
with William Dean Howells, Mark Twain, or Henry James and
to come off with the better of the comparison. His publishers

repeatedly urged him to drive his pen faster, for they considered him one of their most valuable authors for either magazine or book publication. In addition Cable had become a popular reader of his own works on the platform and had found that his manager could sell as much of his time as he could spare for public readings.

It was not Cable's nature, though, to hesitate when he saw a way to work for public improvement. Personal popularity and material success such as were now his could give him untarnished satisfaction only if as a result he was the better prepared, he once wrote his wife, to strive "for the advancement of truth and righteousness." He felt a particular obligation to speak and write on the Southern problem, he said, because he was a Southerner and by descent and his own participation was involved with the institutions and attitudes belonging to the South.

He had been born in New Orleans, October 12, 1844, of parents who owned slaves and apparently felt in no way out of sympathy with the beliefs and activities around them. The father prospered in business for a time, was a staff officer in the state militia, and had a part of some prominence in civic and social affairs. He later suffered reverses and at his death in 1859 left a widow and four children to find their own means of support. Cable, fourteen years old, left high school to begin work. During the Civil War the Cable family showed themselves to be among the staunchest Confederates. After New Orleans had fallen to the Union forces, Cable's mother and two sisters were among the relatively few residents who refused to take the oath of allegiance but instead declared themselves enemies of the United States and were banished into Confederate territory. Cable, not yet of age, accompanied them into Mississippi, where he later enlisted in the Confederate cavalry.

He was twice wounded in battle, and back in New Orleans at the close of the war he was as pleased as anyone else when he heard "The Bonnie Blue Flag" sung on the street or in the theater, or when he learned that Democratic party candidates were elected to office. In the grim, caustic years after Appomattox he witnessed at close hand a social and political order in upheaval. There was bloody rioting in 1866; twice afterward citizens of New Orleans fought federal troops in the streets. According to statements Cable made later in life, it was in this period of turmoil and struggle for survival that he began to think and to revise attitudes which had come to him as a part of his heritage. A humanitarian concern for others had shown itself during his months in the cavalry. So it was at least that his messmates remembered him. One of them recalled after fifty years how Cable, a clerk of nineteen years and a hundred pounds, had joined a seasoned company and soon had won their affection through the habitual cheerfulness with which he encouraged the wounded and the disheartened in the last months of the war. A religious devotion and a sympathy for the debased and dispossessed prompted him in New Orleans after the war to work in his church and its mission school among the poor of the city. His wife had similar inclinations, and they made together an almost formal dedication of themselves to humanitarian causes.

In the years following the war, when the very sills of the Southern social, economic, and political edifice were awash, Cable felt a desperate need for bearings, and in his search he did not hesitate to question inherited attitudes and established institutions. Continuing the self-education he had carried on earlier in studying his books between cavalry raids, he sought in history and the fundamental documents of American government for the guides he needed. It became his habit to reduce any question to ethical considerations, and while others debated technicalities of legality and constitutionality, he searched for the ethical and moral answers. It would be foolish, he thought, to suppose that laws and constitutions could not be adjusted as needed. He came to see all history as a continuum, and as he studied local history he observed the early growth of traditions and beliefs still prevalent in the South. Convinced as he was by the early 1870s that slavery had been a great moral wrong and sharply aware that the effects of slavery reached down to his own time, he took the attitude of one sincerely contrite for the errors of the society to which he belonged and eager to make whatever amends might be possible. At the least, he believed, the Freedman should have in full measure the rights guaranteed to American citizens in the Constitution and its amendments. Any other attitude would not have seemed to him Christian.

His was the type of mind, as it began to develop, which demanded consistency and logic. He had no patience with mere expediency, and though he insisted that any policy or procedure must be practical, he insisted with equal firmness that no course of action could be practical unless it was founded in morality and justice.

Cable proceeded cautiously, and several years elapsed before he was ready to open a campaign for extending full civil rights to the Freedmen, though his fiction made amply clear what his attitudes were. Believing in "the sovereignty of matured thought," as he phrased it in 1882, he was confident that whenever he chose to make the attempt he could win others to his position. He was by no means inexperienced in public reform. In writing a column in the New Orleans *Picayune* in 1870 and 1871, he had touched on several of the local matters most inviting to a reformer. His touch was light and casual, but it became clear that he would have more to say later. Immediately afterward, when he was asked to write in the newspaper with all the virulence he could command attacking the Louisiana Lottery Company, he produced two editorials which reflected solid conviction and also an effective polemic manner. Though the Lottery Company was so firmly entrenched both financially and politically as to remain invulnerable until it was destroyed in 1892 by federal enactment, and though the *Picayune* came under the sway of the Lottery Company as a result of the editorial attack, Cable learned from the experience.

Two newspaper letters written in 1875, one published and

the other rejected by two editors, tore from him prematurely, as it were, a statement condemning segregation in the schools before he was ready to take a positive stand before the public. When he wrote these letters, Cable may have remembered the concessions white Democrats in New Orleans had been willing to make two years earlier in an attempt to win the support of Negroes in the next election. A committee of fifty prominent whites and fifty Negroes had drawn up an agreement which pledged that the coalition party thus to be formed would oppose all race prejudice and violence and would recognize equal rights of the races in schools and all other public institutions, in resorts and travel, in business and employment, and in the holding of public office. The agreement was approved in an open meeting and was endorsed by the Catholic archbishop and the *Picayune*, the organ of the conservative Democrats. Though the consolidation of the whites and the Negroes was not actually effected, perhaps mainly because of poor management, Cable might have seen the episode as evidence that under proper leadership the white Democrats would be willing to end segregation and guarantee full public rights to the Freedman.

After writing the newspaper letters in 1875, Cable left the subject alone for almost ten years and gave his attention to such uncontroversial matters as the humanitarian programs of his church. Following a term of grand jury duty in 1881, he set out to organize citizen groups to compel reform in local prisons and asylums. The chief of the city newspapers, the *Times-Democrat*, made his program its own cause, and the success of the effort surpassed anything that could have been expected. The membership in his organization read like a roster of the leading business and professional men of the city; ordinances which he and his associates drafted were adopted by the city; and the legislature provided facilities in state institutions to relieve the demands on the city. In various ways the program was satisfying. For one thing, it aligned Cable with the most substantial elements in his community in a campaign which had almost universal endorsement.

Cable's next step brought him from the local to the national scene as a reformer. In preparing his argument for prison reform in New Orleans, he had studied reports of prisons in other states and other countries as well, and in the reports from the Southern state penitentiaries he had encountered the convict lease system, which carried with it horrors of a degree to dwarf the abuses he had found in the local jails. Here was a topic inviting him still more urgently to speak out, as he did in 1883. His earlier efforts had taught him that he had a real talent for swaying others to his views. Early in their acquaintance Mark Twain wrote of him: "He is a marvelous talker on a deep subject. I do not see how even [Herbert] Spencer could unwind a thought more smoothly or orderly, and do it in a cleaner, clearer, crisper English."

One step led to another, Cable said. In the New Orleans jails he had found that a man of means could have room and bedding and food far different from what indigent prisoners were furnished, but the inequality had been a matter of individuals. In the state penitentiaries, however, he discovered far greater inequalities which were more reprehensible, he thought, because they represented mass discrimination on the basis of class or caste. The information convinced him that the discrimination which admittedly existed in schools, libraries, and other public institutions was carrying over into the administration of justice. At first he had intended to introduce this matter in dealing with the convict lease system, but he had decided to omit it, feeling that it would obscure his main argument. And besides, he was not ready to challenge public sentiment in the South by broaching the topic. He could not stay silent long, however, and soon he presented his case, "The Freedman's Case in Equity," in a lecture and an essay.

After this essay had been published, other steps came more rapidly and under greater compulsion. It elicited replies which demanded extended argument; new angles brought into the

discussion required elaboration. Cable believed that much had
been accomplished simply by opening the subject for discussion, and he welcomed opinions of all varieties.

Believing that peace and prosperity depended on a solution
of the race question, and convinced that only a solution based
on right and justice could be tolerated, Cable used every
means at his disposal to further this cause: He lectured, wrote
for newspapers and magazines, and published two volumes of
essays, *The Silent South* (1885) and *The Negro Question*
(1890). He distributed his and other essays to hundreds of
readers; he traveled extensively in the South, and he corre-
sponded widely to collect information and to sample the attitudes on current issues and happenings. At one time he
brought together into a loose organization, the Open Letter
Club, something over two dozen prominent men whose purpose was to write on current Southern problems, exchange
their papers for suggestions and revisions, and then publish
the results.

Scholarly by nature and habit and most comfortable even
in writing fiction when he was buttressed by authenticated
facts, he collected information on multiple aspects of Southern
affairs, with the result that he could discuss current matters
from a fund of substantial knowledge which few if indeed any
others of his time possessed. From Booker T. Washington he
learned about the crop liens and the movements of Negroes
within the South. He studied the state constitutions adopted
at the close of the Civil War, those adopted under carpetbagger dominance, and those adopted when the Democrats
regained control. Similarly he made comparative studies of
penitentiary reports, publications of the state superintendents
of education, and statistics on taxation, revenues, and appropriations. He could speak with assurance on illiteracy, school
attendance, school property evaluations, crime rates, court
sentences, crop statistics, and industrial developments.

Scarcely any angle of the total problem escaped Cable's attention: the right to vote, to hold office, and to serve on juries;

justice in the courts and intimidation by public officials and
mobs; segregation or exclusion in transportation, schools, libraries, and churches; civil equality and social equality, race
instinct, race prejudice, miscegenation; federal aid to schools
and federal intervention to protect constitutional rights; African colonization, migration within the Southern states and to
states outside the South, the attractiveness of the South to immigrants and investment capital, the convict lease system, the
crop lien laws.

Several themes echo from one to another of the dozen major
addresses and like number of essays on the Southern question
which Cable produced in what was almost literally an individual crusade: "The safety of society lies in the elevation of the
masses." "The Negro must be educated as the South is reconstructed." ". . . if they could realize what millions of solid
public wealth it is costing to suppress the self-regard and aspirations of one third of their whole population." There is no
such thing as social equality; private social affairs will remain
within the choice of individuals. "The public school relation
is not a private social relation." "I have never yet spoken first
in this matter, save under the conviction that silence was treason to the South. It is treason." The best minds must study
the problem; there must be free, open discussion without any
kind of real or implied threat. Restrictions aimed at the Negro
fall only slightly less heavily on the poor white, especially in
public education. The Negro must never himself draw the
color line. All questions must be referred to the will of the
majority, not of any minority. No two races have ever amal-
gamated except when one was the oppressor.

From the beginning Cable had hoped to argue the Freedman's case before a wide audience and to win a following that
would influence policy and practice in the South. But his hope
was partially denied at once by newspaper opposition. Southern editors cried out that he advocated social equality—in the
face of his statements to the contrary—and that to countenance
his views would be to invite disaster. On February 2, 1885,

a month after "The Freedman's Case in Equity" had appeared, the New Orleans *Times-Democrat* quoted from nine newspapers attacking Cable; later it asserted that not a single Southern newspaper had defended Cable's position. The editorial attacks were often sarcastic; they often sounded a note of ironic condescension. Much of this comment was irresponsible, Cable knew, but he knew also that it of course closed the minds of many readers against his appeal. Within a few weeks it became clear that the public opinion which had a voice in the newspapers and in the political arena was uniform in the aim to discredit Cable and disparage his ideas. He never believed for a minute, however, that this voice spoke for the mass of Southern people, and he felt sure that he was himself speaking for the Silent South. If he had not believed firmly in the Silent South, he could not have thought it worth while to continue the debate another ten years.

In his earlier efforts to lead the public in reform Cable had received the warm support of the prominent citizens of his community. His first essay on the Freedman, in contrast, left him standing at once virtually alone and the object of attacks against which there was no effective defense. Many who agreed with him he knew could not afford to speak out for fear of antagonizing employers or patrons or others on whom they were in some way dependent. Spokesmen for progress in the South, such as Henry W. Grady, Joel Chandler Harris, and Henry Watterson, gave him support only part way. They asked that the Freedman be given better treatment; and they might accept specific goals which Cable set if they could be sure that no change would be hurried; but they would make no compromise on the doctrine of race supremacy and as a consequence they would leave the Negro, Cable thought, only the shell of the freedom supposedly brought by emancipation and confirmed in subsequent constitutional amendments.

During more than fifty years of Cable's active life there was no time when he did not have a leader's role in some program for public betterment. Self-criticism, strict self-discipline, and modest self-assessment were natural to him, and a genuine pride in his community or his city or his section could not be separated in his mind from an obligation to expose and eliminate flaws in the society about him. When he took up the cause of Negro rights in 1885, he did so, he said, because the need was greater than any other at the time. To the campaign he brought the habits of thoroughness and the unsparing dedication which he had already displayed; and with an equanimity not possible to most men under such abuse and vilification as was poured upon him, he proceeded to marshal the facts and to present the arguments which he thought would bring acceptance of the views he had reached. With a calm logic and a tolerance of opposing opinions and an absolute refusal to answer personal attacks in kind, he debated the issues, firm in the conviction that with enough light would come understanding, and with understanding would come in turn a just solution. Above all, he thought, the Southern problem must remain open to untrammeled discussion; progress toward a solution would stop if the time should come when men did not feel free to state unpopular views and defend them.

Cable's determination and hopefulness were sufficient to keep him active in the Southern debate until the cause of Negro rights was as a practical matter lost. By 1890 state laws were being enacted which would restrict the Freedman's civil rights and channel his public activities. Fewer Negroes were voting each year, and there seemed little hope that the trend would be reversed. The Open Letter Club had failed because its members had come to realize that in effect the problems most needing solution could no longer be discussed freely. Furthermore, those living outside the South were inclined now to say that progress had been as rapid as could be expected and that the matter should be left to the Southern states. Within the South and outside as well, those from whom Cable might expect support were now prepared to believe that time would bring a solution to the Southern problem. He was no less certain than he had been all along that expediency and gradualism were false hopes. Whether he had held to his position because he believed those hopes to be false or because he chose to crusade for human rights, his arguments have a prophetic quality which has been authenticated in the years since he stated them.

Cable was reluctant to withdraw from the debate. He completed and published in 1892 two essays he had been writing on education, and in 1894 he published a novel, *John March, Southerner,* in which he marshaled for close study the main problems confronting the South. Then he abandoned the Southern controversy and directed his efforts for reform into non-controversial channels at Northampton, Massachusetts, where he had settled in 1885 and where during the next third of a century he won gratifying public approval for his success in organizing and leading reform programs. He was not bitter over his apparent failure with the Southern problem. He visited the South almost every year and the books he published continued to deal with the South, but he handled the controversial topics only with the lightest touch. He remained confident that in time the Negro would have full public rights and that the related problems would find a solution. He could be confident also that in his long campaign for right and justice in the treatment of the Freedman he had contributed to the final solution.

The Negro Question

My Politics

[On December 22, 1888, Cable was on his way home after lecturing at Cleveland the day before on "Moral Elements in Politics" and at Chicago a week earlier on the subject "Can the Nation Afford a Suppressed Vote?" Seated in his railway car, he wrote in a pocket notebook the first pages of an essay which he called from the outset "My Politics."

He had been embroiled in the Southern controversy almost four years. When he began arguing the Freedman's case, he had expected to meet emotional opposition from many quarters in the South, but he had not anticipated the personal abuse which had been poured into the columns of Southern newspapers. His opinions and his proposals had not received a fair hearing, he believed, because of the charges made over and over that he had answered to Puritan blood in his veins and turned traitor to his section for gain which came in money paid for his books. (The Puritan reference was to his mother, who had been born in Indiana of New England stock. His father had been born in Virginia, where his ancestors had settled before the Revolution.) More than one newspaper editor had advanced such assertions and let them stand as argument sufficient to discredit his views.

It was both to answer personal attacks and to win acceptance for his ideas, therefore, that Cable wanted to make it clear that he was a native of a Southern city and that his attitudes and beliefs had evolved in the South without any external or nefarious promptings. Friends and relatives encouraged him to believe that if the facts were known, his motives would no longer be questioned and his writings would convince more readers. He believed further that a calm discussion such as he hoped to stimulate would produce an answer to "the great sore question." Thus it was that he decided to write a sort of apologia which might be published first in a magazine and then as an introduction to a new edition of his collection of essays, *The Silent South*. While on the road again in January 1889, he completed the draft in his notebook, and in February a revised version went to his editors in New York. Three of them, friends of his a dozen years or longer, agreed that it was too personal to be printed at the time but should be laid away for posthumous publication. The new edition of *The Silent South* in 1889 was introduced by only a short note.

The manuscript of this essay is in the Tulane University Library. Excerpts from it appear in L. L. C. Biklé, *George W. Cable: His Life and Letters*, New York, 1928.]

My Politics

When Abraham Lincoln was elected President of the United States I was just sixteen years old, as ignorant of the world as most boys of thirteen, and reeking with patriotism of the strongest pro-slavery type.

I took great interest in the things we find in books, and absolutely none in newspapers. Principles, especially principles of life, of conduct public and private, were everything to me; mere news was nothing. History, however, was a delight. At ten I had read Hume's *England*, but at nine I was memorizing the Declaration of Independence under a mother's promise of an American flag for reward. I never quite memorized its assertions of the mere facts of British oppression, but I never forgot its great principles, least of all the inherent equality of all men in civil and political rights, rights to which all men are born and which are not something earned by, and only by, bloody wars.

Even then I remember I was puzzled to know how men could declare such ideal truths and yet hold other men in slavery. I was slow to learn what boundless ability men and communities everywhere have for deceiving themselves, and for blowing hot for themselves and cold for others. Nations at birth are supremely heroic, and, lifting their best voices, set up ideals to which afterward they have not the heroism to live up, but only at best to legislate toward and approach by gradual steps with often painful and costly delays. But I did not recognize these simple facts when I was winning my flag, and had no one to tell me why there was such a sad step backward and downward between the Declaration and the Constitution.

At sixteen I was for Union, Slavery, and a White Man's Government! Secession, when it came, seemed a dreadful thing and I wondered at men and women, even if it was a necessity, rejoicing in it. Yet I had not really begun to think for myself and I soon learned to hurrah with a devout fervor for Jeff. Davis and the "Stars and Bars." They seemed to me to stand for the right "to dissolve the political bonds which connected us with another, and to assume among the powers of the earth a separate and equal station, to which the laws of nature and nature's God entitled us"! And I could sing the right of secession, too, "and nail't wi' scripture." All the easier for that by and by I was under Butler's rule in New Orleans. I wonder to this day which of the two, Jeff. Davis or Ben Butler, tried hardest to make the United States Government hateful to the people of that city.

My sisters, two harmless girls of twenty-two and twenty, registered as "enemies of the United States," intimidated by vague threats of imprisonment against all who did not either do this or swear allegiance to the national government. For this they were banished into the starving Confederacy, almost absolutely penniless. I looked so incapable of military duty that I was allowed to accompany them, but a few months later I joined the Confederate cavalry, a division left to protect the railroads in Mississippi after the fall of Vicksburg. In Feb-

ruary 1864, I was wounded in a skirmish. I had hardly recovered from my wound when my horse was stolen and I was
permanently dismounted; for the Confederate cavalryman had
to supply his own mount. I applied to be transferred to in-
fantry and meantime became attached as a clerk—clerks were
scarce and much in demand—to the field staff of Major General
Wirt Adams; afterward for a short time to the field staff of
Lieut. General Forrest.

This connection with headquarters under the slack discipline of that part of the Confederate Army brought me much
into contact with men of choice intelligence. Always fond of
debate, I now began, at last, at nineteen, nearly twenty, to
have thoughts and convictions of my own. The tragic times
had even given me a greed for news and I often saw Northern
as well as Southern newspapers. One of the first things I
learned without being taught was the proneness of public sentiment to be wrong as to the facts, or the principles, involved
in any case.

One morning when we had had a very slight brush with the
enemy and were marching again a group of us, messmates,
fell to chatting over a bit of headquarters gossip. The rumor
was that Toombs and others, of Georgia, were threatening
their state's secession from the Confederacy. My silence was
remarked and I was "bantered"—as the Mississippians say—
to speak.

"This shows me," I replied, "that we are fighting to establish
a scheme of government that will work our destruction as sure
as we succeed. We shall go to pieces as soon as we are safe
from outside enemies."

"Then why do you fight for it?"

"Because I am a citizen of this government, a soldier by its
laws, sworn into service and ordered, not to think, but to fight."

But if I saw the unwisdom of secession, I saw no unright-
eousness in fighting for slavery. Scarce a month before, in
charge of some Negro non-combatant prisoners taken on a
dash of one of our brigades into the enemy's lines, two of those

prisoners having escaped, I had taken part in their recapture with a zest that I now confess only for the sake of candor. At twenty I was still, in far too many things, a very child for thoughtlessness.

One thing I knew; that there were plenty of men over on the other side who loved the Negro as little as our brutal wagon master did. That same morning, I had seen a poor black camp-cook shot at by an Indiana bluecoat in the most shameless wantonry.

When the war ended I came back to New Orleans a paroled prisoner, without one spark of loyalty to the United States Government.

I remember my second dissent from popular opinion quite as clearly as my first. Study was always my natural impulse; I carried books with me in the saddle and studied in camp. But when the war ended I had begun to add *thought* to the study of books. Pretty soon the newspapers all over the South began to pipe a strange, new tune. They began to say diligently that the question of the right of secession had been forever negatived by the arbitrament of the sword, and that to this the Southern people—Negroes were not counted as people—yielded gracefully and once for all. I revolted.

I said to myself, The *power* to secede or prevent secession is all that the "arbitrament of the sword" can decide. The sword can never make right wrong or wrong right. I went too far; for I suspected that whole press of conscious insincerity. I had not learned yet that the great mass of mankind unconsciously adjust their convictions to the ends they have in view; often to the most shortsighted notions of self-interest or the moment's emergency. I believe that in my politics I have always considered insincerity as detestable as it really is; but I have also learned that the mere *feeling* sincere is but an easy virtue; true sincerity is a condition, not a mere feeling.

However: if men, sincerely or insincerely, could so lightly part with a conviction of right and rights, I asked myself, "Was there ever a *right* of secession at all?" I believed there was.

But I borrowed "Story on the Constitution" and began to study the question; not blindly, not even docilely, but weighing every sentence, every word, every implication; for I had fought for this "right" when I did not believe in the wisdom of its exercise, and was angered now to see it renounced as a principle.

I rose at last from this study indignant against the propagators of that doctrine. I knew it had been believed by thousands of good men, but it seemed, and still seems, to me a perfidious doctrine. How, I queried, could good men—not boys, as I was—ever accept so shallow a piece of pettifogging literalism? What use or need had there been to set up such a doctrine and waste three hundred thousand young men's lives in its defense? There could be but one answer; it was to protect slaveholding. Did that shock me? Not at all. Secession was rebellion and revolution; but rebellion and revolution might be right, if only slaveholding was right. *Was* it right? I turned to look into that.

I had never seen a book or tract opposed to slavery except that when barely nine years old I had read *Uncle Tom's Cabin* but had preserved no impressions from it except a tearful longing to marry any girl who resembled Eva and would promise not to die. I had never known an abolitionist, save one man, a German, whose belief was kept carefully under a bushel and who never, to me, used any arguments except the unfairness of his having to compete with the slave in the labor market.

Books being beyond reach—even pro-slavery books being scarce—I could only ponder the matter. But this I did with great diligence and growing uneasiness. Slaveholding did not *seem* right. What held me fast, though, was the "Divine right" of which I had heard so much. One day there fell into my hands a Scotch magazine. Glancing at random, I noticed three or four pages on the epistle to Philemon. I had heard many a sermon on the case of Onesimus, but all from one point of view; here was a word from the other side. I took the scriptures and the little sermon and studied epistle, sermon and my own earlier convictions carefully side by side. The Onesimus argument for slavery went to pieces, and my ponderings had so ripened my convictions against slaveholding that when that bit of sophistry gave way I found that my belief had been hanging only by that last thread.

Not that the letter to Philemon was all the scripture I had heard used to justify slave keeping, but that now I could have no further confidence in like arguments from other parts of scripture. They all yielded to scrutiny, and betrayed a literalism combined, strangely enough, with a violence of inference that made them worthless.

So much for theory. But in the practical daily experiences of life I saw the Freedman in all his offensiveness; multitudinous, unclean, stupid, ugly, ignorant, and insolent. Maybe it was not so bad as it looked to me; I am telling how it looked. If the much feared "war of races" should come—no matter how—I was going to be in the ranks of the white race fighting for the subjugation of the blacks.

And yet I began to see that these poor fellow creatures were being treated unfairly. Military protection saved them from serious oppression in New Orleans; but the pro-Southern papers—I saw no others those days—gave much unconscious evidence to a state of feeling, and of affairs, in the tributary country of Louisiana and Mississippi, that profoundly offended my notions of fair play and human rights. To pass over graver instances, there began to be much talk about "our black peasantry." My gorge rose against that. I had joined a debating society which later furnished some valuable men to New Orleans—Parker, Hester, William Houston, Walker, Whitney, and others—and among these companions I spoke with abhorrence against this un-American, un-Democratic, and tawdry delusion. I made it my private maxim, "There is no room in America for a peasantry."

Did I become a Republican? Nay, I had not yet so much as taken the "oath of allegiance." I could not! Before I had quite digested the Thirteenth Amendment, here came the

8   THE NEGRO QUESTION

Fourteenth! If both had come at once I could have mastered both with the one same contortion of throat and stomach. But Andrew Johnson—in my present view one of the worst enemies the South ever had—had spoiled me, and I was having privately a great deal of mental distress. Mr. C. Harrison Parker, now editor of the New Orleans *Picayune*, Mr. Henry G. Hester, now Superintendent and Secretary of the New Orleans Cotton Exchange, and I were meeting together every evening in an upper story of the *Price Current* to read Bancroft's *United States* and unconsciously—in my case, at least—absorbing much good political ethics; and I was fast growing heartily ashamed of my political attitude. I was accepting the protection and benefits of a government to which I gave no hearty allegiance; and yet I privately repudiated the politics of my "own people." Their boasted policy of "masterly inactivity" meant, in plain English, to withhold the co-operation of society's best wealth, intelligence, and power from all attempts to re-establish order and safety on the basis of the amended Constitution, and leave this colossal task to the Freedman with none to aid his clumsy hand save here and there a white man heroic enough or shameless enough to laugh at a complete and ferocious ostracism. Thus the policies of emancipation and enfranchisement were to be brought into melancholy ridicule before the nation, and the rule of the Southern states handed back in despair to "white men governments" holding the blacks in arbitrary political subjugation. I could not see in this openly avowed policy anything less than a new phase of revolutionary disloyalty. And yet *I* showed an inactivity in which there was not one ray of masterliness.

This is not a sketch of my life, and I have not encumbered the pages with any account of my work for livelihood. During the most of these years I was a counting-room clerk. But now I had got employment as reporter for the ancient and honorable *Picayune*. The Superintendent of Public Schools under the Republican regime called a "Teachers' Institute." I was sent to report its proceedings and was the first to notice and

publish in resentful terms the fact that this official had required compulsory attendance of all teachers of those schools
and had thus compelled whites and blacks to sit together under one roof, in one room, on terms of equality. The equality,
it is true, was public, not private, but I saw no difference then
and Southerners recognized none save in the horsecars, when
General Beauregard as a railway president had forced it upon
them. The other papers joined the hue and cry and I—suddenly weakened, slackened, ceased.

I did not see that I was wrong. I only saw that there were
two sides to the question and much doubted which side was
least right. Naturally the proprietor of the *Picayune* was
greatly vexed at me for losing the lead in this exhilarating
chase. I was living from hand to mouth those days. My household consisted óf a widowed mother, a young wife entirely
without fortune but unused to a poor man's life, and our infant
daughter. I did not feel like losing my place, but I submit
the fact to the thousands who have since then accused me of
pitching my public utterances to suit the popular ear that I
neglected to do it then. I did not lose the place at that time,
nor at last for political reasons; but then and there I permanently lost grace with my employer.

Shortly after this I was ordered to report day by day an
annual examination of the city's public schools. In pursuance
of this duty I saw, to my great and rapid edification, white
ladies teaching Negro boys; colored women showing the
graces and dignity of mental and moral refinement, ladies in
everything save society's credentials; children and youth of
both races standing in the same classes and giving each other
peaceable, friendly, effective competition; and black classes,
with black teachers, pushing intelligently up into the intricacies of high-school mathematics. But I saw through and beyond these things. I saw that while private society always must
and can take care of itself and its own complete defense, the
day must come when the Negro must share and enjoy in
common with the white race the whole scale of *public* rights

and advantages provided under American government; that
public society must be reconstructed on this basis; that the
Negro must come under this process, must decline and disappear where he proves himself incapable, in a condition of
American freedom, of rising to it; that numerously he has the
ambitions and capacity to rise; that the political party that
seeks to prevent this revolution or even artificially to retard it
was the South's worst enemy; and that reconstruction on this
basis was the only way to come once more into harmony with
those great first principles of government on which the nation
has been founded and from which slaveholding and the doctrines it set up in its own defense had dragged us. I saw more
plainly than ever before that the so-called Democratic party
of the South was really bent upon preserving the old order—
minus slavery only—the old rule by race and class and was
hopelessly at variance with the national scheme; and that over
against this "radical" platform—rightly enough called radical
since it alone went to the root of the difficulty—was not for
black rule and white subjugation, but against the rule of any
race over any other, simply and arbitrarily race by race, or
even class by class.

I reached these conclusions without being discipled by any
one. In that week's reporting tour I was daily with Republicans as well as Democrats. But I represented a Democratic
newspaper; they represented, to me, the party of thievery and
"social equality," and personally were covered with the mud
of partisan abuse. How much had been only thrown upon
them, and how much they had themselves wallowed in, I had
no convenient way of knowing. To the best of my recollection
no word of political discussion passed between us.

By and by I lost my place. I was naturally and emphatically
unfit for the work of gathering up and throwing down hetero-
geneous armloads of daily news. I had neither the faculty for
getting mere news, nor the relish for blurting out news for
news' sake after it was got. Had I possessed these equipments
in any excellent degree, I need never have lost my place be-

cause—as has been printed of me—I would not violate my conscientious scruples, or, more strictly, the tenets of my church,
by going to a theater to report a play. The fact is I had no
strong reportorial value in me to offset this sometimes vexa-
tious scrupulosity.

Those were the fiercest days of Reconstruction. The city
newspapers were intensely partisan. I credited nothing they
said, on either side, against their opponents, but only what
they let slip against themselves and their own side. I learned,
then, in debate with relatives and nearest friends, the power
of arguing entirely from such admissions; it is getting the
enemy to furnish the ammunition.

I had to return to counting-room work. But I soon conceived
a sincere affection for my two employers, if not for my work.
The senior was a man of great public value, a proverb for
integrity, deliberate, sagacious, willing to serve, and a true
lover of the people—according to his idea of what and who
the people were. He held many important and unremunerated
public trusts. The best, wisest, and most powerful merchants,
financiers, and lawyers were daily visitors at the desk where
he sat "not caring," he said, "to get any richer"; which was
true, although he was not modernly rich. These visitors came
often on important public errands, and were—virtually all of
them—"Democrats." I was as much his private secretary as I
was the firm's cashier and so daily heard, in favor of pro-
Southern principles and policies, the best that could be said
by the best men who could say it. Nothing was kept from me
save what "the machine" kept from them.

Many a debate I had with him when work was slack and
no visitor near. Often at such times this noble gentleman, the
soul of kindness, cool in council, clear in thought and speech,
pure in heart, and narrow only in his traditions, would fairly
lose command of himself to find himself checkmated in three
moves; for often we agreed, and when we did not I loved and
revered him too much to offer to wrangle with him, but approached him in debate only when he had got himself into a

cul-de-sac, and then quietly shut him in with three modest questions: 1. Tit?—He replied kindly: 2. Tat?—He answered calmly: 3. Toe?—I had him! It was like catching a whale.

"I'll have you understand this is a Democratic counting room, sir!"

I always took up my hat in silence and walked downstairs and out into the street, loving him still, but burning with indignation, and taking all too much comfort in the knowledge that my dear friend was suffering more than I.

"Democrat!" Wasn't I a Democrat? No. In Connecticut or New Jersey I could have passed muster, but not in Louisiana. What, then, was I; a Republican—a Radical—a Scallawag? I shuddered. As far as I knew I had not a friend on earth in the Republican party. I sought none. Yet I lacked not friends. There was scarcely a dozen prominent merchants and financiers in New Orleans with whom I was not at least cordially acquainted.

The *Picayune* changed hands but became more a "Democratic" organ than ever. I was invited to write some historical sketches for it of the principal churches and charities of the city. For while in commerce I was only a cashier and secretary, to the newspapers I was still "our talented fellow townsman whose facile pen," etc., notwithstanding I charged for whatever I wrote.

My counting-room work was not so engrossing but I could accept this invitation, and the better to qualify I began to study the colonial history of Louisiana. I became deeply interested; wrote the sketches, and still studied on. I was moved at last to write some short stories of old New Orleans. But I did not at that time seek a publisher; I laid them aside. In my reading I came to the old Black Code. In sheer indignation I wrote a story which years afterward became the foundation for the episode of Bras Coupé in my novel, *The Grandissimes*. In summer hours, when the counting room was idle, I went to the city archives and read hundreds of old newspapers. Here I got my inspiration for " 'Tite Poulette," written in sympathy for the fate of the quadroon caste. And here, too, I conceived the entirely unpolitical story of "Posson Jone'." All this time months—years—were passing. I met Edward King, visiting Louisiana and writing the "Great South" papers, and he encouraged me to offer my stories to *Scribner's Monthly,* now the *Century Magazine.* Some of them were accepted. But I did not press my success; I neglected it. I was preoccupied in the counting room, wrote little, and offered nothing to Northern publishers that bore any distinct political character or even tincture. In 'Tite Poulette I portrayed a white girl *falsely* supposed to be of Negro extraction, suffering the semi-outlawry to which quadroons and octoroons were condemned by society and the laws in Louisiana during the early years of the present century. But the situation was chosen for its romantic value, a value always recognized in that condition, throughout the South as well as elsewhere; and the story received unstinted praise from the whole New Orleans press, except *L'Abeille,* the organ of the Creoles. The two or three short stories with which I leisurely followed up my success had not a shade of political quality. I state these small matters preliminary to showing the why, when, and how of my distinctly political writing.

Time wore on. A fracas occurred in the Central Boys' High School. A graduate of the École Polytechnique, Paris, had been made teacher of mathematics. There was but one objection urged against him; he was a mulatto. The boys mutinied, the public and the newspapers applauded, and the appointment was withdrawn. Soon after came the first attempt—it failed—to capture the "Radical" state government by force, and the high-school boys, badly spoiled, proceeded to evict the colored girls from the female grammar and high schools. Applause again. A mass meeting was held in Lafayette Square to denounce the contact of the two races in school relations. The New Orleans *Bulletin* strongly supported the movement.

I wrote to that paper, taking open ground against the popular action and sentiment. My communication was signed "A

Southern White Man," but I gave my own name, of course, to the editor. Indeed I handed it to him in person; he was an old acquaintance. It was printed, prefaced by an editorial repudiation as long as itself. In my letter I maintained that there is sufficient antagonism between races to keep them, in the main, pure, without the aid of onerous civil distinctions. In his prefatory condemnation the editor maintained that "Between whites and Africans there is now and has always been an antipathy of instincts. These instincts appear under all conditions, and no familiarity or social blending, or unnatural hybridity, can conquer the inborn, centrifugal, and mutually repellent propensity which causes the two races to shun each other." I came back to him with a brief written reply, in which I made the point that if such a statement as that was offered as a reason for a compulsory legal separation of the two races in school, it was an argument which boldly and openly cut its own throat. He declined to print it. I took it to the *Picayune;* it was declined again. I put it into my desk, and there it has lain for over thirteen years.

I value this mention because in this my first public political utterance, made in my native New Orleans, where dwelt ninety-nine hundredths of all my friends and acquaintances; opposed point-blank to their sentiments and to the sentiments of almost the whole white population; with the whole people in a frenzy of political agitation and on the verge of an armed and bloody revolution; I took the farthest ground I have ever found occasion to take in any treatment of the Southern question. And again I value this mention because it includes the fact that I did not turn and seek a hearing in any Republican publication. I had won my place in the literary world without "catering to Northern prejudices," and I had never then, and I have never since, advanced so much as one item of political theory in or to the North that I had not already uttered in and to the South.

I had not yet thought of ever being in any degree a political writer. I was still occupied, when the counting-room work would allow, with the short stories that make up *Old Creole Days*. I was just writing the last of them, "Café des Exilés."[1] When it was done I ceased for a long time to write anything for magazine publication. My counting-room duties filled my time and I merely wrote a little now and then for the *Picayune* on some unpolitical subjects and sold it as editorial matter. But in 1878, being quite unexpectedly invited by *Scribner's Monthly* to furnish a serial novel, I hired assistance at one of my office desks, and fell to work to write *The Grandissimes*.

In fact that novel was already partly written. The editors knew nothing of this, much less that the work I should by and by send them was going to have any political character. But that was now well nigh inevitable. It was impossible that a novel written by me then should escape being a study of the fierce struggle going on around me, regarded in the light of that past history—those beginnings—which had so differentiated the Louisiana civilization from the American scheme of public society.

I meant to make *The Grandissimes* as truly a political work as it ever has been called. But whether it furthered or hindered the moment's fortune of either political party I cared the very least in the world. In Louisiana both parties were unutterably corrupt, and although I always voted, I rarely voted a "straight ticket," and, whichever ticket I dropped into the box, feared I ought rather to have voted the other. I was still very slowly and painfully guessing out the riddle of our Southern question. During all the time when the national majority was intensely interested in enforcing the principles and scheme of Reconstruction, my writings for Northern publication were unpolitical; and only just when the Reconstruction idea fell most hopelessly out of favor in the national mind I began to ap-

[1] *Madame Delphine* was not written until several years later and was at first a volume by itself. [This is Cable's note, as are the other footnotes in this volume.]

prove and advocate those principles; but always first in the South and then in the North.

My friends and kindred looked on with disapproval and dismay, and said all they could to restrain me.

"Why wantonly offend thousands of your 'own people'?"

But I did not intend to offend. I wrote as near to truth and justice as I knew how, upon questions that I saw must be settled by calm debate and cannot be settled by force or silence; questions that will have to be settled thus by the Southern white man in his own conscience before ever the North and South can finally settle it between them. This was part of my politics and as a citizen I wrote.

I did not know at that time that I had any effective power of public speech. But, such as I have, I now began to discover it. At a public meeting of New Orleans Sunday-school workers I was one of two or three appointed to treat from the platform the parable of the Good Samaritan. I had not yet the courage of my own voice, but read from manuscript the few points I had to offer. That manuscript, still unprinted, dated April 1881, lies before me. A paragraph from it will show why I felt, in those days, impelled to write as I did:

"The Samaritans were a mongrel, half-idolatrous race upon whom the Jews looked down as emphatically their inferiors. Our Samaritan is Chinese, Indian, Irish, Negro. Do we love *this neighbor* as ourselves? Do we do altogether *likewise* to this Samaritan? Do we run great risks both with and for him? Do we give him our seat in God's house? Or do we tell him to go to the gallery? When he makes his peace with God, does he take the blessed cup and bread with us or after us? Have we, in short, and have we unimpeachably, a brother love for the Samaritans of our land and of our times?"

Now, I did not, myself, feel a brother love for the South's Samaritan, but I believed it my duty not to wait for that belated feeling, but to act as if I had it.

That was one reason. Another was the trust that the South would read from a Southern man patiently what it would only resent from a Northerner. These reasons for writing became my reasons for speaking as I wrote; especially when I could speak in the South.

In 1882 I was invited to address the graduating class of the University of Mississippi. A paragraph or two near its close will show yet a further motive:

"When the whole intellectual energy of the Southern states flew to the defense of that one institution which made us the South, we broke with human progress. We broke with the world's thought. We have not entirely in all things joined hands with it again. When we have done so we shall know it by this—there will be no South. We shall be Virginians, Texians, Louisianians, Mississippians, and we shall at the same time and over and above all be Americans. But we shall no more be Southerners than we shall be Northerners. The accidents of latitude shall be nothing to us. We shall be the proud disciples of every American alike who adds to the treasures of truth in American literature, and prouder still if his words reach the whole human heart and his lines of light run through the varied languages of the world. Let us hasten this. Let us hasten to be no longer a unique people. Let us search provinciality out of the land as the Hebrew housewife purged her dwelling of leaven on the eve of the Passover. . . .

"We cannot suppose that our community would hold a servile race in domestic subjection for a century and a half without producing a more lasting effect on the master race than a few subsequent years of partial change could dissipate. Hence search should be made for the flaws that must in that long period have crept into many of our views and into our temper. And who should we expect to do this? Certainly not outsiders. Certainly ourselves. And who among ourselves if not those who expect to be readers, and especially those whose ambition prompts them to be writers. . . . We want, if there is to be no part of our nation that is not self-governed, to write as well as read our share of the nation's literature. And if we are to do this we can avoid final failure only by writing either abreast or ahead of the latest knowledge of truth and beauty that the world possesses."

I longed to see the emancipation of literature in the South. It is not yet complete.

In December 1879, the senior of our firm had died. I never lost a dearer friend. I had tarried two or three months to make his affairs intelligible to his executors and then withdrew finally from counting-house work. I retained a certain salaried secretaryship but I now set about to make myself able to resign that also. I hoped to make literature my sole calling.

Literature meant, to me, belles-lettres, not essays whether political or other. Yet I had made an odd digression from belles-lettres, for all that. The government had commissioned Col. George E. Waring, Jr., to gather the "social statistics of cities," to consist of an untabulated, encyclopedic report from a selected expert in each of the great cities of the Union. On starting for New Orleans a friend of his handed him *Old Creole Days* to read on the train. On reaching the scene of those tales he sought their author and offered him the commission for reporting New Orleans. It was accepted. Against every effort the work expanded as I wrote. The editors of *Scribner's Monthly*, seeing me so deeply immersed, proposed that on finishing for the government I expand the work into an illustrated history of the Louisiana Creoles.

Again I consented, well pleased to write historically of a people whom I was accused of misrepresenting in fiction, and wrote *The Creoles of Louisiana*. It is odd that although this work has never been out of print a day, not one of the writers who have accused me of slandering the Creoles has considered, either in the government report or in the expanded volume, this, my only effort or pretense at a full and historical treatment of the subject.

I think I was still engaged on this work when I was invited to write another novel of the same length—no other feature was ever conditioned—as *The Grandissimes*. I began to write *Dr. Sevier*. An experience told me by Dr. D. W. Brickell, of

New Orleans, had moved me to write this story. An item in
it was the brutal treatment of a young man in our old Parish
Prison or *Calaboose*. My attention had hardly thus been called
to the city's horrid prison system when I was pressed into
grand jury service, was made secretary of the jury and made
a careful tour and report of the city's charities and corrections.
And so the novel was not enough. I caught an ambition to
do my native town a distinguished service and determined to
attempt to establish prison and asylum reform in New Orleans.

I easily gathered into an executive board seven or eight of
the city's best and busiest men, taking, myself, the unpaid office of secretary, with power to employ an assistant at sixty
dollars a month, and beginning at once an energetic newspaper crusade against the most conspicuous evils of the established system. It is my politics that a man *belongs* to the
community in which he lives to whatever extent he can serve
it, consistently with the fact of equal moment that he belongs
to his nation and the human race to the extent of his power
to serve them. Maybe I have never quite lived up to this fine
theory; but in something of its spirit I pressed prison reform;
and my paid secretary worked far better than I did. Owing
to my literary preoccupations he must sometimes have been
idle had he not filled such intervals by gathering the official
literature of his subject. He reached out beyond the city, and
presently beyond the state, and at length collected the latest
annual reports of all the state prisons in the Union. I had him
tabulate these reports, and thus I came upon the whole horrible convict lease system peculiar to our Southern states and
cordially detested by their best citizens.

I do not stop to tell of our local efforts for specific practical
reforms. Some succeeded; others were defeated by a ring of
sheriffs, deputies, and their confederates, whose pockets were
directly involved. The comparative study of prison systems in
other states was but incidental to these efforts. I had heard
and read of this Southern system, told in the loose and vanish-
ing way that belongs to the haste of the daily press; but

now my secretary laid it before me in all its hideous official arithmetic.

He urged me to write a paper on the subject; but I was engrossed with *Dr. Sevier*. One day, however, I received by mail an invitation from the officers of the National Prison Congress, which was appointed to meet in Louisville, Kentucky, urging me to treat that very subject before them, because Southerners would take from a Southerner and in the South— I do not believe much in that now.

The convention would be entirely unpolitical—in the common acceptance of the word. The subject seemed equally so. I was planning a visit to New York and could go by way of Louisville. And so I wrote and read my essay on "The Convict Lease System in the Southern States." To my agreeable surprise I sold it to the *Century Magazine*. But the editors, as well as my own bent, urged me back to novel writing, and I began, even that early, *Bonaventure,* though with a very good notion to write one more essay on a point I had in mind.

The calls of the public platform had already begun to encroach upon my literary production. In the previous winter or early spring, maybe, I had visited Baltimore to read six lectures on the literary art, under the auspices of Johns Hopkins University, and there discovered a new ability of which I had known nothing, and met my earliest success as a reader of my own stories. Returning home, I addressed the graduating class of the academic department of the University of Louisiana. Then to Louisville as already stated, and to New York and Boston, where, having finally resigned all commercial and financial business I openly took the platform on my own risks and spent the winter, '83–'84, not lecturing, but "reading" from my works of fiction.

In writing "The Convict Lease System," I had come upon certain features in that system, which embodied one of the Negro's grossest wrongs; his unequal chances in the courts of law. I pointed these out in my essay, but to avoid all political bias I withdrew the page or two thus occupied, and laid them away. I might never have used them, but on my way to Louisville I saw that incident which is narrated on page 67, of "The Freedman's Case in Equity," and I resolved there and then to tell, first to the South and then to the world, what I had seen, and demand a trial of the Freedman's case in the world's court on its equities. Conversing on this subject with a leading member of the American Social Science Association, he pressed me to make it the subject of a paper and read it the next September 1884 at the Association's annual meeting, in Saratoga. I would not promise. I wanted to enter my charges first before a Southern audience.

That opportunity soon came. As commencement season again approached I was invited to address the graduates of the University of Alabama, and accepted. I went to the platform in Tuscaloosa ready to appeal more boldly to the candor and progressive spirit of our Southern youth and scholarship than I had ever done before. First, I saw the Southern problem and its solution more clearly than ever. At the University of Mississippi I had been told on leaving the platform that I "would not have been allowed to make that speech there five years earlier"; but those five years were now seven and I allowed for further progress. In the third place the nation had largely surrendered the Southern problem to the South. Northern indifference had grown so great that it seemed to me one could not, even by passionate resentment, be charged with "catering to Northern prejudice." There had not been, for thirty years, so little Northern interest in the matter. And then, besides: in North and South for some years great talk had been made of progress in Alabama resultant upon the opening of her mineral treasures and the inpour of capital and immigration, and I had unconsciously taken up the popular error that material gains and thrift produce a general advance in civil and political thought. Every one of these four assumptions I found, too late, was a mistake.

I quote a paragraph simply to show what my politics then were, in the South and spoken to Southerners. I took great pains throughout to use a tone not of superior censure but of confession, and when I had made that intention plain, ventured to say:

"What our fathers called their 'peculiar institution' tended, when it was in force, to promote in us a certain spirit of command—of dictation—that made our wills seem to us nearly or quite as authoritative as the laws, and sometimes more so. We were a race of masters. We were dictators. The main thing to be kept in sight was the discipline of the plantation. Hence a most lamentable laxness of parental discipline; a similar laxness of that defensive discipline by which society lays down its conditions of membership; and, springing distinctly from these deficiencies, a group of outrageous vices: shameless hard drinking, the carrying of murderous weapons, murder, too, and lynching at its heels, the turning of state and county prisons into slavepens, the falsification of the ballot, night riding and whipping, and all the milder forms of political intolerance. Now, I maintain, without fear of offending any one here whose good opinion I can honestly afford to cling to, that we owe it to the parents who, along with all the moral evils that naturally found harbor under the institution of Negro slavery, have left us still a Christianity that not even slaveholding in the nineteenth century could destroy, to rise to such an acuteness of moral sense—to acquire and agree upon such a moral standard—that from one end of this land to the other there shall be lifted against these crimes an outcry of shame and condemnation so long and so loud that it shall divide asunder those who wink at such things from those who do not, even though it split every social circle and every church and every family in the land. We have been silent long enough."

For the first time in my experience the local press met my utterances entirely without commendation. Yet of private expressions of approval and accord I had no lack, and I returned to New Orleans more deeply convinced than ever before that, behind all the fierce conservatism of a noisier element there was a silent South needing to be urged to speak and act.

The ill health of one of my family demanding a radical change of climate, I took my household to spend a summer and fall in a village of Connecticut. I was glad to become a resident student and observer of that kind of American civilization founded on the Village, the antipode of the Plantation. I doubted not I should see the faults of this system also, and even hoped that in their light—or shadow—the errors of our Southern system would be less glaring. All my life I had seen the South near by and the North afar off; now the case would be reversed. Even as a novelist I felt bound to study social science from as many points of view as I could.

But hardly was I settled at my new desk when I was again, and yet again, urged to write "that paper" for the Social Science Association. And this time I reluctantly consented. Reluctantly, however, only because I was immersed in a couple of magazine articles on nothing nearer politics than the ancient slave dances and songs of Louisiana. I finished these and then wrote and in September (1884) read at Saratoga "The Freedman's Case in Equity." It was published the following January in the *Century Magazine*.

I treated the subject as a question, not of party policy, but of political ethics, and throughout the entire North and West the paper met the widest commendation. Only in the South did it meet censure. There the denunciation was a storm. There came to me unsought more than one hundred pages of adverse, and for the most part unparliamentary, criticism. But in quite another tone Mr. H. W. Grady, editor of the Atlanta *Constitution*, replied in the April *Century* (1885), and one of my purposes was attained; the subject was drawn into the forum of literary debate before the nation and the world.

In the preceding month I had gone South. The whole winter had been spent on the platform reading only my pages of fiction; but in the South, as far as my notoriety went at all, the word spread that I was reaping golden harvests by haranguing Northern audiences on the fascinating subject of Southern sins. My journey South—I visited nearly every Southern state—was to note what changes might be taking place, necessary to notice if I should write again on Southern political conditions. Moreover, as literature and the lecture platform was now my only calling and it was therefore idle to retain my residence in New Orleans, more than fifteen hundred miles from my publishers and the center of the lecture field, I had determined to make my home, for some years at least, conveniently near New York City. And so I went South also because I saw that only by wide and studious tours there should I now keep up with all the changes in Southern affairs. Since then I have made repeated tours in the South, and seen it more widely and often than in any similar length of time. Besides which I have visited every state in the Union save Kansas, Arkansas, and Texas, and every territory except Arizona, the Indian Territory, and New Mexico.

I felt that I belonged, still, peculiarly to the South. I had shared in every political error of the "Southerner," and had enjoyed whatever benefits the old slaveholding civilization had to offer. A resultant duty bound me to my best conception of the true interest of the South as a whole—the whole South, white and black. This, aside from the fact that the Negro question is a national question which it is particularly the duty of men of the South to solve; a duty from which they are not released by moving North. My reply to Mr. Grady was "The Silent South." I wrote it in May; it appeared in the *Century* in September. In June I spent several days in Kentucky and addressed the graduates of Berea College. Then I returned to my study table in Connecticut, and from notes made in Louisiana wrote "Grande Pointe" and began "Carancro." About the first of October I removed my family to Northampton, Massachusetts, an old educational center, seat of a noted female college—I have five daughters—a place whence one can visit either Boston or New York and return the same day, and in the heart of the national lecture field. Here I took up my permanent residence. I give room to such details because many kind Southern friends have urged me to state them in

deference to others who, with no wish to be unjust, have misconstrued my removal from the South. And at this point I
may say farther that my politics have always been national. I
think I still owe my native Louisiana a sympathetic interest in
her state affairs. I owe the same, no doubt, by virtue of my
present residence, to Massachusetts. But the nation is more to
me than any one state. I have never in any state where I was
not a citizen spoken in public criticism of any matter not of
national concern. Still less, if possible, have I ever stood in one
state and pointed such criticism against another. Nay, I have
never spoken on a Northern platform about Southern affairs
save when pointedly asked to do so; and the whole number of
times I have thus spoken is just fourteen and no more, out of
some two hundred and fifty appearances on the platform.

After writing "The Silent South," I produced no political
writings, save one or two brief Open Letters in the *Century*
in reply to critics, until three summers after, although constantly busy with my pen when not filling platform appointments—which, I fear, take up too much of my time. But in
June 1887 I addressed the graduates of Vanderbilt University,
Nashville, Tennessee, in an unwritten effort on "The Faith"—
meaning the early political ideals—"of Our Fathers." In it I
tried to show that the true solution of the Southern question
calls simply for the South's return to and fulfillment of the
original principles of government that our Northern and
Southern fathers had together declared when they founded
the nation.

Immediately afterward the London *Contemporary Review*
invited me to write on "The Negro Question in the United
States." I accepted promptly, hoping to gain a larger and
kinder attention through an English review than I could
through a New York or Boston magazine. I did more; wishing
to say in the South itself whatever I had to say on the Southern
problem, I tried to arrange for simultaneous publication in
American newspapers, waiving further compensation for myself but securing it to the English editors. A New York news-

paper syndicate tried to arrange this, especially with Southern newspapers, but got no reasonable offer save from the New York *Tribune* claiming exclusive rights in the East and the Chicago *Inter-Ocean* with like monopoly in the West. I had never published a line in a Republican party organ in my life, but in this case I let the paper appear in London, New York, and Chicago simultaneously and remitted the proceeds of its American sale to the London editors.

The article was an expansion of my Nashville address, and so had been given first in the South; twice, in fact, for I gave it also at Fayetteville, Tennessee. And it reached the South last, also. For it was presently reprinted, not by or for me, in pamphlet form, and distributed by thousands in the Southern states. Rightly enough, too, for I have never written on any phase of the Southern question but I wrote most of all for Southern readers.

Very soon after this I was invited to address a "National League" of colored men in Boston. I spoke to them, not of rights, but of duties, under the subject, "What Shall the Negro Do?" and, the *Forum* inviting me a few days later to contribute an essay, I resolved the meager notes of that address into a careful paper. A few months later Senator Eustis, of Louisiana, printed an essay in the *Forum* on "Race Antagonism in the South," and, being invited to reply, I decided to review the papers of four Southern writers eminent in politics, written within a year. The result was my essay "A Simpler Southern Question."

Such is a summary of my political writings and an account of how they came to be. I have never shaped them to the needs of any political party. Never since I began to write them have I been in accord with all the declarations of any party. I have always made it a point of duty to vote. I have rarely voted the Republican ticket; but I have voted it in Louisiana in the most violent days of insurrectionary strife. I have never voted with a third or fourth party, though I have often voted a "scratched" ticket, and have cared little or nothing for party names and phrases. The Democratic party holds to one or two practical ideals for which I shall always vote when measures pointing experimentally toward those ideals are made the main issue of a canvass. The Republican holds to one or two other practical ideals for which I shall always vote when measures pointing experimentally toward those ideals are made the main issue. But both these great parties are—unless I am greatly mistaken—negligent of one or two ideals of American government for which I shall vote whenever practical measures pointing experimentally toward those ideals are made the main issue, even if to do so I have to vote with a third party.

So much as to my vote. As to my pen I dedicate it to that great question—not of party exigency but of political ethics—on which I can best speak and write, to which as a native Louisianian and "ex-Confederate" I am duty bound, and which is still the most serious and urgent question before the nation: a peaceable renaissance of the Southern states upon the political foundations laid by the nation's fathers, Northern and Southern, when they rose above the dictates of established order, the temptations of the moment's comfort, and the fear to take risks for the right, and gave to their children and the world the Declaration of Independence as an ultimate ideal to be daily and yearly striven toward with faith, diligence, and courage.

With this explanation I again submit these essays to public consideration, ready to welcome any criticism that will help to establish that true and lasting national peace, fellowship, and wealth which can never stand on other foundations than equal justice and equal liberty to all the people.

Segregation
in the Schools

[I. Letter to the Editor, New Orleans *Bulletin*, September 26, 1875.

In the old French Quarter of New Orleans the visitor today will find on Royal Street, a dozen blocks below Canal Street, a large square-shouldered house standing close against the narrow sidewalk. This is the Haunted House which received its ghosts, supposedly, from the famed Madame Lalaurie's torturing her slaves within its walls. In "The 'Haunted House' in Royal Street," which Cable published in his *Strange True Stories of Louisiana* (1889), he retold from the newspaper accounts and documents of the time how a mob, after learning of the horrors concealed in the house, stormed it with such fury in the year 1834 that Madame Lalaurie barely made her escape and fled to France. In the same story Cable told how the house was occupied during Reconstruction days by a girls' high school attended by both white and Negro pupils, how he visited it as a newspaper reporter to hear the annual examinations, and how in December 1874 a mob appeared at the school and evicted all of the girls who had—or could not prove that they did not have—Negro blood in their veins.

The eviction was but one event in the tense struggle between the Radical party and the Democratic party for control in the city. The Negro pupils were soon in the school again and remained until Radical control ended in 1877. Page M. Baker, editor of the New Orleans *Bulletin*, had made his paper into a frenzied organ of attack on the mixed schools, and for that reason Cable wrote his letter to the *Bulletin*.]

Segregation in the Schools

Mr. Editor:

Believing in the good effect of public discussion through the newspapers, and asking the courtesy of a place in your widely read columns, I beg to ask . . . whether we have not all along been making too much ado over this matter of mixed schools.

Our children reach school at about 8½ A.M. and return at about 3 P.M. They are thus in contact with their schoolmates seven hours a day for five days in the week. Most of the time, however, is devoted to silent study. Of playtime there is the half hour before school, the half hour of recess, and let us say another half hour of stolen moments, including the breaking up of school; in all, one hour and a half in the twenty-four, admitting the pupils to free contact with each other. Counting the net school year at forty weeks, and the school week at five days, we find that this opportunity for "mixing" amounts to something less than 1/29th part of the time.

But "not so fast," some will say. At school companionships are formed which reach beyond school hours and into social life. True enough. Our children will do as we did when we were in school. They will select and confer free companionship upon certain playmates, according to their own and their parents' ideas of mental caliber, moral worth, and social position, and the rest of the school may go its way. This fact, then, is rather an argument against our hostility. The schoolroom neither requires nor induces social equality. Social equality is a matter of personal preference, which preference must be mental before the social equality can begin to exist.

But here the *argumentum ad hominem* is thrust in: "How

would you like your son or daughter to sit at a desk with a
Negro?" Should we ask "What harm?" we are quickly answered, "Harm enough! The Negro is an inferior being."
"How do you know?" "Why, he belongs to an inferior race."
Ah! so he does; yet he might be superior to my son and help
him do his sums for all that. But suppose him to be inferior.
After all my boy may go to public school, mixed or unmixed,
for twenty years, and never happen to sit with an exact equal,
either physically, socially, mentally, or morally; however if he
behaves himself, he will most likely have a deskmate of his
own selection. Let us at this point note particularly that for
generations parents have been sending their children to our
public schools, recognizing with impunity the fact that their
children there meet schoolmates too far beneath them in the
social scale to admit of a speaking acquaintance beyond the
walls of the schoolyard.

The opponents of mixed schools propose to afford equal but
separate advantages to each race distinctively. It behooves
them to show that it can be done without great additional expense. But after all, do what we can, the distinction is odious;
for though accommodations were every whit equal in two sets
of schools, should one set be closed against any other class
other than the blacks, as (for example merely) the Irish, I
need not say what indignation would be aroused, nay, what
blood would be shed, nor how quickly the closed doors would
be battered in. And yet whatever our good Hibernian citizens
may think, there are few Anglo-Saxons, be they ever so mistaken, who do not consider the Anglo-Saxon race superior to
the Celtic. The question of superiority of race, I take it, is not
sufficient cause for separating children where contact does not
and cannot place them on an equality.

You, Mr. Editor, have not space, nor I leisure, to discuss the
question of colored teachers. It is not the main issue. But I
can say in passing that hundreds of demurring parents among
our people have had their children nourished at the breast of
Negro nurses—for these parents to object to their children

being taught by an educated and polite mulatto is rather illogical.

A word upon the school tax. This ought never to be considered an expense. It is an investment, and the most paying public investment that is made. It is every citizen's interest to have the masses educated. Inestimably more expensive will it be for us to refuse to provide for, or for us to hinder, the elevation of the many thousands among us whose dense ignorance and incapacity is today the greatest incubus that lies on the material interests of the state. If we withdraw our children from the public schools on the color line, thousands of poor parents will follow the example and their children will go to that school of depravity, the street, whose diploma at best is a shaved head and a striped suit. I would rather pay for schools than prisons, though I and all my kin were childless.

There is much said about race antipathy. I believe in it more strongly than do the opponents of a mixed school system. But see our dilemma: if there is no mutual antipathy between the races we have no right to make one; "lest haply," as Gamaliel said, "we be found warring against God"; but, and if there is this native antagonism, I have that confidence in the Caucasian race to believe it will preserve its purity without the bolstering aid of mass meetings or the expulsion of well-behaved children from the schools where they are now attendant without injury to any person concerned.

If the race is inferior, we can the better afford to give them an even start. If any child, colored or colorless, is dirty or vicious, the rules of the school will compel his expulsion. If he is not, I ask, and appeal to each reader's sense of fairness for his answer, what harm will the child do?

Yes, the black race is inferior to the white. The Almighty has established inequality as a principle in nature. But the lesson it teaches is magnanimity, not scorn. To apply the words of Coleridge:

> The great God who loveth us,
> He made and loveth all.

How aptly might the quotation lately made by the Hon. Mr. Gladstone from Tennyson's "Guinevere" be repeated to us:

> For in those days
> No knight of Arthur's noblest dealt in scorn;
> But if a man were halt or hunched, in him
> By those whom God had made full-limbed and tall
> Scorn was allowed as part of his defect,
> And he was answered softly by the King
> And all his table.

A SOUTHERN WHITE MAN

[II. Letter to the Editor, rejected by the New Orleans *Bulletin* and the New Orleans *Picayune*, September 1875.

In printing Cable's letter on September 26, Page M. Baker accompanied it with an editorial in which he assured his readers, who he felt certain would be unbelieving, that the author of the letter was actually a Southern white man. He made his own position clear: "The only condition under which the two races can co-exist peacefully is that in which the superior race shall control and the inferior race shall obey. . . . For our part we hope never to see the white boys and girls of America forgetful of the fact that Negroes are their inferiors." He affirmed his belief in race instinct, and he called Cable's reference to Negro wet nurses his "lacteal argument," professing to see no "foul contact" in such a relationship comparable to that existing in a mixed schoolroom.

Baker declined to publish the second letter, predicting that if Cable would put it by and read it after ten years he would be ashamed of himself. Cable attached a note to the manuscript when he laid it away, "I predict that the opinions embodied in it will then be adopted by a majority of the people."

A. M. Holbrook, proprietor of the *Picayune,* also declined to publish the letter.

General P. G. T. Beauregard, a New Orleans Creole, was an honored citizen and a prominent financier in the years following the Civil War. The clamor for separate cars on the street railways had been denied for reasons of economy.

The manuscript of this letter is in the Tulane University Library.]

Mr. Editor:

In my communication which you were so good as to publish Sunday morning I advanced certain statements which I beg leave to condense into the following propositions; and very briefly, but, I hope, fairly, to answer your criticisms upon them. For I take it for granted that what our people want is the whole truth and nothing else, and hence obtrude myself a second time upon you, pleading the right and usefulness of free discussion for a place in your journal; feeling assured, as you have rightly intimated, that so I shall reach many readers.

My first proposition was, in brief, that:

1. In mixed schools the opportunity for social contact with colored children would be afforded our children only 1/29th part of the whole time, and even then *not forced upon them;* for—

2. School children select their intimates *out from* the mass of the school, according to their own and their parents' social affinities.

To this argument you answer that a foul contact is bad for 1/29th part of the time. It is unjust to assume that the contact is always necessarily foul or that it is compulsory during that small fraction of time. But let that pass; your answer is at best a terrible rebuke to the vast majority of our good Southern people who have for so many generations, not in the country alone, but largely in the cities also, allowed their children to make constant playmates of slave children whose highest aspirations were (necessarily from their condition of slavery) low and mean. If I with my 1/29th of the time make "an attack upon human instincts," what do you charge this majority of the Southern people with, with their *four-fifths* of the time?

I appeal to your readers to say whether our children, as a body, ever have been quite free from this contact; and also whether the public schools will be purged of moral uncleanness simply by the expulsion of the blacks; or whether, instead, every respectable pupil will not still have white schoolmates unfit for them to associate with and whom they will be at perfect liberty to shun.

My second proposition was: That if the so-called equitable separation between the blacks and whites should be attempted against any considerable class of our community *other than the blacks*, it would be resented to the extremity of bloodshed.

This, I believe, is one of my statements (heretical I think you call them) which you had not room to answer. I foresaw as much when I wrote it; and I fear you will be too crowded to grapple it for a long time to come.

But I said also: That there is an antagonism between races of men, not violent, but instinctive and universal. That *therefore* the Caucasian race will preserve its high purity without the aid of onerous civil distinctions, and that Caucasian superiority calls, instead, for the most exalted magnanimity.

To this I need add only your own words, found, oddly enough, in the very article in which you condemn my attitude. Your own words are that "Between whites and Africans there is now and has always been an antipathy of instincts. These instincts appear *under all conditions*" (excuse my italics), "and no familiarity or social blending, or unnatural hybridity, can conquer the inborn, centrifugal, and mutually repellent propensity which causes the two races to shun each other."

Good for the *Bulletin!* Let the public say, after that, what
they need fear from mixed schools, social intercourse (per-
missible, not compulsory) confined to 1/29th part of the time.
O, sir, is it not a little bit unreasonable?

In the fourth place I asserted: That a school tax is not only
a public benefaction but an investment for the benefit of every owner of property, childless or otherwise, as well as of the
non-taxpaying and the poor. Your response is a pungent denunciation of the manner of raising our school tax, while my
statement goes unanswered. I repeat that, notwithstanding the
popular notion that the school tax is a charity which only the
donors have the right to administer, the fact remains; it is an
investment for the benefit of everybody, and *pays the taxpayer
a hundredfold.*

Now for my "lacteal argument." (I shall not spring back
upon you with a retort about *milk-and-water* arguments.) I
said, merely, that "Parents who have had their children nourished by Negro nurses cannot logically object to those children being taught by a polite and competent mulatto." Mr.
Editor, tell me frankly; if anyone was in the habit of bringing
his cow into the house and letting his infants fasten to her
udder, would it not give said infants a pretty fair passport to
the stable? But badinage aside; they pass from infancy to and
through the impressible and educable years of childhood still
in the nurse's care and frequently in company with the nurse's
children. What reason, then, is there in likening a few minutes
of possible contact (foul contact as the fashion is to call it)
at the recess hour of the public schools to "breathing mephitic
exhalations."

No, Mr. Editor, this is only the old Star-car trouble expand-
ing to ghostly proportions. But I beg you to remember that
that difficulty was settled, not by legislation nor yet by mass
meeting, but by the quiet good sense of our railroad presidents
headed by General Beauregard. The result? New Orleans has
suffered from the "foul contact" at least as little as from the

fragrant proximity of the somnolent sons of Gascony whom she never dreamed of cramping into special, equal, separate accommodations. Let her now come out magnanimously and be the first to do the "fair thing" in the schools.

A SOUTHERN WHITE MAN

The Good Samaritan

[From an address delivered before the New Orleans Sunday-School Association, April 4, 1881.

The letters Cable wrote to the newspaper on school segregation in 1875 were evidence that such efforts could hope to accomplish but little and would alienate many who held opposing views. Both editors who rejected the second of his letters had been friends of his for several years.

In 1877 the military occupation ended, the Radical party fell from power, and Democrats occupied state and local offices. A period of adjustment followed, before the policies of the new governments became clear. During that period Cable did not challenge openly again the prevailing views of the white Democrats, but in the fiction he published there was evidence that he was doing his own thinking on current problems. Two stories, "Belles Demoiselles Plantation" and "'Tite Poulette," both published in 1874 and later included in *Old Creole Days* (1879), reflected obvious sympathy for the tragic bearers of mixed blood in New Orleans. *The Grandissimes* (1880) has its setting in slave days, but no reader could fail to see that the comment on class and caste and race was meant to apply no less to the South of the author's own time than to Louisiana at the time of the purchase. *Madame Delphine*, a novelette published in 1881, could be said to plead the cause of the quadroon women represented by the title character and her daughter.

More directly than in his fiction and yet not in a way to invite opposition, Cable's address before the Sunday-School Association asked for a degree of charity and magnanimity toward the Freedmen, the Samaritans of his day and region, which he did not find about him.

The manuscript of this address is in the Tulane University Library.]

The Good Samaritan

. . . Have you never tried to paraphrase the teachings of Christ by clothing them in the garb of our modern everyday life? You often get new lights by this method.

A certain family moved down from a church neighborhood into a disreputable district, made unfortunate acquaintances, and one and all went to the bad and by and by were stripped of everything but a few rags.

And by chance there came down a minister of the gospel. And when he saw these people he avoided them.

And likewise a layman—a trustee, probably, or a vestryman. He stopped at their door, looked in on them, and after pondering the matter well went away, saying to himself, "The trouble with that class of people is they are almost certain to impose on you"—the very thing we do to God's mercy every day.

But, my fellow workers, God does not judge people by classes, any more than he saves them by classes; he makes them one by one and judges them one by one, and as surely as he is our pattern we ought to wipe that phrase out of Christian speech. The parable points the finger of condemnation directly at it. Class? That class? Our circle? Their circle? The Christian circle is the circumference of the earth—at the equator; where it is the biggest. But we go on with the paraphrase.

But a certain person of doubtful social standing came where this family was. He was part Chinese, part Indian, part Irish, and part Negro, and was nominally and by superstition a Roman Catholic. He stopped, looked in, entered, and had compassion on them, clothed them, fed them, and took them to

God's house. Does this finish the story? No. The parable stands among all the rest as peculiarly the unfinished parable; so left by the divine art of the Savior who calls upon each and all of us to finish it in our hearts; and if we are taking the word of God like little children, like little children we shall ask, What did the wounded man do? And the hope will rise that he lived ever after on the assumption that if a Samaritan could do thus to him he could do likewise to a Samaritan.

But let us remember what this resolution would involve. The Samaritans were a mongrel, half-idolatrous race upon whom the Jews looked down as emphatically their inferiors. So in our paraphrase we have made our Samaritan Chinese, Indian, Irish, and Negro. Do we love *this neighbor* as ourselves? Do we do altogether *likewise* to this Samaritan? Do we run great risks both with and for him? Do we give him our seat in God's house? Or do we tell him to go to the gallery? When he makes his peace with God, does he take the blessed cup and bread with us or after us? Have we, in short, and have we unimpeachably, a brother love for the Samaritans of our land and of our times? God demands the answer. Let the answer be to God. . . .

Literature in
the Southern States

[From a commencement address at the University of Mississippi, June 28, 1882.

In this address Cable asked for a national rather than a sectional literature. In that request he had the agreement of others in the South, Mark Twain and Joel Chandler Harris among them; but he was ready to protest more forcefully than the others, perhaps because he had already encountered the same restrictions which he believed had denied a great literature to the ante-bellum South. He had been taxed with offending in his fiction the sectional bias which he felt still plagued Southern letters.

When he went to the platform at Oxford, Mississippi, Cable could draw courage from the fact that he was the most prominent novelist then writing in the South, and from the same fact he derived a sense of obligation to speak out. He knew that his strictures on slavery and caste and the plantation might cause offense in the home state of Jefferson Davis, who was busy at the time defending the Lost Cause with his pen. His shrewd assessment of the audience and the occasion is attested by the fact that his utterances were not challenged in the press but were commended warmly in a number of papers in the region. The address is clear evidence, moreover, of the facility and assurance with which he could deal with both historical and current aspects of the South. He was constructing in his mind a frame of reference for studying the crucial problems of the contemporary South.

In writing "My Politics," Cable had the manuscript of this address open before him, but in quoting from it (pages 15 and 16 of this volume), he made several minor revisions.

This address remained unpublished until 1955, when it was printed in the *Tulane Studies in English* in an article entitled "George W. Cable's Revolt Against Literary Sectionalism."]

Literature in the Southern States

. . . My friends, I have proposed to myself to speak to you on the subject of "Literature in the Southern States." I do not say the South. The day must come when that word shall have receded to its original meaning of mere direction and location; but for the present, causes have made it necessary for us to be regarded as a distinct section of the American Union and to be studied by ourselves and others as presenting a unique phase of American life and thought. If I touch the secret spring of this unfortunate singularity, it must be only for a moment, & with tenderness and filial reverence.

In our wide country two different ideas of social organization began from the first to grow and to move apart. In the Southern colonies the separation from the mother country had not been such a total disruption from all its social traditions as in the Northern. . . . In the main the Southern idea of popular liberty was, or soon became, in certain aspects, more constrained than the Northern.

It could not but be so. We know how soon in the North the question of slaveholding in its moral aspect began to agitate the public mind. And we know how profoundly was the American mind in the South impressed with the belief that slavery was vitally necessary to the existence of society.

And truly, one of the cornerstones of our social edifice, *as it stood,* was this principle and practice of slaveholding. It established caste. It made a fixed aristocracy and a fixed peas-

antry and weakened the vitality of the idea that self-government is an inalienable right of all mankind. From such an
aristocracy there could be no fear of falling. From such a peasantry there was no hope of rising. Thus in the very foundations
of our society some of the finest springs of human endeavor
were mired and choked. The Americans of the South were
presently a people without a middle class. What rejected matter its aristocracy did throw off sank even into the contempt
of its peasantry; and from the ranks of that peasantry there
was no extrication more than nominal so long as a drop of its
blood was discernible in the veins. Such rudimentary show as
there was of a middle class was found either in the overseer
or the immigrant of the cities. But the cities were few, towns
were far apart and small, and the typical life was that of the
plantation.

Let me say to those before me who are of senior years that
it is not my intention to analyze the deplorable error which in
all its aspects we can now so plainly see was our crime and
our curse. I have alluded to it in order to show the cause of
our early estrangement from the only literature the world had
to offer us which it was even presumable might be adapted
to our intellectual needs.

Soon, indeed, we found something in that literature from
which we turned with a loss of appetite. Around and beyond
our borders our brethren had no more got rid of the questions
of *social rank* than had we. No people ever will. They are
healthful and ever-vital questions. But among themselves, as
modern speech has it, they got those questions out of politics.
They got them out of the statute book. They were rooting
their conventional phrases and titular distinctions out of popular speech. Here was a great victory—a great development, in
which *we* did not fully and with hearty sympathy share; *we*
had reduced these questions to a single crude one of race and
had stamped its answer upon the statute book in black letter.

Already, therefore, the life northward and northeastward of
us was more truly and peculiarly the typical civilization of the

continent—the outcome of the Revolution—than that of Canada, for instance, could possibly be, or than ours was. And therefore it was the civilization, more than these others, that demanded and could foster and cherish a new literature.

Its people had less time to read than we, but they read more and far more of them read. There was intellectual fermentation from the very highest down to the very lowest. Naturally, then, the infant literature of the nation chose the cities of the North for its birthplace. In that direction, town life increased; a life not so favorable to authorship, it may be, as to the production of a reading public and the multiplication of libraries. Education not merely commanded great appreciation, it had also great positive and practical value. No man's status was fixed by his birth; the faces of land and sky were not too indulgent; and in the race of life, education offered any man tremendous advantages. But the pursuit of elementary knowledge produced a widespread taste for polite literature, and that ambition of the pen, which few students fail to experience and which there ran from the top of the social scale to the very bottom.

With us the case was different. Race was rank. Few conditions qualified it except the question of actual slaveholding. This settled status. The earth was generous. The toil of the slaves made the ease of the planter. The life was what we loved to style "baronial." Education was an equipment not strenuously called for by any actual necessity of life, comfort, or profit. The plantation life did not demand it, or at least could easily dispense with it. Agriculture, a primitive art, employing the African, a primitive workman, took on the most primitive character. *All* the stimulants to intellectual fruition were heavily discounted. The order of society, for instance, was, as we have said, fixed, immovable, iron-bound; there was no question of pre-eminence to settle. No moral question was open for public discussion. All was isolation. The whole South, except in the cities, was turned by the plantation idea into a vast archipelago of patriarchal estates whereof every one was

a complete empire within itself and looked to its neighbors
for little else than to supply matrimonial alliances to its imperial family.

Learning soon began to take the aspect of a merely orna-
mental accomplishment. The land was inherited, the labor was
owned, the art of livelihood was comprised in the simple traditions of agriculture by the dullest of hand labor and the equally
simple and traditional government of slaves. There was no
more social agitation, no more rush for preference, no more
struggle for room, than if each homestead had been a separate
island in the Pacific. As to climate, so much has been said
and said so often on that score that I shall only ask you to
make the allowance for that influence which you have long
ago decided to be proper.

Let us turn to the results. Did education fall into complete
neglect? No. *"Noblesse oblige."* But it became antique. The
planter was contented with the world as it was, and there was
not and could not be any friction or lifting from below to disturb him in his contentment. The people—that part of the population which allowed only itself to be so called—became filled
with conservatism; the desire to conserve—to preserve—to perpetuate matters as they stand. We became distended—mired
and stuffed with conservatism to the point of absolute rigidity.
Our life had little or nothing to do with the onward movement
of the world's thought. We were in danger of being a civilization that was not a civilization, because there was not in it the
element of advancement.

Under these conditions how could we produce or even receive a new literature. We were used to the old. We were not
widowed from the past; how could we wed the present or
affiance ourselves to the future? Our country was America, but
the impulses of our thought still found the old highways of
English literature running nearly enough in our desired direction to beguile us from the arduous paths of the uncleared
wilderness. Our book reading ran down the scale of time to
1800 and there it stopped. Irvings and Coopers and Bryants

might arise and shine without great notice from a people satisfied with Fieldings and Sternes and Popes.

That the Southern mind was incapable of literary production is not only not to be supposed, but it is refuted by facts. In those branches of intellectual endeavor related to the fundamental motives and needs of man, and therefore comprised within the practical professions, the South had always sons to bring her honor. We lacked neither great jurists nor great senators, divines, theologians, physicians, or captains. But in the rare ether of abstract research and imaginative creation, where toil has no claim but its own charms, we set few stars. Of historians, philosophers, poets, fictionists, dramatists, and their like, the very fewest appeared who cast other than a feeble or else a lurid light. Labor, the lot of the slave, was lightly honored. The toil that accompanied professional rank alone escaped contempt, and pure literature to be entirely respectable had to be mentioned apologetically as a pastime that could not entertain offers of compensation.

And yet, despite all this, the Southern states did contribute to the nation's literature, though not in the quantity we would have liked to record. With new thoughts moving in more new directions there would have been more writing of the kind that gives light and heat and that lives. Where we had new thoughts, in the departments of civil government and of jurisprudence, the South gave to American literature some of the brightest lights in its sky. And whenever and wherever the eloquence of the bar is brought to remembrance, Americans will not forget the name of Seargent S. Prentiss of Mississippi.

By and by came the verdict of the world against the holding of slaves. Alackaday! Would it had then and there been the verdict of our Southern states. In earlier days the best minds of the South had spoken apologetically of the institution, as one speaks of some small vice which he would like to quit if he could, and still promises his friends at some indefinite day to break from. But when censure came from without, the whole intellectual life of the South started fiercely up. It found itself on an island. The great moral question ran like a stream of lava down upon and across the whole plain of Anglo-Saxon letters. The American of the South could not turn a fresh page or open a newspaper received across the border or from beyond the Atlantic, but he was likely to confront the exasperating accusation that his life and the order of society in his land was a crime against heaven and humanity. And so it came about that that very principle in the Southern life which had all along impeded literature was that which now called for a literature of its own.

The voice of that young American literature, which had never strongly allured us, was now a perpetual affront. The contemporaneous literature of England was equally repulsive, and the youth of the South sought his latest illuminations on the bookshelves of his grandfather's library and sat down in spectacles to defend with a sputtering pen the divine right and political economy of our melancholy mistake.

So then was heard a call for a literature in America and for Americans that was to be something different from what the world was beginning to recognize as American literature and the farthest possible from being a part of it. Its mission did not contemplate the evolution of one new idea. It was to uphold the old. It was to cut by the old patterns. It was to steer by the old lights. It was to echo the old voices.

Well, without sufficient reason for being—for it had absolutely no revelation to make—this literature came. . . .

My kind friends, I have a word to say—but how shall I say it? Venerating the past as I must; honoring the graves of our fathers as I do; cherishing the memory of the intellectual giants whose bones lie under our sods; and gratefully culling from their wisdom the thoughts that are good for all times; how can I say it?

I cannot pitch my utterance in unison with tradition, nor if the dead could speak from their graves would they have us do so. Their muffled voices would come up commanding us to go on—to go on—to look not behind, but to push on up the winding stream of thought, nearer and nearer, as fast as strength and sight will let us, toward the pure headwaters of truth. They would demand—they would have a right to demand—that, starting where they made their last camp, we should leave their unconscious errors behind and make new discoveries farther on, in justice and liberty and duty and all excellence, humbly mindful that they who shall come after us must do the same for us. What I would say then I say humbly and reverentially; it is this:

When the whole intellectual energy of the Southern states flew to the defense of that one institution which made us the South, we broke with human progress. We broke with the world's thought. We have not entirely in all things joined hands with it again. When we have done so we shall know it by this—there will be no South. We shall be Virginians, Texians, Louisianians, Mississippians, and we shall at the same time and over and above all be Americans. But we shall no more be Southerners than we shall be Northerners. The accidents of latitude shall be nothing to us. We shall be the proud disciples of every American alike who adds to the treasures of truth in American liturature, and prouder still if his words reach the whole human heart and his lines of light run through the varied languages of the world. Let us hasten to be no longer a unique people. Let us search provincialism out of the land as the Hebrew housewife purged her dwelling of leaven on the eve of the Passover.

There is a newly-coined name that most agreeably tickles the ear of the young citizen in our Southern states, but which I would gladly see met with somewhat of disrelish: the New South. It is a term only fit to indicate a transitionary condition. What we want—what we ought to have in view—is the No South! Does the word sound like annihilation? It is the farthest from it. It is enlargement. It is growth. It is a higher life.

Young sons of Mississippi, a little while within the pleasant walls of this university and you pass out into citizenship. The time approaches when you must begin to hear the appeals of those who seek to be your public servants. As well as they studying your minds can guess your thoughts, those appeals will be addressed to your leading motives—to your ruling sentiments. What they will be I do not know; I can only hope. But I trust the time is not far away when anyone who rises before you and addresses you as "Southrons" shall be stared at as the veriest Rip Van Winkle that the times can show. When you shall say, "Southerners? South? New South? Sir, your words are not for us. Mississippians we are. State boundaries we know, acknowledge, and preserve. As to the Union of States, God bless it! God save it! But the league of any one group of them under any name of North or South or East or West is an invasion of freemasonry into our family circle. We are Americans. Go you to Mexico. That is the New South. And make haste, friend, or they will push you on into South America, where we have reshipped the separate sort of books printed for the Southern market."

Well, now, the question must come up, seeing war has purged us of the great differentiating element in our social life, what changes of direction must there be in our intellectual movement if we would, with our best intelligence, participate in the nation's reading and writing? For we must know that war's cinders are still in our path, clogging our wheels and breaking our order of march. And a preliminary question must be, Have we the courage to be iconoclasts in our own homes? Can we give such fealty to Truth and Candor and Right that we can lop off and pull down and dig out as those three stern fates may command us? For we cannot but have some deep-rooted and overgrown ideas to prune to truer proportions before we can read and write abreast of the pioneers of thought. I shall mention one or two.

The plantation idea is a semi-barbarism. It is the idea of the old South with merely the substitution of a Negro tenantry for Negro slaves. It is a pathetic and senile sentiment for the maintenance of a landed aristocracy in a country and in times that have outgrown that formidable error in political economy; an idea branded as an error as far back as the days of Moses, and that shows itself a lamentable evil today—I will not say in unhappy Ireland, but in happy England. The landlord—the landlord, in all ages, has been a burden to the land wherever he has lorded it. I pray you, let your endeavor be to set the sentiment and the conviction of your community emphatically against it. Whoever is able to be a landlord is able to be something more valuable to himself and to the masses less fortunate than he. Landlordism kept the South poor one century, and just as sure as it survives it will keep her poor another.

Another idea which must be sloughed away is that of caste. Why?—tell us why we should not send that unmanly and inhuman tyranny back to India and Africa? Why should not that which we still call the "Southern mind" rise to the moral dignity of distinguishing between man and man by such rules only as bear the strain of clear, conscientious logic? Why should we, who are given minds, still expatiate upon our *instincts* and go on holding our unproven *therefores* at the expense of our fellow creatures and in the face of the world's best enlightenment? Is that the "Southern mind"? Is the "Southern" instinct not cunning enough to snuff out the stupid wickedness of exalting and abusing our fellow humans class by class and race by race instead of man by man? God forbid! But if so, let us give instinct to the brutes and be guided henceforth by reason.

I know that more or less the tendency to establish and maintain caste obtains everywhere; and I will call your attention to the fact that the supremacy of class over class is one of the chief blemishes in the social organism of a superb people on whose order of society I find we of the South in particular are prone to lavish our admiration; I mean the British people. It is very human for the stronger classes of society to assume that the classes below should allow the stronger to think and act for them. As truth loves to present herself hooded in the cloak of paradox, so tyranny, in the mask of protection. The

challenge is often heard among us, albeit we are Americans,
"Who—if not the intelligent—are to rule?" I will answer you in
one word, and I adjure you as American readers and writers,
build it into your convictions: *All!* All are to rule. That order
of society is best, and that order of society only is American,
where the intelligent are so hemmed in with the unintelligent
that they cannot afford to let them rest in their unintelligence.
"Not fit for self-government?" replied a living American writer
to a despondent Spanish patriot. "No people is fit for any
other."

We cannot suppose that our community could hold a servile
race in domestic subjection for a century and a half without
producing a more lasting effect on the master race than a few
subsequent years of partial change could dissipate. The statement is almost axiomatic. Hence search should be made for
the flaws that must in that long period have crept into many
of our views and into our temper. And who should we expect
to do this? Certainly not outsiders. Certainly ourselves. And
who among ourselves if not those who expect to be readers
and especially those whose ambition prompts them to be
writers. You know how large a part of the governing of a people consists in the directing of its thought. What says the old
writer so often quoted?

"I knew a very wise man," he says, "that believed that, if
a man were permitted to make all the ballads, he need not
care who should make the laws of a nation."

We want, if there is to be none in our nation that is not
self-governed, to write as well as read our share of the nation's
literature. And if we are to do this we can avoid final failure
only by writing either abreast or ahead of the latest knowledge
of truth and beauty that the world possesses. And to do this
we must write from thorough and correct convictions, from
right hearts and in loving and lovable spirits. . . .

The Due Restraints
and Liberties
of Literature

[From a commencement address at the University of Louisiana, June 15, 1883.

Speaking in his home city, Cable picked up the subject where he had left off a year earlier and asked that authors be allowed the freedom he thought essential in the handling of local and sectional matters.

This address was printed separately by the University of Louisiana, New Orleans, 1883.]

The Due Restraints and Liberties
of Literature

. . . Who can say but there may be one, if no more, among our young student friends, waiting to ask us, with an equally noble concern, what exactions and limitations we are going to lay upon his pen when the electric spark of inspiration poises on its point, and what liberties and rewards we are going to accord him? What would our answer be to such an inquiry? . . .

Are we going to demand, he asks, that he shall bow down to our crotchets and whims? Admitted, he says, that the old, open, and shameless cringing to individual generalissimos of patronage is no longer required or tolerated, will he not be expected to practice certain amiable and cowardly oversights and silences in order to smooth the frowns of sections and parties and pacify the autocratic voice of ruling classes and established ideas? . . .

We need, therefore, to assure the young man whose foot points outward on the threshold of this university today, and who feels himself a possible literary producer, that, from us at least, he shall not encounter the oppression of these unjust demands; but that our exactions and limitations shall be such only as are consistent with the perfection of candor and good faith in him and us. . . .

Literature, even from the pen of the poet or the fictionist, is almost a religion. It must be free; free to study principles for themselves; to present and defend truth; to assert rights; to dissolve and sublimate and re-crystallize all that is best of old or new; to rectify thoughts, morals, manners, society, even though it shake the established order of things like an earthquake.

Friends, I ask your leave to say that we offer *these* liberties to literary utterance among us. That we lay no other exactions, no other limitations upon the literary ambition of our academic youth than are in these conditions. That we throw our society, our section, our institutions, ourselves wide open to their criticism and correction, reserving the right to resent only what we can refute.

. . . They will be faithful and bold, while they are still reverential, filial. They will remember, moreover, that literature, like charity, "begins at home"; will write about their own state, their own town, possibly even their own little neighborhoods; but they will never conceive of their audience as less than their entire nation, and will write remembering that in these days the whole enlightened world is one vast whispering gallery. The stroke of their pen must now and then cross out some notion that some one loves better than truth, and they may from certain quarters even be denounced as turbulent overturners of order, as mischievous innovators and disturbers

of the peace; but their only reply will be the gentle retort of
the great Bacon: "a stubborn retention of customs is a turbulent thing, no less than the introduction of new"; and they
will rest in quiet assurance that, sooner or later, society will
pay into their bosom its gratitude, its love, and its honors.

The Freedman's
Case in Equity

[An address delivered before the American Social Science Association at Saratoga, New York, September 11, 1884; adapted from a commencement address at the University of Alabama on June 18, 1884.

Cable's work for prison reform had begun with his term on a grand jury in 1881. By initiating and directing citizens' organizations in New Orleans, he had secured gratifying results in the prisons and asylums and orphanages, and he had been applauded widely for his work. The thoroughness which was habitual with him had led him to study reports from the state penitentiaries, and thus it was that he encountered the convict leases then in force in twelve Southern states. Invited to address the National Conference of Charities and Correction on the subject, he wrote "The Convict Lease System in the Southern States" for delivery at Louisville on September 26, 1883. The address was published in the *Century Magazine*, February 1884, and in *The Silent South*, 1885.

Of the convict lease paper Cable wrote afterward, "Nothing I have ever written has gained me so many friends among the best people of the South." A few sentences from Henry Watterson's newspaper, the Louisville *Courier-Journal*, will suggest something of Cable's literary reputation at the time and also the approval given his address:

"Mr. Cable is the ablest writer the South has had since Poe, and ranks as a novelist with Howells and James. . . . He reads unusually well, and throws a fire and intensity into his reading that one would hardly think him capable of from his slender frame. His paper lasted two hours, and it is safe to say that during that time not a man but kept his eyes fixed on the speaker. It is needless to say that the Southern author received an ovation. He was applauded time and again, and at the conclusion of the reading there was a storm of hand-clapping."

With this paper Cable had stepped from the local to the national scene as a reformer, respected for his motives and admired for his effectiveness.

"The Convict Lease System in the Southern States" was the logical climax to Cable's work for prison reform. Similarly, he had reached the point in 1884 when it was appropriate, if not indeed necessary, for him to take up the question of Negro rights. Since becoming convinced that the Civil War had been in fact a war over slavery and that the usual defenses of slavery, the Biblical defense along with the others, were shoddy at best, he had little patience with beliefs and institutions founded on assumptions of caste and race superiority. If the Negro had been the victim of a wrong centuries old, then were not the whites, he asked, morally obligated to make restitution, even at great cost? Thus when he found what to him was evidence that the Freedman did not receive justice in the courts of law, he was ready to appeal the case to the public conscience.

"The Freedman's Case in Equity" was written with no less care to the implications than to the facts of the case. Holding to calm and reasoned argument, the author made it plain that he was himself a Southerner and that he saw the problem as one to be worked out in the South. His hope, it is clear, was to raise the ethical questions and push them forward for discussion, hoping to avoid inciting the kind of resentment which would be sure to follow a more specific recital of grievances. He had profited from his experiences in swaying public opinion to the cause of reform. This essay reflected neither sharp indignation such as that of the newspaper letters of 1875 nor the particular indictments of the address at the University of

Mississippi, but it brought into direct focus several ironies and inconsistencies inherent in the Southern attitude toward race, such as the acceptance of Negroes in public accommodations if they came as servants and not as free citizens. Such observations as this punctuated the broader generalizing and theorizing of the essay, serving as barbs to make sure that it would not be piously approved and then ignored, as might otherwise have been its fate.

This essay was published in the *Century Magazine,* January 1885, and in *The Silent South.*]

The Freedman's Case in Equity

I. THE NATION'S ATTITUDE

The greatest social problem before the American people today is, as it has been for a hundred years, the presence among us of the Negro.

No comparable entanglement was ever drawn round itself by any other modern nation with so serene a disregard of its ultimate issue, or with a more distinct national responsibility. The African slave was brought here by cruel force, and with everybody's consent except his own. Everywhere the practice was favored as a measure of common aggrandizement. When a few men and women protested, they were mobbed in the public interest, with the public consent. There rests, therefore, a moral responsibility on the whole nation never to lose sight of the results of African-American slavery until they cease to work mischief and injustice.

It is true these responsibilities may not fall everywhere with the same weight; but they are nowhere entirely removed. The original seed of trouble was sown with the full knowledge and consent of the nation. The nation was to blame; and so long as evils spring from it, their correction must be the nation's duty.

The late Southern slave has within two decades risen from slavery to freedom, from freedom to citizenship, passed on into political ascendency, and fallen again from that eminence. The amended Constitution holds him up in his new political rights as well as a mere constitution can. On the other hand, certain enactments of Congress, trying to reach further, have lately been made void by the highest court of the nation. And another thing has happened. The popular mind in the old free states, weary of strife at arm's length, bewildered by its complications, vexed by many a blunder, eager to turn to the cure of other evils, and even tinctured by that race feeling whose grosser excesses it would so gladly see suppressed, has retreated from its uncomfortable dictational attitude and thrown the whole matter over to the states of the South. Here it rests, no longer a main party issue, but a group of questions which are to be settled by each of these states separately in the light of simple equity and morals, and which the genius of American government is at least loath to force upon them from beyond their borders. Thus the whole question, become secondary in party contest, has yet reached a period of supreme importance.

II. OLD SOUTH AND NEW

Before slavery ever became a grave question in the nation's politics—when it seemed each state's private affair, developing unmolested—it had two different fates in two different parts of the country. In one, treated as a question of public equity, it withered away. In the other, overlooked in that aspect, it petrified and became the cornerstone of the whole social structure; and when men sought its overthrow as a national evil, it first brought war upon the land, and then grafted into the citizenship of one of the most intelligent nations in the world six millions of people from one of the most debased races on the globe.

And now this painful and wearisome question, sown in the

African slave trade, reaped in our Civil War, and garnered in the national adoption of millions of an inferior race, is drawing near a second seedtime. For this is what the impatient proposal to make it a dead and buried issue really means. It means to re-commit it to the silence and concealment of the covered fur-row. Beyond that incubative retirement no suppressed moral question can be pushed; but all such questions, ignored in the domain of private morals, spring up and expand once more into questions of public equity; neglected as matters of public equity, they blossom into questions of national interest; and, despised in that guise, presently yield the red fruits of revolution.

This question must never again bear that fruit. There must arise, nay, there has arisen, in the South itself a desire to see established the equities of the issue; to make it no longer a question of endurance between one group of states and another, but between the moral debris of an exploded evil and the duty, necessity, and value of planting society firmly upon universal justice and equity. This, and this only, can give the matter final burial. True, it is still a question between states; but only secondarily, as something formerly participated in, or as it concerns every householder to know that what is being built against his house is built by level and plummet. It is the interest of the Southern states first, and *consequently* of the whole land, to discover clearly these equities and the errors that are being committed against them.

If we take up this task, the difficulties of the situation are plain. We have, first, a revision of Southern state laws which has forced into them the recognition of certain human rights discordant with the sentiments of those who have always called themselves the community; second, the removal of the entire political machinery by which this forcing process was effected; and, third, these revisions left to be interpreted and applied under the domination of these antagonistic sentiments. These being the three terms of the problem, one of three things must result. There will arise a system of vicious evasions eventually

ruinous to public and private morals and liberty, or there will
be a candid reconsideration of the sentiments hostile to these
enactments, or else there will be a division, some taking one
course and some the other.

This is what we should look for from our knowledge of men
and history; and this is what we find. The revised laws, only
where they could not be evaded, have met that reluctant or
simulated acceptance of their narrowest letter which might
have been expected—a virtual suffocation of those principles
of human equity which the unwelcome decrees do little more
than shadow forth. But in different regions this attitude has
been made in very different degrees of emphasis. In some the
new principles have grown, or are growing, into the popular
conviction, and the opposing sentiments are correspondingly
dying out. There are even some districts where they have received much practical acceptance. While, again, other limited
sections lean almost wholly toward the old sentiments; an easy
choice, since it is the conservative, the unyielding attitude,
whose strength is in the absence of intellectual and moral
debate.

Now, what are the gains, what the losses of these diverse
attitudes? Surely these are urgent questions to any one in our
country who believes it is always a losing business to be in
the wrong. Particularly in the South, where each step in this
affair is an unprecedented experience, it will be folly if each
region, small or large, does not study the experiences of all
the rest. And yet this, alone, would be superficial; we would
still need to do more. We need to go back to the roots of
things and study closely, analytically, the origin, the present
foundation, the rationality, the rightness of those sentiments
surviving in us which prompt an attitude qualifying in any
way peculiarly the black man's liberty among us. Such a treatment will be less abundant in incident, less picturesque; but
it will be more thorough.

III. THE ROOTS OF THE QUESTION

First, then, what are these sentiments? Foremost among them stands the idea that he is of necessity an alien. He was brought to our shores a naked, brutish, unclean, captive, pagan savage,[1] to be and remain a kind of connecting link between man and the beasts of burden. The great changes to result from his contact with a superb race of masters were not taken into account. As a social factor he was intended to be as purely zero as the brute at the other end of his plowline. The occasional mingling of his blood with that of the white man worked no change in the sentiment; one, two, four, eight multiplied upon or divided into zero still gave zero for the result. Generations of American nativity made no difference; his children and children's children were born in sight of our door, yet the old notion held fast. He increased to vast numbers, but it never wavered. He accepted our dress, language, religion, all the fundamentals of our civilization, and became forever expatriated from his own land; still he remained, to us, an alien. Our sentiment went blind. It did not see that gradually, here by force and there by choice, he was fulfilling a host of conditions that earned at least a solemn moral right to that naturalization which no one at first had dreamed of giving him. Frequently he even bought back the freedom of which he had been robbed, became a taxpayer, and at times an educator of his children at his own expense; but the old idea of alienism passed laws to banish him, his wife, and children by thousands from the state, and threw him into loathsome jails as a common felon for returning to his native land.[2]

It will be wise to remember that these were the acts of an enlightened, God-fearing people, the great mass of whom have passed beyond all earthly accountability. They were our fa-

[1] Sometimes he was not a mere savage but a trading, smithing, weaving, town-building, crop-raising barbarian.
[2] Notably in Louisiana in 1810 and subsequently.

thers. I am the son and grandson of slaveholders. These were their faults; posterity will discover ours; but these things must be frankly, fearlessly taken into account if we are ever to understand the true interests of our peculiar state of society.

Why, then, did this notion, that the man of color must always remain an alien, stand so unshaken? We may readily recall how, under ancient systems, he rose, not only to high privileges, but often to public station and power. Singularly, with us the trouble lay in a modern principle of liberty. The whole idea of American government rested on all men's equal, inalienable right to secure their life, liberty, and the pursuit of happiness by governments founded in their own consent. Hence, our Southern forefathers, shedding their blood, or ready to shed it, for this principle, yet proposing in equal good conscience to continue holding the American black man and mulatto and quadroon in slavery, had to anchor that conscience, their conduct, and their laws in the conviction that the man of African tincture was, not by his master's arbitrary assertion merely, but by nature and unalterably, an alien. If that hold should break, one single wave of irresistible inference would lift our whole Southern social fabric and dash it upon the rocks of Negro emancipation and enfranchisement. How was it made secure? Not by books, though they were written among us from every possible point of view, but, with the mass of our slaveowners, by the calm hypothesis of a positive, intuitive knowledge. To them the statement was an axiom. They abandoned the methods of moral and intellectual reasoning and fell back upon this assumption of a God-given instinct, nobler than reason, and which it was an insult to a free man to ask him to prove on logical grounds.

Yet it was found not enough. The slave multiplied. Slavery was a dangerous institution. Few in the South today have any just idea how often the slave plotted for his freedom. Our Southern ancestors were a noble, manly people, springing from some of the most highly intelligent, aspiring, upright, and refined nations of the modern world; from the Huguenot, the

French chevalier, the Old Englander, the New Englander. Their acts were not always right; whose are? But for their peace of mind they had to believe them so. They therefore spoke much of the Negro's contentment with that servile condition for which nature had designed him. Yet there was no escaping the knowledge that we dared not trust the slave caste with any power that could be withheld from them. So the perpetual alien was made also a perpetual menial, and the belief became fixed that this, too, was nature's decree, not ours.

Thus we stood at the close of the Civil War. There were always a few Southerners who did not justify slavery, and many who cared nothing whether it was just or not. But what we have described was the general sentiment of good Southern people. There was one modifying sentiment. It related to the slave's spiritual interests. Thousands of pious masters and mistresses flatly broke the shameful laws that stood between their slaves and the Bible. Slavery was right; but religion, they held, was for the alien and menial as well as for the citizen and master. They could be alien and citizen, menial and master, in church as well as out; and they were.

Yet over against this lay another root of today's difficulties. This perpetuation of the alien, menial relation tended to perpetuate the vices that naturally cling to servility, dense ignorance, and a hopeless separation from true liberty; and as we could not find it in our minds to blame slavery with this perpetuation, we could only assume as a further axiom that there was, by nature, a disqualifying moral taint in every drop of Negro blood. The testimony of an Irish, German, Italian, French, or Spanish beggar in a court of justice was taken on its merits; but the colored man's was excluded by law wherever it weighed against a white man. The colored man was a prejudged culprit. The discipline of the plantation required that the difference between master and slave be never lost sight of by either. It made our master caste a solid mass, and fixed a common masterhood and subserviency between the ruling and

the serving race.[3] Every one of us grew up in the idea that
he had, by birth and race, certain broad powers of police over
any and every person of color.

All at once the tempest of war snapped off at the ground
every one of these arbitrary relations, without removing a single one of the sentiments in which they stood rooted. Then,
to fortify the Freedman in the tenure of his new rights, he was
given the ballot. Before this grim fact the notion of alienism,
had it been standing alone, might have given way. The idea
that slavery was right did begin to crumble almost at once.
"As for slavery," said an old Creole sugar planter and former
slaveowner to me, "it was damnable." The revelation came
like a sudden burst of light. It is one of the South's noblest
poets who has but just said:

> I am a Southerner;
> I love the South; I dared for her
> To fight from Lookout to the sea,
> With her proud banner over me:
> But from my lips thanksgiving broke,
> As God in battle-thunder spoke,
> And that Black Idol, breeding drouth
> And dearth of human sympathy
> Throughout the sweet and sensuous South,
> Was, with its chains and human yoke,
> Blown hellward from the cannon's mouth,
> While Freedom cheered behind the smoke![4]

IV. WHAT THE WAR LEFT

With like readiness might the old alien relation have given
way if we could only, while letting that pass, have held fast

[3] The old Louisiana Black Code says, "That free people of color
ought never to . . . presume to conceive themselves equal to the
white; but, on the contrary, that they ought to yield to them in
every occasion, and never speak or answer to them but with respect,
under the penalty of imprisonment according to the nature of the
offense." (Section 21, p. 164.)

[4] Maurice Thompson, in the *Independent*.

by the other old ideas. But they were all bound together. See
our embarrassment. For more than a hundred years we had
made these sentiments the absolute essentials to our self-
respect. And yet if we clung to them, how could we meet the
Freedman on equal terms in the political field? Even to lead
would not compensate us; for the fundamental profession of
American politics is that the leader is servant to his followers.
It was too much. The ex-master and ex-slave—the quarterdeck
and the forecastle, as it were—could not come together. But
neither could the American mind tolerate a continuance of
martial law. The agonies of Reconstruction followed.

The vote, after all, was a secondary point, and the robbery
and bribery on one side, and whipping and killing on the other
were but huge accidents of the situation. The two main questions were really these: on the Freedman's side, how to establish republican state government under the same recognition of his rights that the rest of Christendom accorded him;
and on the former master's side, how to get back to the old
semblance of republican state government, and—allowing that
the Freedman was *de facto* a voter—still to maintain a purely
arbitrary superiority of all whites over all blacks, and a purely
arbitrary equality of all blacks among themselves as an alien,
menial, and dangerous class.

Exceptionally here and there some one in the master caste
did throw off the old and accept the new ideas, and, if he
would allow it, was instantly claimed as a leader by the newly
liberated thousands around him. But just as promptly the old
master race branded him also an alien reprobate, and in ninety-
nine cases out of a hundred, if he had not already done so,
he soon began to confirm by his actions the brand on his cheek.
However, we need give no history here of the dreadful episode
of Reconstruction. Under an experimental truce its issues
rest today upon the pledge of the wiser leaders of the master
class: Let us but remove the hireling demagogue, and we will
see to it that the Freedman is accorded a practical, complete,
and cordial recognition of his equality with the white man be-

fore the law. As far as there has been any understanding at
all, it is not that the originally desired ends of Reconstruction
have been abandoned, but that the men of North and South
have agreed upon a new, gentle, and peaceable method for
reaching them; that, without change as to the ends in view,
compulsory Reconstruction has been set aside and a voluntary
Reconstruction is on trial.

It is the fashion to say we paused to let the "feelings engendered by the war" pass away, and that they are passing.
But let not these truths lead us into error. The sentiments we
have been analyzing, and upon which we saw the old compulsory Reconstruction go hard aground—these are not the
"feelings engendered by the war." We must disentangle them
from the "feelings engendered by the war," and by Reconstruction. They are older than either. But for them slavery
would have perished of itself, and emancipation and Reconstruction been peaceful revolutions.

Indeed, as between master and slave, the "feelings engendered by the war," are too trivial, or at least were too short-
lived, to demand our present notice. One relation and feeling
the war destroyed: the patriarchal tie and its often really tender and benevolent sentiment of dependence and protection.
When the slave became a Freedman, the sentiment of alienism
became for the first time complete. The abandonment of this
relation was not one-sided; the slave, even before the master,
renounced it. Countless times, since Reconstruction began, the
master has tried, in what he believed to be everybody's interest, to play on that old sentiment. But he found it a harp
without strings. The Freedman could not formulate, but he
could see, all our old ideas of autocracy and subserviency, of
master and menial, of an arbitrarily fixed class to guide and
rule, and another to be guided and ruled. He rejected the over-
ture. The old master, his well-meant condescensions slighted,
turned away estranged, and justified himself in passively withholding that simpler protection without patronage which any
one American citizen, however exalted, owes to any other,

however humble. Could the Freedman in the bitterest of those
days have consented to throw himself upon just that one old
relation, he could have found a physical security for himself
and his house such as could not, after years of effort, be given
him by constitutional amendments, Congress, United States
marshals, regiments of regulars, and ships of war. But he could
not; the very nobility of the civilization that had held him in
slavery had made him too much a man to go back to that
shelter; and by his manly neglect to do so he has proved to
us who once ruled over him that, be his relative standing
among the races of men what it may, he is worthy to be free.

V. FREED—NOT FREE

To be a free man is his still distant goal. Twice he has been
a Freedman. In the days of compulsory Reconstruction he was
freed in the presence of his master by that master's victorious
foe. In these days of voluntary Reconstruction he is virtually
freed by the consent of his master, but the master retaining
the exclusive right to define the bounds of his freedom. Many
everywhere have taken up the idea that this state of affairs
is the end to be desired and the end actually sought in Reconstruction as handed over to the states. I do not charge such
folly to the best intelligence of any American community; but
I cannot ignore my own knowledge that the average thought
of some regions rises to no better idea of the issue. The belief
is all too common that the nation, having aimed at a wrong
result and missed, has left us of the Southern states to get now
such other result as we think best. I say this belief is not universal. There are those among us who see that America has
no room for a state of society which makes its lower classes
harmless by abridging their liberties, or, as one of the favored
class lately said to me, has "got 'em so they don't give no
trouble." There is a growing number who see that the one
thing we cannot afford to tolerate at large is a class of people
less than citizens; and that every interest in the land demands

that the Freedman be free to become in all things, as far as
his own personal gifts will lift and sustain him, the same sort
of American citizen he would be if, with the same intellectual
and moral caliber, he were white.

Thus we reach the ultimate question of fact. Are the Freedman's liberties suffering any real abridgment? The answer is
easy. The letter of the laws, with a few exceptions, recognizes
him as entitled to every right of an American citizen; and to
some it may seem unimportant that there is scarcely one public relation of life in the South where he is not arbitrarily and
unlawfully compelled to hold toward the white man the attitude of an alien, a menial, and a probable reprobate, by reason of his race and color. One of the marvels of future history
will be that it was counted a small matter, by a majority of
our nation, for six millions of people within it, made by its
own decree a component part of it, to be subjected to a system
of oppression so rank that nothing could make it seem small
except the fact that they had already been ground under it
for a century and a half.

Examine it. It proffers to the Freedman a certain security
of life and property, and then holds the respect of the community, that dearest of earthly boons, beyond his attainment.
It gives him certain guarantees against thieves and robbers,
and then holds him under the unearned contumely of the mass
of good men and women. It acknowledges in constitutions and
statutes his title to an American's freedom and aspirations, and
then in daily practice heaps upon him in every public place
the most odious distinctions, without giving ear to the hum-
blest plea concerning mental or moral character. It spurns his
ambition, tramples upon his languishing self-respect, and indignantly refuses to let him either buy with money, or earn
by any excellence of inner life or outward behavior, the most
momentary immunity from these public indignities even for
his wife and daughters. Need we cram these pages with facts
in evidence, as if these were charges denied and requiring to

be proven? They are simply the present avowed and defended state of affairs peeled of its exteriors.

Nothing but the habit, generations old, of enduring it could make it endurable by men not in actual slavery. Were we whites of the South to remain every way as we are, and our six million blacks to give place to any sort of whites exactly their equals, man for man, in mind, morals, and wealth, provided only that they had tasted two years of American freedom, and were this same system of tyrannies attempted upon them, there would be as bloody an uprising as this continent has ever seen. We can say this quietly. There is not a scruple's weight of present danger. These six million Freedmen are dominated by nine million whites immeasurably stronger than they, backed by the virtual consent of thirty-odd millions more. Indeed, nothing but the habit of oppression could make such oppression possible to a people of the intelligence and virtue of our Southern whites, and the invitation to practice it on millions of any other than the children of their former slaves would be spurned with a noble indignation.

Suppose, for a moment, the tables turned. Suppose the courts of our Southern states, while changing no laws requiring the impaneling of jurymen without distinction as to race, etc., should suddenly begin to draw their thousands of jurymen all black, and well-nigh every one of them counting, not only himself, but all his race, better than any white man. Assuming that their average of intelligence and morals should be not below that of jurymen as now drawn, would a white man, for all that, choose to be tried in one of those courts? Would he suspect nothing? Could one persuade him that his chances of even justice were all they should be, or all they would be were the court not evading the law in order to sustain an outrageous distinction against him because of the accidents of his birth? Yet only read white man for black man, and black man for white man, and that—I speak as an eyewitness—has been the practice for years, and is still so today;

an actual emasculation, in the case of six million people both as plaintiff and defendant, of the right of trial by jury.

In this and other practices the outrage falls upon the Freedman. Does it stop there? Far from it. It is the first premise of American principles that whatever elevates the lower stratum of the people lifts all the rest, and whatever holds it down holds all down. For twenty years, therefore, the nation has been working to elevate the Freedman. It counts this one of the great necessities of the hour. It has poured out its wealth publicly and privately for this purpose. It is confidently hoped that it will soon bestow a royal gift of millions for the reduction of the illiteracy so largely shared by the blacks. Our Southern states are, and for twenty years have been, taxing themselves for the same end. The private charities alone of the other states have given twenty millions in the same good cause. Their colored seminaries, colleges, and normal schools dot our whole Southern country, and furnish our public colored schools with a large part of their teachers. All this and much more has been or is being done in order that, for the good of himself and everybody else in the land, the colored man may be elevated as quickly as possible from all the debasements of slavery and semi-slavery to the full stature and integrity of citizenship. And it is in the face of all this that the adherent of the old regime stands in the way to every public privilege and place—steamer landing, railway platform, theater, concert hall, art display, public library, public school, courthouse, church, everything—flourishing the hot branding iron of ignominious distinctions. He forbids the Freedman to go into the water until *he* is satisfied that he knows how to swim and, for fear he should learn, hangs millstones about his neck. This is what we are told is a small matter that will settle itself. Yes, like a roosting curse, until the outraged intelligence of the South lifts its indignant protest against this stupid firing into our own ranks.

VI. ITS DAILY WORKINGS

I say the outraged intelligence of the South; for there are
thousands of Southern-born white men and women, in the
minority in all these places—in churches, courts, schools, libraries, theaters, concert halls, and on steamers and railway
carriages—who see the wrong and folly of these things, silently blush for them, and withhold their open protests only
because their belief is unfortunately stronger in the futility
of their counsel than in the power of a just cause. I do not
justify their silence; but I affirm their sincerity and their goodly
numbers. Of late years, when condemning these evils from the
platform in Southern towns, I have repeatedly found that those
who I had earlier been told were the men and women in whom
the community placed most confidence and pride—they were
the ones who, when I had spoken, came forward with warmest
hand grasps and expressions of thanks, and pointedly and
cordially justified my every utterance. And were they the
young South? Not by half. The graybeards of the old times
have always been among them, saying in effect, not by any
means as converts, but as fellow discoverers, "Whereas we
were blind, now we see."

Another sort among our good Southern people make a similar but feeble admission, but with the timeworn proviso that
expediency makes a more imperative demand than law, justice,
or logic, and demands the preservation of the old order. Some-
body must be outraged, it seems; and if not the Freedman,
then it must be a highly refined and enlightened race of people
constantly offended and grossly discommoded, if not imposed
upon, by a horde of tatterdemalions, male and female, crowding into a participation in their reserved privileges. Now look
at this plea. It is simply saying in another way that though
the Southern whites far outnumber the blacks, and though we
hold every element of power in greater degree than the blacks,
and though the larger part of us claim to be sealed by nature

as an exclusive upper class, and though we have the courts completely in our own hands, with the police on our right and the prisons on our left, and though we justly claim to be an intrepid people, and though we have a superb military experience, with ninety-nine hundredths of all the military equipment and no scarcity of all the accessories, yet with all these facts behind us we cannot make and enforce that intelligent and approximately just assortment of persons in public places and conveyances on the merits of exterior decency that is made in all other enlightened lands. On such a plea are made a distinction and separation that not only are crude, invidious, humiliating, and tyrannous, but which do not reach their ostensible end or come near it; and all that saves such a plea from being a confession of driveling imbecility is its utter speciousness. It is advanced sincerely; and yet nothing is easier to show than that these distinctions on the line of color are really made not from any necessity, but simply for their own sake—to preserve the old arbitrary supremacy of the master class over the menial without regard to the decency or indecency of appearance or manners in either the white individual or the colored.

See its everyday working. Any colored man gains unquestioned admission into innumerable places the moment he appears as the menial attendant of some white person, where he could not cross the threshold in his own right as well-dressed and well-behaved master of himself. The contrast is even greater in the case of colored women. There could not be a system which when put into practice would more offensively condemn itself. It does more: it actually creates the confusion it pretends to prevent. It blunts the sensibilities of the ruling class themselves. It waives all strict demand for painstaking in either manners or dress of either master or menial, and, for one result, makes the average Southern railway coach more uncomfortable than the average of railway coaches elsewhere. It prompts the average Southern white passenger to find less offense in the presence of a profane, boisterous, or unclean

white person than in that of a quiet, well-behaved colored man
or woman attempting to travel on an equal footing with him
without a white master or mistress. The holders of the old sentiments hold the opposite choice in scorn. It is only when we
go on to say that there are regions where the riotous expulsion
of a decent and peaceable colored person is preferred to his
inoffensive company that it may seem necessary to bring in
evidence. And yet here again it is prima-facie evidence; for
the following extract was printed in the Selma (Alabama)
Times not six months ago,[5] and not as a complaint, but as a
boast:

"A few days since, a Negro minister, of this city, boarded
the eastbound passenger train on the E. T., V. & G. Railway
and took a seat in the coach occupied by white passengers.
Some of the passengers complained to the conductor and
brakemen, and expressed considerable dissatisfaction that they
were forced to ride alongside of a Negro. The railroad officials
informed the complainants that they were not authorized to
force the colored passenger into the coach set apart for the
Negroes, and they would lay themselves liable should they do
so. The white passengers then took the matter in their own
hands and ordered the ebony-hued minister to take a seat in
the next coach. He positively refused to obey orders, where-
upon the white men gave him a sound flogging and forced
him to a seat among his own color and equals. We learned
yesterday that the vanquished preacher was unable to fill his
pulpit on account of the severe chastisement inflicted upon
him. Now [says the delighted editor] the query that puzzles
is, 'Who did the flogging?'"

And as good an answer as we can give is that likely enough
they were some of the men for whom the whole South has
come to a halt to let them get over the "feelings engendered
by the war." Must such men, such acts, such sentiments stand
alone to represent us of the South before an enlightened world?
No. I say, as a citizen of an extreme Southern state, a native of

5 In the summer of 1884.

Louisiana, an ex-Confederate soldier, and a lover of my home, my city, and my state, as well as of my country, that this is not the best sentiment in the South, nor the sentiment of her best intelligence; and that it would not ride up and down that beautiful land dominating and domineering were it not for its tremendous power as the *traditional* sentiment of a conservative people. But is not silent endurance criminal? I cannot but repeat my own words, spoken near the scene and about the time of this event. Speech may be silvern and silence golden; but if a lump of gold is only big enough, it can drag us to the bottom of the sea and hold us there while all the world sails over us.

The laws passed in the days of compulsory Reconstruction requiring "equal accommodations," etc., for colored and white persons were Freedmen's follies. On their face they defeated their ends; for even in theory they at once reduced to half all opportunity for those more reasonable and mutually agreeable self-assortments which public assemblages and groups of passengers find it best to make in all other enlightened countries, making them on the score of conduct, dress, and price. They also led the whites to overlook what they would have seen instantly had these invidious distinctions been made against themselves: that their offense does not vanish at the guarantee against the loss of physical comforts. But we made, and are still making, a mistake beyond even this. For years many of us have carelessly taken for granted that these laws were being carried out in some shape that removed all just ground of complaint. It is common to say, "We allow the man of color to go and come at will, only let him sit apart in a place marked off for him." But marked off how? So as to mark him instantly as a menial. Not by railings and partitions merely, which, raised against any other class in the United States with the same invidious intent, would be kicked down as fast as put up, but by giving him besides, in every instance and without recourse, the most uncomfortable, uncleanest, and unsafest place; and the unsafety, uncleanness, and discomfort of most of these places are a shame to any community pretending to practice public justice. If any one can think the Freedman does not feel the indignities thus heaped upon him, let him take up any paper printed for colored men's patronage, or ask any colored man of known courageous utterance. Hear them:

"We ask not Congress, nor the Legislature, nor any other power, to remedy these evils, but we ask the people among whom we live. Those who *can* remedy them if they *will*. Those who have a high sense of honor and a deep moral feeling. Those who have one vestige of human sympathy left. . . . Those are the ones we ask to protect us in our weakness and ill-treatments. . . . As soon as the colored man is treated by the white man as a *man*, that harmony and pleasant feeling which should characterize all races which dwell together shall be the bond of peace between them."

Surely their evidence is good enough to prove their own feelings. We need not lean upon it here for anything else. I shall not bring forward a single statement of fact from them or any of their white friends who, as teachers and missionaries, share many of their humiliations, though my desk is covered with them. But I beg to make the same citation from my own experience that I made last June[6] in the far South. It was this: One hot night in September of last year[7] I was traveling by rail in the state of Alabama. At rather late bedtime there came aboard the train a young mother and her little daughter of three or four years. They were neatly and tastefully dressed in cool, fresh muslins, and as the train went on its way they sat together very still and quiet. At the next station there came aboard a most melancholy and revolting company. In filthy rags, with vile odors and the clanking of shackles and chains, nine penitentiary convicts chained to one chain, and ten more chained to another, dragged laboriously into the compartment of the car where in one corner sat this mother and child, and

[6] 1884.
[7] 1883.

packed it full, and the train moved on. The keeper of the convicts told me he should take them in that car two hundred miles that night. They were going to the mines. My seat was not in that car, and I staid in it but a moment. It stank insufferably. I returned to my own place in the coach behind, where there was, and had all the time been, plenty of room. But the mother and child sat on in silence in that foul hole, the conductor having distinctly refused them admission elsewhere because they were of African blood, and not because the mother was, but because she was *not*, engaged at the moment in menial service. Had the child been white, and the mother not its natural but its hired guardian, she could have sat anywhere in the train, and no one would have ventured to object, even had she been as black as the mouth of the coalpit to which her loathsome fellow passengers were being carried in chains.

Such is the incident as I saw it. But the illustration would be incomplete here were I not allowed to add the comments I made upon it when in June last I recounted it, and to state the two opposite tempers in which my words were received. I said: "These are the facts. And yet you know and I know we belong to communities that, after years of hoping for, are at last taking comfort in the assurance of the nation's highest courts that no law can reach and stop this shameful foul play until we choose to enact a law to that end ourselves. And now the East and North and West of our great and prosperous and happy country, and the rest of the civilized world, as far as it knows our case, are standing and waiting to see what we will write upon the white page of today's and tomorrow's history, now that we are simply on our honor and on the mettle of our far and peculiarly famed Southern instinct. How long, then, shall we stand off from such ringing moral questions as these on the flimsy plea that they have a political value, and, scrutinizing the Constitution, keep saying, 'Is it so nominated in the bond? I cannot find it; 'tis not in the bond.'"

With the temper that promptly resented these words

through many newspapers of the neighboring regions there can be no propriety in wrangling. When regions so estranged from the world's thought carry their resentment no further than a little harmless invective, it is but fair to welcome it as a sign of progress. If communities nearer the great centers of thought grow impatient with *them,* how shall we resent the impatience of these remoter ones when their oldest traditions are, as it seems to them, ruthlessly assailed? There is but one right thing to do: it is to pour in upon them our reiterations of the truth without malice and without stint.

But I have a much better word to say. It is for those who, not voiced by the newspapers around them, showed both then and constantly afterward in public and private during my two days' subsequent travel and sojourn in the region, by their cordial, frequent, specific approval of my words, that a better intelligence is longing to see the evils of the old regime supplanted by a wiser and more humane public sentiment and practice. And I must repeat my conviction that if the unconscious habit of oppression were not already there, a scheme so gross, irrational, unjust, and inefficient as our present caste distinctions could not find place among a people so generally intelligent and high-minded. I ask attention to their bad influence in a direction not often noticed.

VII. THE "CONVICT LEASE SYSTEM"

In studying, about a year ago, the practice of letting out public convicts to private lessees to serve out their sentences under private management, I found that it does not belong to all our once slave states nor to all our once seceded states.[8] Only it is no longer in practice outside of them. Under our present condition in the South, it is beyond possibility that the individual black should behave mischievously without offensively rearousing the old sentiments of the still dominant white

[8] See "The Convict Lease System in the Southern States," in [the *Century* for Feb. 1884].

man. As we have seen, too, the white man virtually monopolizes the jury box. Add another fact: the Southern states have
entered upon a new era of material development. Now, if with
these conditions in force the public mind has been captivated
by glowing pictures of the remunerative economy of the
convict lease system, and by the seductive spectacle of mines
and railways, turnpikes and levees that everybody wants and
nobody wants to pay for, growing apace by convict labor that
seems to cost nothing, we may almost assert beforehand that
the popular mind will—not so maliciously as unreflectingly—
yield to the tremendous temptation to hustle the misbehaving
black man into the state prison under extravagant sentence and
sell his labor to the highest bidder who will use him in the
construction of public works. For ignorance of the awful condition of these penitentiaries is extreme and general, and the
hasty half-conscious assumption naturally is that the culprit
will survive this term of sentence, and its fierce discipline
"teach him to behave himself."

But we need not argue from cause to effect only. Nor need
I repeat one of the many painful rumors that poured in upon
me the moment I began to investigate this point. The official
testimony of the prisons themselves is before the world to establish the conjectures that spring from our reasoning. After
the erroneous takings of the census of 1880 in South Carolina
had been corrected, the population was shown to consist of
about twenty blacks to every thirteen whites. One would therefore look for a preponderance of blacks on the prison lists;
and inasmuch as they are a people only twenty years ago released from servile captivity, one would not be surprised to
see that preponderance large. Yet, when the actual numbers
confront us, our speculations are stopped with a rude shock;
for what is to account for the fact that in 1881 there were
committed to the state prison at Columbia, South Carolina,
406 colored persons and but 25 whites? The proportion of
blacks sentenced to the whole black population was one to
every 1488; that of the whites to the white population was

but one to every 15,644. In Georgia the white inhabitants decidedly outnumber the blacks; yet in the state penitentiary October 20, 1880, there were 115 whites and 1071 colored; or if we reject the summary of its tables and refer to the tables themselves (for the one does not agree with the other), there were but 102 whites and 1083 colored. Yet of 52 pardons granted in the two years then closing, 22 were to whites and only 30 to blacks. If this be a dark record, what shall we say of the records of lynch law? But for them there is not room here.

VIII. IN THE SCHOOLHOUSE

A far pleasanter aspect of our subject shows itself when we turn from courts and prisons to the schoolhouse. And the explanation is simple. Were our educational affairs in the hands of that not high average of the community commonly seen in jury boxes, with their transient sense of accountability and their crude notions of public interests, there would most likely be no such pleasant contrast. But with us of the South, as elsewhere, there is a fairly honest effort to keep the public-school interests in the hands of the state's most highly trained intelligence. Hence our public educational work is a compromise between the unprogressive prejudices of the general mass of the whites and the progressive intelligence of their best minds. Practically, through the great majority of our higher educational officers, we are fairly converted to the imperative necessity of elevating the colored man intellectually, and are beginning to see very plainly that the whole community is sinned against in every act or attitude of oppression, however gross or however refined.

Yet one thing must be said. I believe it is wise that all have agreed not to handicap education with the race question, but to make a complete surrender of that issue, and let it find adjustment elsewhere first and in the schools last. And yet, in simple truth and justice and in the kindest spirit, we ought to

file one exception for that inevitable hour when the whole
question must be met. There can be no more real justice in
pursuing the Freedman's children with humiliating arbitrary
distinctions and separations in the schoolhouses than in putting them upon him in other places. If, growing out of their
peculiar mental structure, there are good and just reasons for
their isolation, by all means let them be proved and known;
but it is simply tyrannous to assume them without proof. I
know that just here looms up the huge bugbear of Social
Equality. Our eyes are filled with absurd visions of all Shanty-
town pouring its hordes of unwashed imps into the company
and companionship of our own sunny-headed darlings. What
utter nonsense! As if our public schools had no gauge of clean-
liness, decorum, or moral character! Social Equality! What a
godsend it would be if the advocates of the old Southern regime could only see that the color line points straight in the
direction of social equality by tending toward the equalization
of all whites on one side of the line and of all blacks on the
other. We may reach the moon some day, not social equality;
but the only class that really effects anything toward it are
the makers and holders of arbitrary and artificial social distinctions interfering with society's natural self-distribution. Even
the little children everywhere are taught, and begin to learn
almost with their A B Cs, that they will find, and must be
guided by, the same variations of the social scale in the public
school as out of it; and it is no small mistake to put them or
their parents off their guard by this cheap separation on the
line of color.

IX. THE QUESTION OF INSTINCT

But some will say this is not a purely artificial distinction.
We hear much about race instinct. The most of it, I fear, is
pure twaddle. It may be there is such a thing. We do not
know. It is not proved. And even if it were established, it
would not necessarily be a proper moral guide. We subordi-

nate instinct to society's best interests as apprehended in the
light of reason. If there is such a thing, it behaves with strange
malignity toward the remnants of African blood in individuals
principally of our own race, and with singular indulgence to
the descendants of—for example—Pocahontas. Of mere race
feeling we all know there is no scarcity. Who is stranger to it?
And as another man's motive of private preference no one has
a right to forbid it or require it. But as to its being an instinct,
one thing is plain: if there is such an instinct, so far from ex-
cusing the malignant indignities practiced in its name, it furnishes their final condemnation; for it stands to reason that
just in degree as it is a real thing it will take care of itself.

It has often been seen to do so, whether it is real or imagi-
nary. I have seen in New Orleans a Sunday-school of white
children every Sunday afternoon take possession of its two
rooms immediately upon their being vacated by a black school
of equal or somewhat larger numbers. The teachers of the
colored school are both white and black, and among the white
teachers are young ladies and gentlemen of the highest social
standing. The pupils of the two schools are alike neatly at-
tired, orderly, and in every respect inoffensive to each other.
I have seen the two races sitting in the same public high-
school and grammar-school rooms, reciting in the same classes,
and taking recess on the same ground at the same time, without one particle of detriment that any one ever pretended to
discover, although the fiercest enemies of the system swarmed
about it on every side. And when in the light of these observations I reflect upon the enormous educational task our Southern states have before them, the inadequacy of their own
means for performing it, the hoped-for beneficence of the general government, the sparseness with which so much of
our Southern population is distributed over the land, the thousands of school districts where, consequently, the multiplication of schools must involve both increase of expense and
reductions of efficiency, I must enter some demurrer to the enforcement of the tyrannous sentiments of the old regime until

wise experiments have established better reasons than I have
yet heard given.

X. THE CASE SUBMITTED

What need to say more? The question is answered. Is the
Freedman a free man? No. We have considered his position in
a land whence nothing can, and no man has a shadow of right
to drive him, and where he is being multiplied as only oppression can multiply a people. We have carefully analyzed his
relations to the finer and prouder race, with which he shares
the ownership and citizenship of a region large enough for ten
times the number of both. Without accepting one word of his
testimony, we have shown that the laws made for his protection against the habits of suspicion and oppression in his late
master are being constantly set aside, not for their defects, but
for such merit as they possess. We have shown that the very
natural source of these oppressions is the surviving sentiments
of an extinct and now universally execrated institution; sentiments which no intelligent or moral people should harbor a
moment after the admission that slavery was a moral mistake.
We have shown the outrageousness of these tyrannies in some
of their workings, and how distinctly they antagonize every
state and national interest involved in the elevation of the colored race. Is it not well to have done so? For, I say again,
the question has reached a moment of special importance. The
South stands on her honor before the clean equities of the issue. It is no longer whether constitutional amendments, but
whether the eternal principles of justice, are violated. And the
answer must—it shall—come from the South. And it shall be
practical! It will not cost much. We have had a strange experience: the withholding of simple rights has cost much blood;
such concessions of them as we have made have never yet
cost a drop. The answer is coming. Is politics in the way? Then
let it clear the track or get run over, just as it prefers. But,
as I have said over and over to my brethren in the South, I

take upon me to say again here, that there is a moral and intellectual intelligence there which is not going to be much longer beguiled out of its moral right of way by questions of political punctilio, but will seek that plane of universal justice and equity which it is every people's duty before God to seek, not along the line of politics—God forbid!—but across it and across it and across it as many times as it may lie across the path, until the whole people of every once slaveholding state can stand up as one man, saying, "Is the Freedman a free man?" and the whole world shall answer, "Yes."

The Silent South

[When "The Freedman's Case in Equity" appeared Cable was on the road with Mark Twain, near the mid-point of a four months' tour on which they gave platform readings from their works. His popularity with the audiences was not much less than Mark Twain's, all considered, and frequently the newspaper reporters favored him over his companion. With the publication of his new novel, *Dr. Sevier,* during the tour the critical approval of his literary work reached new heights, and after the essay on the Freedman was in print he was surrounded by interviewers wherever he went. From one quarter, however, the South, the response was anything but favorable.

Cable had known that to argue for Negro rights was to invite opposition in the South; relatives and friends had warned him. But he had not expected the flood of protest and abuse elicited by "The Freedman's Case in Equity." The New Orleans newspapers hesitated before taking up the cry but soon were leading the pack. Some of the Creoles had been displeased with the portrait Cable drew of them and their ancestors in his fiction; now they joined with others in calling him a traitor to his section. Page M. Baker, editor of the *Bulletin* in 1875 and now editor of the *Times-Democrat,* steered that paper into a vigorous attack on Cable. It had been the *Times-Democrat* which a few years earlier, under a different editor, championed Cable's prison reform work.

The *Century Magazine* received a flurry of letters on Cable's essay. The editors decided that instead of culling among them for the few they had space to print they would choose someone to sum up the opposing views in a single article, to which

Cable would then write a rebuttal. Henry W. Grady, editor of the Atlanta *Constitution* since 1881, wrote for the opposition. A spokesman for rebuilding and reconciliation, for diversified industries and crop rotation, he had emerged as the apostle of progress and the New South. His essay in the *Century* of April 1885, with the title "In Plain Black and White," was in a sense a composite reply, for he wrote it with the advice of others in the South.

Grady insisted on saying, over the editors' objection, that, because of New England blood reaching Cable through his mother, he had never been sympathetic to the Southern way of life. Except for this remark and another to the effect that if anyone in the South should subscribe to Cable's ideas, he would be a dreaming theorist, Grady held the discussion to the issues and avoided personal recrimination. He believed in race instinct and would not compromise by one jot his insistence on white supremacy, saying that the whites must rule because they have "intelligence, character, and property." The remoteness of his position from Cable's is suggested by his declaration, "Nowhere on earth is there kindlier feeling, closer sympathy, or less friction between two classes of society than between the whites and the blacks of the South today." Grady did not doubt that the Negro had been given the ballot permanently, but he did doubt the wisdom of it.

The four pages first allotted Cable for his reply grew to seventeen finally, and his article, "The Silent South," did not appear in the issue with Grady's as intended but five months later. Several of Cable's friends read his manuscript and offered suggestions, and when it appeared they were elated, believing that it made his position amply clear and left no room for the sort of personal charges that had been leveled against him. Charles Scribner, one of Cable's publishers in New York, wrote him:

"I can hardly express how greatly I was stirred by it. . . . I do not see how any reply *can* be even attempted; but it was not even that that moved me so much. There is some-

thing truly ennobling in your discussion of the subject; you lift
the whole question into a higher moral plane. It is an article
which must do great good and the constant tributes of gratitude which you will receive must make it one of the proudest
achievements of your life. You know that I do not often overflow in this way but I really cannot help writing this to you."

In "The Freedman's Case in Equity" Cable had skirted the
most controversial aspects of the subject, but those aspects had
been introduced by his opponents in such lurid and frighten-
ing terms that now he took them up for calm consideration.
He believed that those who had voices, the journalists and the
politicians, were not speaking for the majority of the Southern
people, who he thought could be depended on for kindness
and fair play and justice if they were not persuaded to other
courses by their leaders. He believed that he could speak for
this majority, the "Silent South," and he felt an obligation to
do so. As a consequence this essay states his views more fully
and more clearly than the first essay. It is masterly in handling
the detailed argument, and yet it holds steadily to the moral
issues he thought fundamental to the discussion.

This essay was published in the *Century Magazine*, September 1885, and in *The Silent South*.]

The Silent South

I. "A TIME TO SPEAK"

In Tivoli Circle, New Orleans, from the center and apex of
its green, flowery mound, an immense column of pure white
marble rises in the fair unfrowning majesty of Grecian proportions high up above the city's housetops into the dazzling sun-
shine and fragrant gales of the Delta. On its dizzy top stands
the bronze figure of one of the world's greatest captains.

He is all alone. Not one of his mighty lieutenants stands
behind or beside him or below at the base of his pillar. Even

his horse is gone. Only his good sword remains, hanging motionless in its scabbard. His arms are folded on that breast that never knew fear or guile, and his calm, dauntless gaze meets the morning sun as it rises, like the new prosperity of the land he loved and served so masterly, above the far distant battle-fields where so many thousands of his ragged gray veterans lie in the sleep of fallen heroes.

Great silent one! who lived to see his standards furled and hung in the halls of the conqueror; to hear the victor's festal jubilations; to behold a redistribution of rights riding over the proud traditions of his people, and all the painful fruits of a discomfited cause shaken to the ground; to hear and see the tempestuous and ofttimes bloody after-strife between the old ideas and the new; to see, now on one side, now on the other, the terms of his own grand surrender and parole forgotten or ignored; to have his ear filled with the tirades and recriminations of journals and parties, and the babble of the unthinking million; to note the old creeds changing, and to come, himself, it may be—God knows—to respect beliefs that he had once counted follies; and yet, withal, never, before the world that had set him aside but could not forget him, never to quail, never to wince, never to redden with anger, never to wail against man or fate, or seek the salve of human praise or consolation; but silently amid the clamor of the times to stand and wait, making patience royal, with a mind too large for murmuring, and a heart too great to break, until a Messenger as silent as his bronze effigy beckoned Robert E. Lee to that other land of light and flowers where man's common inheritance of error is hidden in the merit of his honest purpose, and lost in the Divine charity.

So this monument, lifted far above our daily strife of narrow interests and often narrower passions and misunderstandings, becomes a monument to more than its one great and rightly loved original. It symbolizes our whole South's better self; that finer part which the world not always sees; unaggressive, but brave, calm, thoughtful, broad-minded, dispassionate, sincere,

and, in the din of boisterous error round about it, all too mute.
It typifies that intelligence to which the words of a late writer
most truly apply when he says concerning the long, incoherent
discussion of one of our nation's most perplexing questions,
"Amid it all the South has been silent."

But the times change—have changed. Whatever the merit
or fault of earlier reticence, this mute, firm-rooted figure, with
sheathed sword and folded arms, must yield a step, not backward, but forward. "Where it has been silent it now should
speak." Nay, already it speaks; and the blessing of all good
men should rest on this day if it reveals the Silent South laying
off its unsurrendered sword, leaving brawlers to their brawls,
and moving out upon the plain of patient, friendly debate,
seeking to destroy only error and to establish only truth and
equity and a calm faith in their incomparable power to solve
the dark problems of the future.

Within the last few months the voice of temperate discussion has been heard in well-nigh every quarter of our Southern states on themes that have scarcely been handled with
patience and clemency these forty years. True, there has been
some clamor, throwing stones, and casting dust; but calmer
utterances have come from Memphis, from Louisville, Chattanooga, Lynchburg, Atlanta, Charleston, Dallas, and far San
Angelo; some on one side, some on the other, of the debate,
professing in common at least three quiet convictions: that recrimination and malignment of motive are the tactics of those
who have no case; that the truth is worth more than any man's
opinion; and that the domination of right is the end we are
bound to seek.

Under these convictions the following pages are written;
written in deprecation of all sectionalism; with an admiration
and affection for the South that for justice and sincerity yield
to none; in a spirit of faithful sonship to a Southern state;
written not to gratify sympathizers, but to persuade opponents; not to overthrow, but to convince; and begging that all

harshness of fact or vehemence of statement be attributed entirely to the weight of the interests under debate.

II. POINTS OF AGREEMENT

It is pleasant to note how much common ground is occupied by the two sides in this contest of opinions. By both it is recognized that the fate of the national Civil Rights bill has not decided and cannot dismiss the entire question of the Freedman's relations; but that it puts upon trial in each Southern state a voluntary Reconstruction which can never be final till it has established the moral equities of the whole case. Says one opponent, imputing his words to a personified South, "Leave this problem to my working out. I will solve it in calmness and deliberation, without passion or prejudice, and with full regard for the unspeakable equities it holds."[1] Says Mr. Watterson's paper, in Louisville, "We believe there is a general desire among the people of the South, that the Negro shall have all the rights which a citizen of the United States, whatever be the color of his skin, is entitled to, but we know of no method to argue away or force down what may be called the caste of color. If we did . . . or if anybody else did, the dark problem as to the future of this unfortunate race would be more quickly and more easily solved. None more earnestly than the *Courier-Journal* desires to see this question happily settled."

Is not this progress? It seems scarce a matter of months since we were saying the question was dead and should be buried. Now it rises to demand a wider grave, which both the writers quoted admit it must have, though one thinks nobody knows how to dig it, and another insists it must be dug without cutting away any more ground.

But the common field of assertion and admission broadens as we move on. On this side it has been carefully demonstrated that, not from emancipation or enfranchisement, or anything

[1] "In Plain Black and White," April *Century*, 1885.

else in or of the late war, or of Reconstruction, but from our
earlier relation to the colored man as his master, results our
view of him as naturally and irrevocably servile; and that
hence arises our proneness to confuse his social with his civil
relations, to argue from inferiority of race a corresponding inferiority of his rights, and to infer that they fall, therefore,
justly under our own benevolent domination and, at times,
even our arbitrary abridgment. The point is made that these
views, as remnants of that slavery which, we all admit, has of
right perished, ought to perish with it; and the fact is re-
gretted that in many parts of the South they nevertheless still
retain such force—though withal evidently weakening—that
the laws affirming certain human rights discordant to the
dominant race are sometimes openly evaded and sometimes
virtually suffocated under a simulated acceptance of their narrowest letter. How plainly we feel the date of this discussion
to be 1884–85—not earlier—when we hear this evasion, once
so hotly denied, admitted freely, nay, with emphasis, to be a
"matter of record, and, from the Southern standpoint, mainly
a matter of reputation."

And there are yet other points of agreement. As one who
saw our great Reconstruction agony from its first day to its
last in one of the South's most distracted states and in its largest city, with his sympathies ranged upon the pro-Southern
side of the issue, and his convictions drifting irresistibly to the
other, the present writer affirms of his knowledge, in the initial
paper of this debate, that after we had yielded what seemed
to us all proper deference to our slaves' emancipation and
enfranchisement, there yet remained our invincible determination—seemingly to us the fundamental condition of our self-
respect—never to yield our ancient prerogative of holding
under our own discretion the colored man's *status,* not as a
Freedman, not as a voter, but in his daily walk as a civilian.
This attitude in us, with our persistent mistaking his civil rights
for social claims, this was the taproot of the whole trouble.
For neither would *his* self-respect yield; and not because he

was so unintelligent and base, but because he was as intelligent and aspiring as, in his poor way, he was, did he make this the cause of political estrangement. This estrangement—full grown at its beginning—was the carpetbagger's and scallawag's opportunity. They spring and flourish wherever, under representative government, gentility makes a mistake, however sincere, against the rights of the poor and ignorant. Is this diagnosis of the Reconstruction malady contested by the other side? Nay, it is confirmed. The South, it tells us, "accepted the emancipation and enfranchisement of her slaves as the legitimate results of war that had been fought to a conclusion. These once accomplished, nothing more was possible. 'Thus far and no farther,' she said to her neighbors in no spirit of defiance, but with quiet determination. In her weakest moments, when her helpless people were hedged about by the unthinking bayonets of her conquerors, she gathered them for resistance at this point. Here she defended everything that a people should hold dear. There was little proclamation of her purpose," etc.

Surely hope is not folly, as to this Southern question, when such admissions come from this direction. What salutary clearing of the ground have we here! Our common assertion in the South has long been that the base governments of the Reconstruction period were overturned by force because they had become so corrupt that they were nothing but huge machines for the robbery of the whole public, a tangle of low political intrigues that no human intelligence could unravel; that our virtue and intelligence sought not the abridgment of any man's rights, but simply the arrest of bribery and robbery; that this could be done only by revolution because of the solid black vote, cast, we said, without rationality at the behest of a few scoundrels who kept it solid by playing upon partisan catchwords, or by promise of spoils. And especially among those whose faith is strongest in our old Southern traditions, it always was and is, today, sincerely believed that this was the whole issue. It was this profession that averted the interference of federal arms. It was upon this profession that the manliest youth and intelligence of New Orleans went forth to stake their lives, and some to pour out their hearts' blood in internecine war on the levee of their dear city. Sad sight to those who knew that this was not the whole matter—that the spring of trouble lay yet deeper down. To such it brings no small or selfish gladness to hear, at length—if one may without offense coin a term—to hear Southern *traditionists* admitting a truth which the South has denied with sincere indignation ten thousand times—that in all that terrible era the real, fundamental issue was something else which the popular Southern mind was hardly aware of. "Barely"—say these—"barely did the whispered word that bespoke her [the South's] resolution catch the listening ears of her sons; but for all this, the victorious armies of the North, had they been rallied again from their homes, could not have enforced and maintained among this disarmed people the policy indicated in the Civil Rights bill." This was the point at which, they say, and they say truly, the South "gathered for resistance."

Let us be sure these so gallantly spoken words are not misunderstood. There were two policies indicated in the Civil Rights bill: the policy of asserting congressional jurisdiction in the case; and the policy of legalizing, at all, such rights as it declared. One raised a question of state rights; the other, of human rights. But the state-rights issue, by itself—the mere question of whence the legislation should emanate—could never of itself make fierce strife. Any state could have settled that point by simply stepping ahead of Congress with the same legislation. No; the irreconcilable difference was not as to whence but as to *what* the law should be. The essential odium of the bill lay, not in its origin, but in its definition of the black man's rights. Indeed, the main object of most of those who have written on the other side in the present controversy has been to assert the resolution never to recognize the Freedman's rights upon that definition of them. In the meantime a gentle movement of thought, that sounds no trumpet before it, is gradually pressing toward that very recognition.

III. THE STICKING POINT

But now that we have clearly made out exactly *what* this immovable hostility is, the question follows—and half the nation are asking it today with perplexed brows—*why* is it? Yet the answer is simple. Many white people of the South sincerely believe that the recognition of rights proposed in the old Civil Rights bills or in "The Freedman's Case in Equity" *would pre- cipitate a social chaos.* They believe Civil Rights means Social Equality. This may seem a transparent error, but certainly any community in the world that believed it would hold the two ideas in equal abomination; and it is because of the total un- consciousness and intense activity of this error at the South, and the subtle sense of unsafety that naturally accompanies it—it is because of this, rather than for any lack of clearness in its statement of the subject, that the article on "The Freed- man's Case in Equity" is so grossly misinterpreted even by some who undoubtedly wish to be fair. That this is the true cause of the misinterpretation is clear in the fact that from the first printing of the article until now the misconstruction has occurred only among those whose thinking still runs in the grooves of the old traditions.

Nothing in that paper touches or seeks to touch the domain of social privileges. The standing of the magazine in which it appears is guarantee against the possibility of the paper con- taining any such insult to the intelligence of enlightened so- ciety. Social equality is a fool's dream. The present writer wants quite as little of it as the most fervent traditionist of the most fervent South. The North, the West, the East, and the rest of the intelligent world, want quite as little of it as the South wants. Social equality can never exist where a com- munity, numerous enough to assert itself, is actuated, as every civilized community is, by an intellectual and moral ambition.

No form of laws, no definition of rights, from Anarchy to
Utopia, can bring it about. The fear that this or that change
will produce it ought never to be any but a fool's fear. And
yet there is this to be added; that no other people in America
are doing so much *for* social equality as those who, while they
warmly charge it upon others, are themselves thrusting arbitrary and cheap artificial distinctions into the delicate machinery of society's self-distribution as it revolves by the power of
our natural impulses, and of morality, personal interest, and
personal preferences. This, of course, is not the intention, and
even these persons retard only incidentally, unawares and
within narrow limits, nature's social distributions, while taking
diligent and absolutely needless pains to hold apart two races
which really have no social affinity at all.

Do we charge any bad intention or conscious false pretense?
Not at all! They are merely making the double mistake of first
classing as personal social privileges certain common impersonal rights of man, and then turning about and treating them
as rights definable by law—which social amenities are not and
cannot be.

For the sake of any who might still misunderstand, let us
enlarge here a moment. The family relation has *rights*. Hence
marital laws and laws of succession. But beyond the family
circle there are no such things as social *rights;* and when our
traditionists talk about a too hasty sympathy having "fixed by
enactment" the Negro's *social* and civil rights they talk—unwisely. All the relations of life that go by *impersonal right* are
Civil relations. All that go by *personal choice* are Social relations. The one is all of right, it makes no difference who we
are; the other is all of choice, and it makes all the difference
who we are; and it is no little fault against ourselves as well
as others to make confusion between the two relations. For the
one we make laws; for the other every one consults his own
pleasure; and the law that refuses to protect a civil right, con-
struing it a social privilege, deserves no more regard than if it
should declare some social privilege to be a civil right. Social

choice, civil *rights;* but a civil *privilege,* in America, is simply
heresy against both our great national political parties at once.
Now, "The Freedman's Case in Equity" pleads for not one
thing belonging to the domain of social relations. Much less
the family relation; it does not hint the faintest approval of
any sort of admixture of the two bloods. Surely nothing that
a man can buy a ticket for anonymously at a ticket seller's
handhole confers the faintest right to even a bow of recognition that any one may choose to withhold. But what says the
other side? "The South will never adopt the suggestion of the
social intermingling[2] of the two races." So they beg the question of equity, and suppress a question of civil right by simply
miscalling it "social intermingling"; thus claiming for it that
sacredness from even the law's control which only social relations have, and the next instant asserting the determination of
one race to "control the social relations," so-called, of two. Did
ever champions of a cause with blanker simplicity walk into
a sack and sew up its mouth? Not only thus, but from within
it they announce a doctrine that neither political party in our
country would venture to maintain; for no party dare say that
in these United States there is any room for any one class of
citizens to fasten arbitrarily upon any other class of citizens a
civil status from which no merit of intelligence, virtue, or pos-
sessions can earn an extrication. We have a country large
enough for all the *unsociality* anybody may want, but not for
incivility either by or without the warrant of law.

"What history shows," says a sound little book lately
printed, "is that rights are safe only when guaranteed against
all arbitrary power and all class and personal interest." Class
rule of any sort is bad enough, even with the consent of the
ruled class; un-American enough. But the domination of one
fixed class by another without its consent is Asiatic. And yet it
is behind this error, of Asian antiquity and tyranny, this arbitrary suppression of impartial, impersonal civil rights, that we
discover our intelligent adversaries in this debate fortified, im-

[2] Italicized only here.

agining they have found a strong position! "Neither race wants
it," says one, alluding to that common, undivided participation
in the enjoyment of civil rights, for which the darker race has
been lifting one long prayer these twenty years, and which he
absurdly miscalls "social intermingling." "The interest, as the
inclination, of both races is against it," he adds. "Here the issue
is made up."

But he mistakes. The issue is not made up here at all. It is
not a question of what the *race* wants, but of *what the individual wants and has a right to*. Is that question met? No.
Not a line has been written to disprove the individual Freedman's title to these rights; but pages, to declare that his *race*
does not want them and shall not have them if it does. Mark
the contradiction. It does not want them—it shall not have
them! Argument unworthy of the nursery; yet the final essence
of all the other side's utterances. They say the colored race
wants a participation in public rights separate from the whites;
and that anyhow it has got to take that or nothing; "The
white and black races in the South *must*[3] walk apart." One
writer justifies this on the belief of a natal race instinct; but
says that if there were no such thing the South "would, by
every means in its power, so strengthen the race *prejudice*[3]
that it would do the work and hold the stubbornness and
strength of instinct." Could any one more distinctly or unconsciously waive the whole question of right and wrong? Yet this
is the standpoint on which it is proposed to meet the Freedman's case *in equity*. Under the heat of such utterances how
the substance melts out of their writer's later proposition for
the South to solve the question "without passion or prejudice
and with full regard for the unspeakable equities it holds."

It is not the Louisville gentlemen who are found at this untenable standpoint. They admit the desirability of extirpating
the state of affairs condemned by "The Freedman's Case in
Equity," and merely ask with a smile, "in what manner the
writer expects that evil to disappear before high-sounding im-

[3] Italicized only here.

peratives," etc. As to that we leave others on that side to give
the answer; hear it, from Atlanta: "Clear views, clear statement, and clear understanding are the demands of the hour.
Given these, the common sense and courage of the American
people will make the rest easy."

IV. CIVIL RIGHT NOT SOCIAL CHOICE

Let us then make our conception of the right and wrong of
this matter unmistakable. Social relations, one will say, are sacred. True, but civil rights are sacred, also. Hence social relations must not impose upon civil rights nor civil rights impose
upon social relations. We must have peace. But for peace to be
stable we must have justice. Therefore, for peace, we must find
that boundary line between social relations and civil rights,
from which the one has no warrant ever to push the other; and,
for justice, this boundary must remain ever faithfully the same,
no matter whose the social relations are on one side or whose
the civil rights are on the other.

Suppose a case. Mr. A. takes a lady, not of his own family, to
a concert. Neither one is moved by compulsion or any assertion
of right on the part of the other. They have chosen each other's
company. Their relation is social. It could not exist without
mutual agreement. They are strangers in that city, however,
and as they sit in the thronged auditorium and look around
them, not one other soul in that house, so far as they can dis-
cern, has any social relation with them. But see, now, how
impregnable the social relation is. That pair, outnumbered a
thousand to one, need not yield a pennyweight of social inter-
change with any third person unless they so choose. Nothing
else in human life is so amply sufficient to protect itself as are
social relations. Provided one thing—that the law will protect
every one impartially in his civil rights, one of the foremost of
which is that both men and laws shall let us alone to our personal social preferences. If any person, no matter who or what
he is, insists on obtruding himself upon this pair in the concert

hall he can only succeed in getting himself put out. Why? Because he is trying to turn his civil right-to-be-there into a social passport. And even if he make no personal advances, but his behavior or personal condition is so bad as to obtrude itself offensively upon others, the case is the same; the mistake and its consequences are his. But, on the other hand, should Mr. A. and his companion demand the expulsion of this third person when he had made no advances and had encroached no more on their liberty than they had on his, demanding it simply on the ground that he was their social or intellectual inferior or probably had relatives who were, then the error, no matter who or what he is, would be not his, but theirs, and it would be the equally ungenteel error of trying to turn their social choice into a civil right; and it would be simply increasing the error and its offensiveness for them to suggest that he be given an equally comfortable place elsewhere in the house, providing it must indicate his inferiority. There is nothing comfortable in ignominy, nor is it any evidence of high mind for one stranger to put it upon another.

Now, the principles of this case are not disturbed by any multiplication of the number of persons concerned, or by reading for concert hall either theater or steamboat or railway station or coach or lecture hall or streetcar or public library, or by supposing the social pair to be English, Turk, Jap, Cherokee, Ethiopian, Mexican, or "American." But note the fact that, even so, Mr. A. and his companion's social relations are, under these rulings, as safe from invasion as they were before; nay, even safer, inasmuch as the true distinction is made publicly clearer, between the social and the civil relations. Mr. A. is just as free to decline every sort of unwelcome social advance, much or little, as ever he was; and as to his own house or estate may eject any one from it not of his own family or a legal tenant, and give no other reason than that it suits him to do so. Do you not see it now, gentlemen of the other side? Is there anything new in it? Is it not as old as truth itself? Honestly, have you not known it all along? Is it not actually the part of good breeding to know it? You cannot say no. Then why have you charged us with proposing "to break down every distinction between the races," and "to insist on their intermingling in all places and in all relations," when in fact we have not proposed to disturb any distinction between the races which nature has made, or molest any private or personal relation in life, whatever? Why have you charged us with "moving to forbid all further assortment of the races," when the utmost we have done is to condemn an *arbitrary* assortment of the races, crude and unreasonable, by the stronger race without the consent of the weaker, and in places and relations where no one, exalted or lowly, has any right to dictate to another because of the class he belongs to? We but turn your own words to our use when we say this battery of charges "is as false as it is infamous." But let that go.

Having made it plain that the question has nothing to do with social relations, we see that it is, and is only, a question of *indiscriminative civil rights*. This is what "The Freedman's Case in Equity" advocates from beginning to end, not as a choice which a *race* may either claim or disclaim, but as every citizen's individual yet impersonal right until he personally waives or forfeits it. The issue, we repeat, is not met at all by the assertion that "neither race wants it." There is one thing that neither race wants, but even this is not because either of them is one race or another, but simply because they are members of a civilized human community. It is that thing of which our Southern white people have so long had such an absurd fear; neither race, or in other words nobody, wants to see the civil rewards of decency in dress and behavior usurped by the common herd of clowns and ragamuffins. But there is another thing that the colored race certainly does want: the freedom for those of the race who can to earn the indiscriminative and unchallenged *civil—not social*—rights of gentility by the simple act of being genteel. This is what we insist the best intelligence of the South is willing—in the interest of right, and therefore of both races—to accord. But the best intelligence is not the majority, and the majority, leaning not upon the equities, but the traditional sentiments of the situation, charge us with "theory" and "sentiment" and give us their word for it that "neither race wants it."

Why, that is the very same thing we used to say about slavery! Where have these traditionists been the last twenty years? Who, that lived in the South through those days, but knows that the darker race's demand from the first day of the Reconstruction era to its last was, "If you *will not give us* undivided participation in civil rights, *then and in that case* you must give us equal separate enjoyment of them"; and from the close of Reconstruction to this day the only change in its expression has been to turn its imperative demand into a supplication. This was the demand, this is the supplication of American citizens seeking not even their civil rights entire, but their civil rights mutilated to accommodate, not our public rights, but our private tastes. And how have we responded? Has the separate accommodation furnished them been anywhere nearly equal to ours? Not one time in a thousand. Has this been for malice? Certainly not. But we have unconsciously —and what people in our position would not have made the same oversight?—allowed ourselves to be carried off the lines of even justice by our old notion of every white man holding every Negro to a menial status.

Would our friends on the other side of the discussion say they mean only, concerning these indiscriminative civil rights, "neither race wants them *now*"? This would but make bad worse. For two new things have happened to the colored race in these twenty years; first, a natural and spontaneous assortment has taken place within the race itself along scales of virtue and intelligence, knowledge and manners; so that by no small fraction of their number the wrong of treating the whole race alike is more acutely felt than ever it was before; and, second, a long, bitter experience has taught them that "equal accommodations, but separate" means, generally, accommodations of a conspicuously ignominious inferiority. Are these people op-

posed to an arrangement that would give them instant release
from organized and legalized incivility? —For that is what a
race distinction in civil relations is when it ignores intelligence
and decorum.

V. CALLING THE WITNESSES

There is another way to settle this question of fact. One side
in this debate advocates indiscriminative civil rights; the other,
separate—*racial* civil rights. It is not to be doubted that our
opponents have received many letters from white men and
women full of commendation and thanks for what they have
written. Such, too, has been the present writer's experience.
Such testimonials poured in upon him daily for four months,
from East, West, North, and South. But how about the colored race? Have they written him, begging him to desist because "neither race wants" the equities he pleads for? The
pages of this essay are limited, but we beg room for a few
extracts from colored correspondents' letters, each being from a
separate letter and no letter from any colored person whom the
present writer has ever seen or known. One letter ends, "May
all the spirits that aid justice, truth, and right constantly attend you in your effort." Another, "I hope that you will continue the work you have begun, and may God bless you."
Another, "Accept this, dear sir, as the thanks of the colored
people of this city." Another begins, "I am a Negro. In behalf
of the Negroes and in behalf of equitable fair dealing on the
principle of giving a dollar's worth for a dollar, without any
possible reference to social matters, permit me to tender you
my sincere thanks," etc. Says another, "The judicious fairness
with which you have treated our case renders your thesis
worthy of our adoption as a Bill of Rights." A letter of thanks
from a colored literary club says, " . . . We thank you for
your recognition of our capacity to suffer keenly under the
indignities we are made to endure." A similar society in another town sent a verbal expression of thanks by its president

in person. (Followed since by its committee's formal resolution ornamentally written and mounted.) In Louisville a numerous impromptu delegation of colored citizens called upon the writer and tendered a verbal address of thanks. Another letter says, "If the people of the South will only regard your article in the same spirit as I believe it was intended, then I know, sir, great and enduring good will be accomplished." In Arkansas, a meeting of colored people, called to express approval of the article on "The Freedman's Case in Equity," passed a resolution pronouncing its ideas "consonant with true religion and enlightened civilization," etc. Not one word of adverse criticism, written or printed, has come to him from a person of color. Has the same race given "In Plain Black and White," or "The Freedman's Case in Reality," or any of the less dignified mass of matter on that side of the question, a like cordial ratification? Or has only Mr. Jack Brown sent in his congratulation?[4]

[4] The Selma *Times*, quoted in "The Freedman's Case in Equity" as rejoicing in the flogging of a colored preacher on a railway train for not leaving the passenger coach when ordered out by irresponsible ruffians, has since published a letter purporting to come from one "Jack Brown, colored," of Columbia, South Carolina. The letter denounces the present writer as one of the sort "that has brought on all the trouble between the white and colored people of the South. I do not know his initials or address," it continues, "or I would address him in person, as I am anxious to *test his sincerity*" [so italicized originally]. "Now," says the Selma *Times*, "the above article bears every imprint of honesty and truthfulness. We don't believe any one but a sharp Negro could have written or did write it. The handwriting, the loose grammar, the postmark on the envelope, all mark it as a genuine document coming from the man it purports to have come from. Not only is this true of such external marks as we have named, but so is it likewise of its internal, essential substance. It sounds as if it could have been thought out and written by a Negro *only*. We cannot conceive of a white man's putting himself so thoroughly into the place of a Negro, mentally, as to have executed such a thing as a forgery. We shall find out if there is such a Negro in Columbia, South Carolina, as Brown, and secure other proofs that he wrote it, because we know Mr. Cable and others are sure to challenge its authenticity. We confidently expect to be fully prepared to convince the most skeptical. "The Negro is right. Those of his race who have any sense cannot

But it may be asked, may not a great many individuals, and even some clubs, impromptu delegations, and public meetings called for the purpose, approve certain declarations and yet the great mass of a people not sanction them? Then let us go one step farther. There are, it is said, eighty—some say a hundred—journals published in this country by colored men. They look to the colored race for the great bulk of their readers and subscribers. Hence they are bound to be in large degree the organs of popular thought among the reading part, at least, of that people. But *these papers are a unit for the ideas set forth in "The Freedman's Case in Equity."* Now, to believe the other side we should have to make two impossible assumptions; that among a people treated rigorously as one race, compacted by a common status, the intelligent and comparatively refined part numerous enough to send—in spite of its poverty—*twenty thousand students to normal schools and colleges* and to support eighty newspapers, this portion, moreover, associated with the less intelligent portion more cordially in every interest than two such classes are amongst any other people in the world unless it be the Jews—that such a lump of leaven as this has no power to shape the views of the rest on matters of common public right! Such a thing may be credible on some other planet, not

---

expect what Mr. Cable would give them, do not expect it, and would be unhappy and uncomfortable if, in any way, it could be forced upon them."

So if Jack Brown, colored, were a real person, nothing could be easier than to find him. Writing from a small inland city, getting through one hundred and seventy-five words of his letter before making a grammatical slip, a colored man in sympathy with the tritest sentiment of the dominant race, and with a taste for public questions—such a man could not be hid, much less overlooked, in Columbia. But on the present writer's desk lies his own letter *to* Mr. Jack Brown, colored, stamped "Return to the writer," after having lain in the Columbia post office for nearly a month, unclaimed. An exhaustive search and inquiry amongst the people of both races by a white gentleman resident on the spot fails to find any "Jack Brown" except—to quote the gentleman's letter—"a poor, illiterate fellow, who cannot read or write his name," and who, instead of being "twenty-seven years of age," is—to quote another letter—"an aged man."

on this. And the second impossible assumption: that the intelligent and sensitive portions of a people shall submit to
an ignominious mutilation of their public rights because the
unintelligence of their race chooses (?) to submit to it. This
assumption is a crime against common justice; the other is a
crime against common sense. It is simply a mistake that "the
assortment of the races which has been described as shameful
and unjust . . . commands the hearty assent of both."

True, our traditionist friends, who think they believe it, are
glad to take the witness stand and testify; but surely some of
them should be lawyer enough to know that when they say the
colored race *shall not have* the other thing in any event, their
testimony as to which the colored race prefers is of no further
account. At Atlanta, they are equally unfortunate in another
witness. If the Georgia State Commissioner of Public Education will allow the personal mention from one who has met
and admires him, we may say that throughout the United
States he has won the high regard and praise of the friends of
public education for the exceptional progress he—a man of the
old South—has made in unlearning our traditional Southern
prejudices. He stands a noble, personal refutation of the superficial notion that the world must look to the young South,
only, for progressive ideas of human right among us. Maybe
it was easy to make the mistake of calling this admirable gentleman to testify that "neither race wants it." But see how
quickly Commissioner Orr provokes the reader to dismiss him,
too, from the witness stand: Speaking of mixed schools, which,
he says, "both races would protest against"—but which, mark
it, "The Freedman's Case in Equity" does not ask to have
forced upon any community or forced by either race upon the
other anywhere—Mr. Orr says, "I am so sure of the evils that
would come from mixed schools that, even if they were possible, I would see the whole educational system swept away
before I would see them established."

Ah! gentlemen, you are not before a Congressional investi-
gating committee that gets Republican facts from Republican

witnesses and Democratic facts from Democratic witnesses,
and then makes two reports. You are before the judgment seat
of the world's intelligence; and if you cannot bring for evidence
of a people's feelings their own spontaneous and habitual expressions to those who think with them; and, for the establishment of facts, the unconscious or unwilling testimony of your
opponents, then it is high time you were taking your case out of
this court.[5] As for us we can prove all we need prove by the
gentlemen themselves.

Once only does the opposite side bring forward the actual
free utterance of a colored man professing to express a sentiment of his race; well-nigh a magazine column of "Negro
eloquence" and adulation poured upon a conference of ap-
plauding "Bishops and Brethren" because of the amazing fact
that when in the neighboring vestry room, he had "thought-
lessly asked" the governor of the state if he could get a drink,
that magnate sent for and handed him a glass of water! Unlucky testimony! which no candid mind can deny is an elab-
orate confession of surprised delight at being treated with indiscriminative civility. We are told, however, that it is offered
simply to show the affectionate "feeling of that people toward
their white neighbors." Thus a display of affection is utilized
to give a color of justice to the *mutilation* of just such equal
rights as this one whose unexpected recognition called forth

[5] They might easily have brought in colored schoolteachers.
Many of these favor separate colored schools, for the obvious reason
that those are the only schools they may teach in. They do bring
in just two witnesses from a side avowedly opposed to them; but
it is not our side, either. One is the late Bishop Haven, of whom
we shall speak presently. The other, a young white woman on a
railway train, who—forbidden to enjoy her civil rights and her
peculiar social preferences at the same time—threw away a civil
right to retain the social preference; which was her business, not
ours, and proves nothing whatever for or against anybody else; but
whose expression of *pride* at being mistaken for a quadroon proves
her an extremely silly person. They summon her for "the sole
object" of suggesting that she and such as agree with her—which
lets us out as plainly as it does the other side—are "unsafe as
advisers and unfair as witnesses." Certainly they are.

this display of affection! So they go round and round their tether.

VI. GUNS THAT SHOOT BACKWARD

Our demonstration is complete; but there follows a short corollary: While the colored people always did and still do accept with alacrity an undivided enjoyment of civil rights with the white race wherever cordially offered, they never mistake them for social privileges, nor do they ever attempt to use them to compel social intercourse. We might appeal to the everyday streetcar experience of hundreds of thousands of residents in New Orleans and other Southern cities; or to the uniform clearness with which civil rights are claimed and social advances disclaimed in the many letters from colored men and women that are this moment before the writer. But we need not. We need refer only to our opponents in debate, who bring forward, to prove their own propositions, a set of well-known facts that turn and play Balaam to their Balak. Hear their statement: "They"—the colored people—"meet the white people in all the avenues of business. They work side by side with the white bricklayer or carpenter in perfect accord and friendliness. When the trowel or hammer is laid aside, the laborers part, each going his own way. Any attempt to carry the comradeship of the day into private life would be sternly resisted by both parties in interest."

We prove, by the other side's own arguments, that the colored people always accept the common enjoyment of civil rights and never confound civil with social relations. But in just one phase of life there is a conspicuous exception; and an exception especially damaging to the traditional arguments of our opponents. And who furnishes our evidence this time? Themselves again. We allude to the church relation. We are asked to confront the history of an effort made, they say, many times over, by Bishop Haven and the Northern Methodist Church generally, soon after the late war; an effort to abolish

racial discrimination in the religious worship of the church in
the South composed of Northern whites and Southern blacks;
its constant and utter failure; and the final separation of those
churches into two separate conferences and into separate congregations wherever practicable. These facts are brought forward to prove the existence of race instinct, intending to justify by race instinct the arbitrary control by the whites of the
relations between the two races; and the conclusion is san-
guinely reached at a bound that the only explanation of these
churches' separation on the color line is each race's race instinct, "that spoke above the appeal of the bishop and dominated the divine influences that pulsed from pew to pew." But
the gentlemen are too eager. What in their haste they omit to
do is to make any serious search at all for a simpler explanation.
And how simple the true explanation is! Bishop Haven and his
colleagues, if rightly reported, ought to have known they
would fail. They were attempting under acute disadvantages
what none of the Protestant churches in America, faithfully as
they have striven for it, has ever been able extensively to accomplish. That is, *to get high and low life to worship together*.
The character of much ritual worship and of nearly all non-
ritual worship naturally and properly takes for its standard the
congregation's average intelligence. But this good process of
assortment, unless held in by every proper drawback, flies off
to an excess that leaves the simple and unlearned to a spiritual
starvation apparently as bad as that from which non-ritual worship, especially, professes to revolt. Bishop Dudley, of Kentucky, has lately laid his finger upon this mischief for us with
great emphasis. But, moreover, as in society, so in the church,
this intellectual standard easily degenerates toward a standard of mere manners or station. Thus the gate is thrown wide
open to the social idea, and presently not our Dorcases only,
but at times our very bishops and elders, are busy trying to
make the social relation co-extensive with the church relation.
With what result? Little, generally, save the bad result of congregations trimming themselves down to fit the limitations of

social fellowship. See the case cited. Here were whites, cultured, and counting themselves, at least, as good as the best in the land; and here was an ignorant, superstitious race of boisterous worshipers just emerged from slavery; one side craving spiritual meat, the other needing spiritual milk, and both sides beset by our prevalent American error that social intimacy is one of the distinct *earnings* of church membership. Of course they separated.

It is but a dwarfed idea of the church relation that cramps it into the social relation. The church relation is the grandest fraternity on earth.[6] Social relations are good and proper, but can the social relation grasp all these conditions in one embrace? Can any one social circle span from the drawing room to the stable, from the counting room or professional desk to the kitchen, from the judge's bench to the tailor's and cobbler's, from the prince's crown to the pauper's bowl? Yet without any social intimacy the prince may be the pauper's best friend, and even the pauper the prince's; and the church relation ought to be so wide and high that all these ranks might kneel abreast in it in common worship, and move abreast in it in perfect, active, co-laboring fraternity and regard, gathering any or every social circle into its noble circumference, never pressing one injuriously upon another, and above all things never letting in the slender but mischievous error of confusing Christian fraternity with social equality. Yet the high and low nigh all our country over are kept apart in divine worship by just this error or the fear of it. Fifty thousand Bishop Havens could not, until they had overthrown the domination of this mistake, get the lofty and the lowly to worship together. How could they but separate? And the dragging in of a race instinct to account for the separation is like bringing a pole to knock down strawberries. Other things *will*, but a belief in instinct will *not*, keep the races apart. Look at the West Indies. But not even miscegena-

[6] "There is neither Jew nor Greek, there is neither bond nor free, there is neither male nor female." Galatians 3:28.

tion—may the reader forgive us the bedraggled word—could have saved such a scheme from failure.

The gentlemen prove absolutely nothing for their case, but much against it. For here is shown by actual experiment that even where there is not of necessity a social relation, yet when the social idea merely gets in by mistake of both classes, the effect will not be social confusion, but a spontaneous and willing separation along the strongest lines of social cleavage. The log—the church—will not split the wedge—the social impulse; but the wedge will split the log. The uncultured, be they white or black, in North or South, will break away on one side with even more promptness and spontaneity than the cultured on the other, and will recoil, moreover, to a greater distance than is best for any one concerned. Thus far are we from having the least ground to fear from the blacks that emptiest of phantasms, social aggression. Thus far are we from needing for the protection of social order any assumption of race instinct. And so do the advocates of our traditional sentiments continually establish the opposite of what they seek to prove.

They cite, again, to establish this assumption of race instinct, the spontaneous grouping together of colored people in such social or semi-social organizations as Masonic lodges, military companies, etc. But there is no proscription of whites in the lodges of colored Odd Fellows or Masons. In Georgia, for example, the *law requires* the separation of the races in military companies. The gentlemen forget that the colored people are subject to a strong expulsive power from the whites, which they say must and shall continue whether it is instinct or not; and that the existence of a race instinct can never be proved or disproved until all expulsive forces are withdrawn and both races are left totally free to the influences of those entirely self-sufficient *social* forces which one of the gentlemen has so neatly termed "centripetal." But even if these overlooked facts were out of existence, what would be proved? Only, and for the second time, that the centripetal force of social selection operates so completely to the fulfillment of these gentlemen's wishes that there is no longer any call to prove or disprove the existence of race instinct, or the faintest excuse for arbitrary race separations in the enjoyment of civil rights.

Thus, setting out with the idea that the social integrity of the races requires vigorous protection from without, they prove instead, by every argument brought to establish it, that every relation really social, partially social, or even mistakenly social takes—instinct or no instinct—the most spontaneous and complete care of itself. We are debating the Freedman's title to a totally impersonal freedom in the enjoyment of all impersonal rights; and they succeed only in *saying*, never in bringing a particle of legitimate evidence to prove, that "neither race wants it"; an assertion which no sane man, knowing the facts, can sincerely make until, like these gentlemen, he has first made the most woeful confusion in his own mind between personal social privileges and impersonal civil rights.

VII. THE RIGHT TO RULE

But they have yet one last fancied stronghold. They say, "The *interest* of both races is against it"; that is, against a common participation in their civil rights; and that it is, rather, in favor of a separate enjoyment of them. Now, there are people—but their number is steadily growing less—who would mean by this merely that the interest of both races is against common participation because *they* are against it and have made separate participation the price of peace. But the gentlemen whom we have in view in these chapters, though they must confess their lines often imply this, give a reason somewhat less offensive in its intention. They say common participation means common sociality, and common sociality, race amalgamation. Have we not just used their own facts to show conclusively that this is not what occurs? Yet these two reasons, so called, are actually the only ones that scrutiny can find in all the utterances pledging these gentlemen to "the exactest justice and the fullest equity." Nay, there is another; we must

maintain, they say, "the clear and unmistakable domination of
the white race in the South." —Why, certainly we must! and
we must do it honestly and without tampering with anybody's
natural rights; and we can do it! But why do *they* say we
must do it? Because "character, intelligence, and property" belong pre-eminently to the white race, and "character, intelligence, and property" have "the right to rule." So, as far as the
reasoning is sincere, they are bound to mean that not merely
being white entails this right, but the possession of "character,
intelligence, and property." And the true formula becomes
"the clear and unmistakable domination" of "character, intelligence, and property" "in the South." But if this be the true
doctrine, as who can deny it is? then why—after we have run
the color line to suit ourselves through all our truly social relations—why need we usurp the prerogative to run it so need-
lessly through civil rights, also? It is widely admitted that we
are vastly the superior race in everything—as a race. But is
every colored man inferior to every white man in character,
intelligence, and property? Is there no "responsible and steadfast element" at all among a people who furnish sixteen thousand schoolteachers and are assessed for ninety-one million
dollars' worth of taxable property? Are there no poor and irresponsible whites? So, the color line and the line of character, intelligence, and property frequently cross each other.
Then tell us, gentlemen, which are you really for; the color
line, or the line of character, intelligence, and property that
divides between those who have and those who have not "the
right to rule"? You dare not declare for an inflexible color line;
such an answer would shame the political intelligence of a
Russian.

Another point just here. The right to rule: what is it? It is not
the right to take any peaceable citizen's civil right from him in
whole or in part. It is not the right to decree who may earn or
not earn any *status* within the reach of his proper powers. It is
not the right to oppress. In America, to rule is to serve. There is
a newspaper published in Atlanta called the *Constitution*. The

instrument of which this name is intended to remind us, and of
which it is well to keep us reminded, is founded on a simple
principle that solves the problem of free government over
which Europe sat in dark perplexity for centuries, shedding
tears of blood; the principle that the right to rule is the consent
of the ruled and is vested in the majority by the consent of all.
It took ages of agony for the human race to discover that there
is no moral right of class rule, and that the only safety to human freedom lies in the intelligence, virtue, and wealth of
communities holding every right of every being in such sacred
regard, and all claims for class or personal privilege in such
uniform contempt, that unintelligence, vice, and poverty, having no potent common grievance, shall naturally invest intelligence, character, and property with the right to rule. It took
ages for us to discover the necessity of binding intelligence,
character, and property to the maintenance of this attitude by
giving, once for all, to the *majority* the custody and right of
assignment of this truly precious right to rule. Is this mere
sentiment? A scheme in the clouds? Who says so cannot truly
qualify as a whole American citizen. The safety of American
government is that intelligence, virtue, and wealth dare not
press any measure whose viciousness or tyranny might suspend
the expulsive forces that keep unintelligence, vice, and poverty
divided among themselves; and that intelligence and virtue
hold themselves entirely free to combine now with wealth and
now with poverty as now the lower million or now the upper
ten shows the livelier disposition to impose upon the other.
But the only way to preserve these conditions is to hold sacred
the will and voice of the majority. Of course there are friction
and imperfections in their working; but human wisdom has not
yet found any other scheme that carries us so near to perfect
government. The right to rule is a right to earn the confidence
and choice of the majority of the whole unfettered people. Yet
it is in the face of this fundamental principle of American freedom that our traditionist friends stand, compelling six million
Freedmen to mass together under a group of common griev-

ances, within a wall of these gentlemen's own avowed building, then charging them with being "leagued together in ignorance and irresponsibility," and then talking in large approval about "*minorities*"—not earning, but—"*asserting and maintaining* control." And a proposition to set such antique usurpation of human rights aside, to remove the real grievances that make a common cause for six million distrusted and distrusting people, to pull down that wall of civil—*not social*—distinctions that tends to keep them "leagued together in ignorance and irresponsibility," to open to them the *civil*—not social—rewards of gentility and education, and the responsibilities of knowledge and citizenship, to arouse in them the same concern in common public interests that we feel, and to make all their fortunes subject to the same influences as ours—this, we are told, is "against the interest of both races"! And this we have from men who, claiming a pre-eminent right to speak for the South, claim with it a "right to rule" that fails to signify anything better than the right of the white man to rule the black without his consent and without any further discrimination between intelligence and unintelligence or between responsibility and irresponsibility. In other words, a principle of political and civil selection such as no free man could possibly choose and which cannot be the best interest of any American community. So the other side are our witnesses again. And now we may say to them, as the lawyers do in court, "That will do."

VIII. SUMMING UP

The case is before the reader. The points of fact made in our earlier paper—the privations suffered by the colored people in their matters of civil rights—have been met with feeble half denials equivalent to admissions by opponents in controversy too engrossed with counter statements and arguments, that crumble at the touch, to attend to a statement of facts. In the end they stand thus: As to churches, there are probably not a dozen in the land, if one, "colored" or "white," where a white

person is not at least professedly welcome to its best accommodations; while the colored man, though he be seven eighths
white, is shut up, on the ground that "his race" prefers it, to
the poor and often unprofitable appointments of the "African"
church, whether he like it best or not, unless he is ready to
accept without a murmur distinctions that mark him, in the
sight of the whole people, as one of a despised caste and that
follow him through the very sacraments. As to schooling, despite the fact that he is today showing his eager willingness to
accept separate schools for his children wherever the white
man demands the separation, yet both his children and the
white man's are being consigned to illiteracy wherever they
are too few and poor to form separate schools. In some moun-
tainous parts of Kentucky there is but one colored school district in a *county*. In railway travel the colored people's rights
are tossed from pillar to post with an ever-varying and therefore more utterly indefensible and intolerable capriciousness.
In Virginia they may ride exactly as white people do and in
the same cars. In a neighboring state, a white man may ride in
the "ladies' car," while a colored man of exactly the same dress
and manners—nay, his wife or daughter—must ride in the no-
torious "Jim Crow car," unprotected from smokers and dram
drinkers and lovers of vile language. "In South Carolina," says
the Charleston *News and Courier,* on the other hand, "respectable colored persons who buy first-class tickets on any railroad
ride in the first-class cars as a right, and their presence excites
no comment on the part of their white fellow-passengers. It is
a great deal pleasanter to travel with respectable and well-
behaved colored people than with unmannerly and ruffianly
white men." In Alabama the majority of the people have not
made this discovery, at least if we are to believe their newspapers. In Tennessee the law *requires* the separation of all first-
class passengers by race with equal accommodations for both;
thus waiving the old plea of decency's exigencies and forcing
upon American citizens adjudged to be first-class passengers
an alienism that has thrown away its last shadow of an excuse.

But this is only the law, and the history of the very case alluded to by our traditionist friends, in which a colored woman
gained damages for being compelled to accept inferior accommodation or none for a first-class ticket, is the history of an
outrage so glaring that only a person blinded to the simplest
rights of human beings could cite it in such a defense.

A certain daily railway train was supplied, according to the
law, with a smoking car and two first-class cars, one for colored and one for whites. The two first-class cars were so nearly
of a kind that they were exchangeable. They generally kept
their relative positions on the track; but the "ladies' car" of the
morning trip became the "colored car" of the return, afternoon,
trip, and *vice versa*. But the rules of the colored car were little
regarded. Men, white and black, were sometimes forbidden,
sometimes allowed, to smoke and drink there. Says the court,
"The evidence is abundant to show that the rule excluding
smoking from that car was but a nominal one, that it was often disregarded, that white passengers understood it to be a
nominal rule, and that adequate means were not adopted to
secure the same first-class and orderly passage to the colored
passengers occupying that car as was accorded to the passengers in the rear car. Nor was the separation of the classes of
the passengers complete. There is no evidence tending to show
that the white passengers were excluded from the car assigned
to colored passengers, and it appears that whenever the train
was unusually crowded it was expected that the excess of
white passengers would ride, as they then did ride, in the forward one of the two first-class cars. So, too, it appeared that
persons of color, of whom the plaintiff was one, had several
times occupied seats in the rear car." A certain "person of lady-
like appearance and deportment," one day in September 1883,
got aboard this train with a first-class ticket. She knew the
train, and that, as the court states it, "in the rear car . . . quiet
and good order were to so great an extent the rule that it was
rarely if ever that any passenger gave annoyance by his conduct to his fellow-passengers." In the colored car there was at

least one colored man smoking, and one white man whom she saw to be drunk. She entered the rear car and sat down, no one objecting. She was the only colored person there. The conductor, collecting his tickets, came to her. He was not disconcerted. Not long previously he had forbidden another colored person to ride in that car, who must also have been "of lady-like appearance and deportment," for when he saw this one he "supposed her to be the same person . . . intentionally violating the defendant's (Railroad's) rules and *seeking to annoy his other passengers*." Twice they exchanged polite request and refusal to leave the car; and then, in full presence of all those "other passengers" whom this person of lady-like appearance and deportment was erroneously suspected of seeking to annoy, there occurred a thing that ought to make the nation blush. The conductor laid hands upon this defenseless woman, whose infraction of a rule was interfering neither with the running of the road, the collection of fares, nor the comfort of passengers, and "by force removed her from her seat and carried her out of the car. When near the door of the car the plaintiff promised that she would then, if permitted, leave the car rather than be forcibly ejected; but the conductor, as he says, told her that her consent came too late, and continued to remove her forcibly. On reaching the platform of the car, plaintiff left the train." Judgment was given for the plaintiff. But the point was carefully made that she would have been without any grievance if the "colored car" had only been kept first-class. In other words, for not providing separate first-class accommodations, five hundred dollars' damages; for laying violent hands upon a peaceable, lady-like, and unprotected woman, nothing; and nothing for requiring such a one publicly to sit apart from passengers of the same grade under a purely ignominious distinction. What! not ignominious? Fancy the passenger a white lady, choosing, for reasons of her own, to sit in a first-class "colored car"; infringing, if you please, some rule; but paying her way, and causing no one any inconvenience, unsafety, or delay. Imagine her, on insisting upon her wish to stay, drawn from her seat by force, and lifted and carried out by a black conductor, telling her as he goes that her offer to walk out comes too late. If this is not ignominy, what is it? To the commission and palliation of such unmanly deeds are we driven by our attempts to hold under our own arbitrary dictation others' rights that we have no moral right to touch, rights that in ourselves we count more sacred than property and dearer than life.

But we must not tarry. If we turn to the matter of roadside refreshment, what do we see? Scarcely a dozen railroad refreshment rooms from the Rio Grande to the Potomac—is there one?—where the weary and hungry colored passenger, be he ever so perfect in dress and behavior, can snatch a hasty meal in the presence of white guests of any class whatever, though in any or every one of them he or she can get the same food, and eat with the same knife, fork, and plate that are furnished to white strangers, if only he or she will take a menial's attitude and accept them in the kitchen. Tennessee has formally "abrogated the rule of the common law" in order to make final end of "any right in favor of any such person so refused admission" to the enjoyment of an obvious civil right which no public host need ever permit any guest to mistake for a social liberty. As to places of public amusement, the gentlemen who say that "each [race] gets the same accommodation for the same money," simply—forget. The statement comes from Atlanta. But, in fact, in Atlanta, in Georgia, in the whole South, there is scarcely a place of public amusement—except the cheap museums, where there are no seated audiences—in which a colored man or woman, however unobjectionable personally, can buy, at any price, any but a second-, sometimes any but a third- or fourth-class accommodation. During a day's stay in Atlanta lately, the present writer saw many things greatly to admire; many inspiring signs of thrift, stability, virtue, and culture. Indeed, where can he say that he has not seen them, in ten Southern states lately visited? And it is in contemplation of these evidences of greatness, prosperity, safety, and the desire to be just, that he feels constrained to ask whether it must be that in the principal depot of such a city the hopeless excommunication of every person of African tincture from the civil rewards of gentility must be advertised by three signs at the entrances of three separate rooms, one for "Ladies," one for "Gentlemen," and the third a "Colored waiting room"? Visiting the principal library of the city, he was eagerly assured, in response to inquiry, that no person of color would be allowed to draw out books; and when a colored female, not particularly tidy in dress, came forward to return a book and draw another, it was quickly explained that she was merely a servant and messenger for some white person. Are these things necessary to—are they consistent with—an exalted civilization founded on equal rights and the elevation of the masses?

And the Freedman's rights in the courts. It is regarding this part of our subject that our friends on the other side make a mistake too common everywhere and very common among us of the South. That is, they assume the state of affairs in more distant localities to be the same as that immediately around them. A statement concerning certain matters in Florida or Maryland is indignantly denied in Tennessee or Texas because it is not true of those regions; and so throughout. It is in this spirit that one of these gentlemen explains that in Georgia Negroes are not excluded from the jury lists except for actual incompetency, and thereupon *assumes* that Georgia does not materially differ from the other states." But really, in Tennessee they may not sit in the jury box at all, except that in a few counties they may sit in judgment on the case of a colored person. While in Texas, at the very time of the gentleman's writing, the suggestion of one of her distinguished citizens to accord the right of jury duty to the colored people was being flouted by the press as an "innovation upon established usage," and a "sentimental and utterly impracticable idea." This in the face of a state constitution and laws that give no warrant for the race distinction. So much for assumption.

The same mistake is repeated by the same writer in discussing the question of the Freedmen's criminal sentences. No fact or person is brought forward to prove or disprove anything except for Georgia. And even the prosecuting attorney for the Atlanta circuit, brought in to testify, says, for the state's cities and towns, that the Negro gets there "equal and exact justice before the courts"; but he is not willing to deny "a lingering prejudice and occasional injustice" in remote counties. Why, with nearly six million freed people getting "full and exact justice in the courts whether the jury is white or black," why could there not be found *among them* two or three trustworthy witnesses to testify to this fact? Their testimony would have been important, for these lines are written within hand's reach of many letters from colored men denying that such is the case.

The present writer does not charge, and never did, that our Southern white people consciously and maliciously rendered oppressive verdicts against the Freedman. On the contrary, it is plainly stated by him that they acted "not so maliciously as unreflectingly," and "ignorant of the awful condition of the penitentiaries." His only printed utterance on the subject is on record in "The Freedman's Case in Equity," and is too long to quote; but he cited the *official reports* of our Southern state prisons themselves, and asked how with their facts before us we are to escape the conviction that the popular mind had been seduced—as every student of American prison statistics knows it has—by the glittering temptation of our Southern convict lease system; and not one word of reply have we had, except the assertion, which nobody would think of denying, that the black man, often in Georgia, and sometimes elsewhere, gets an even-handed and noble justice from white juries.

Have our opponents observed the workings of this convict lease system? To put such a system as a rod of punishment into the hands of a powerful race sitting in judgment upon the misdemeanors of a feebler and despised caste would warp the verdicts of the most righteous people under the sun. Examine

our Southern penitentiary reports. What shall we say to such
sentences inflicted for larceny alone, as twelve, fourteen, fifteen, twenty, and in one case forty years of a penal service
whose brutal tasks and whippings kill in an average of five
years? Larceny is the peculiar crime of the poorest classes everywhere. In all penitentiaries out of the South the convicts for
this offense always exceed and generally double the number
of convicts for burglary. Larceny has long been called the
favorite crime of the Negro criminal. What, then, shall we say
to the facts, deduced from official records, that in the Georgia
penitentiary and convict camps there were in 1882 twice as
many colored convicts for burglary as for larceny, and that
they were, moreover, serving sentences averaging nearly twice
the average of the white convicts in the same places for the
same crime? This, too, notwithstanding a very large number
of short sentences to colored men, and a difference between
their longest and shortest terms twice as great as in the case
of the whites. For larceny the difference is five times as great.[7]
Shall we from these facts draw hasty conclusions? We draw
none. If any one can explain them away, in the name of humanity let us rejoice to see him do so. We are far from charging any one with deliberately prostituting justice. We are far
from overlooking "the depravity of the Negro." But those who
rest on this cheap explanation are bound to tell us which shows
the greater maliciousness; for one man to be guilty of hog
stealing or for twelve jurors to send him to the coal mines
for twenty years for doing it? In Georgia outside her prisons
there are eight whites to every seven blacks. Inside, there are
eight whites to every eighty blacks. The depravity of the Negro may explain away much, but we cannot know how much
while there also remain in force the seductions of our atrocious
convict lease system, and our attitude of domination over the
blacks, so subtly dangerous to our own integrity. Here is a
rough, easy test that may go for what it is worth: These crimes

[7] Without counting the exceptional forty years' sentence
mentioned.

of larceny and burglary are just the sort—since they are neither
the most trivial nor the most horrible—to incur excessive verdicts and sentences, if the prejudices of one class against another come into the account. Now, what is the fact in the
prisons we have mentioned? Of all the inmates under sentence
for these crimes nineteen twentieths are classed as of that race
which we "dominate" both out of and in the jury box. We
ask no opinion on these points from the stupid or vicious of
either whites or blacks; but is it wise for us not to consider
what may be their effect upon the minds of the property-
holding, intelligent, and virtuous portion of the "dominated"
race? Is it right?

IX. POLITICAL "SOLIDITY"—WHY
AND TILL WHEN

In the same number of the *Century* that contains "In Plain
Black and White," appears an open letter on "The Solid
South." It tells us that political "solidity," founded on the
merits neither of candidates nor questions, is an emphatic national and still greater local evil; but that the whites of the
South "had to be solid," because they feared, and that they
still fear, the supremacy of the blacks. That if this fear were
removed the whites would divide. Hence, we must first procure the division of the blacks; this is what it calls "the pre-
requisite." Is it? Is that a wise or just arbitration? Must the
side that is immeasurably the weaker begin the disarmament?
Is *"noblesse oblige"* untranslatable into "American"? We are
only told that "once divide the Negro vote and the 'solid
South' is broken." True statement, but sadly antique. An old
catchword pulled out of the rubbish of the Reconstruction
strife. And why was the Negro vote solid? The carpetbagger
and scallawag? It was so believed, and these—the most of them
richly deserving their fate—were suppressed. What then? Less
political activity among the blacks. But division? No. Then
why were the blacks still "solid"? The open letter gives two

causes: first, gratitude to the Republican party; second, fear of the Democratic. But these sentiments, it says, are fading out. Will their disappearance reveal the solid blacks divided? That depends on the matter that forms—what the open letter does not touch—the solid bottom of this question. But the more ambitious article in the same number of the magazine boldly confesses it when it decrees *the subserviency of the Freedman's civil rights to the white man's domination.* As long as that continues to be or to threaten, the blacks will be solid. We—any people—would be so—would have to be so, in their place. Such a decree is equivalent to saying they must and shall be solid. Only let it be withdrawn and the solidity will vanish from the white vote and the black at the same instant.

This is what is coming. There is today no political party in America that is "solid" for this un-American and tyrannical principle; and the reason why the Negro vote is a divided vote in the North today and in the South shows more signs of dividing than ever before is that the Republican party has grown fat and lazy concerning civil rights, while *Democratic* legislatures and governors, North, East, West, have been passing and signing Civil Rights bills, rooting out of the laws and of popular sentiment this heresy of domination by fixed class and race, and throwing to the winds "legal discriminations on account of color [which] are not based on character or conduct and have no relation to moral worth and fitness for civic usefulness, but are rather relics of prejudice which had its origin in slavery. I recommend," says the present Democratic governor of Ohio, from whose message we are quoting, "I recommend their total repeal." It is but little over a year since the Democrats joined the Republicans in the legislature of Connecticut in making liable to fine and imprisonment "every person who subjects or causes to be subjected any other person to the deprivation of any rights, privileges, or immunities secured or protected by the Constitution of the state or of the United States, on account of such person being an alien or by reason of his color or race." The time is still shorter since a Democratic ma-

jority in the legislature of New Jersey passed a bill of civil
rights, as its own text says, "applicable alike to citizens of every race and color." Nor are they afraid of the names of things.
"By direction of Governor Abbett," writes the executive clerk,
"I send you copy of the *Civil Rights bill*[8] as passed by the Legislature and approved by him." In Indiana, while these pages
were being written, Democrats were endeavoring to pass a
civil rights bill. In May of last year the legislature at Albany
passed a bill removing the last remaining civil disabilities from
the colored people in the city of New York, by a *unanimous
vote*, "three fifths being present"; and the governor who signed
the act is now President of the United States.

"Ah!" some will say, "these Northern Democrats do this in
their ignorance; they do not know the Negro." Is this the whole
truth? Do not we forget that they have only gradually put
aside from their own minds the very worst opinion of the Negro that ever we had? To get where they are they have left
behind the very same prejudices and misconceptions of citizens' rights that we are called to lay aside, and no others. Nay,
even we assert facts now that twenty years ago we used to
say no man who knew the Negro could honestly believe.

"But"—the answer comes again—"if they had the Negro
among them numerically powerful, they would not venture to
concede"—etc. Let us see: From Georgia, where, we are told,
the Freedman shall never enjoy "the policy indicated in the
Civil Rights bill," pass across its eastern boundary, and lo, we
are in a state under Southern Democratic rule, where the
blacks are in the majority, yet which is not afraid to leave on
the printed page, from the days of Reconstruction, a civil
rights bill, not nearly so comprehensive, it is true, but "fully
as stringent," says its leading daily journal, "as any that Congress ever placed upon the statute books," and attending
whose enforcement "there is no friction or unpleasantness."
This, in South Carolina!

May the time be not long delayed when her strong, proud

[8] Italicized only here.

people, that are sometimes wrong but ever conscientious and
ever brave, not content with merely not undoing, shall broaden
the applications of that law until it perfectly protects white
man and black man alike in the enjoyment of every civil right,
and their hearts behind the law open to the Freedman equally
with the white man, as far as in him lies to achieve it, every
civil reward of intelligence, wealth, and virtue. Then shall it
still be as true as it is today that "No special harm has come
of it." Not only so; but the Freedman, free indeed, shall along
with his other fetters cast off the preoccupation in this question of civil rights which now engrosses his best intelligence,
and shall become a factor in the material and moral progress
of the whole land. Be the fault now where it may, he will not
then outnumber the white man on the prison rolls eleven to
one. And what is true of one Southern state is true of all. The
temptations to which the Negro—shut out from aspirations—
now yields, will lose their power, and his steps be turned with
a new hope and desire toward the prizes of industry, frugality,
and a higher cultivation. Multiplying and refining his tastes,
the rank energies of his present nature will not, as now, run
entirely to that animal fecundity characteristic of all thriftless,
reckless, unaspiring populations; his increase in civic value will
be quickened, his increase in numbers retarded to a rate more
like our own. And neither all the crops our sun-loved South
can yield, nor all the metals and minerals that are under the
soil made sacred by the blood of her patriots can bring us
such wealth and prosperity as will this change in the hopes
and ambitions of our once unaspiring, time-serving slaves. The
solid black will be solid no longer; but he will still be black.

X. THE GEOGRAPHY OF AMALGAMATION

Is it not wonderful? A hundred years we have been fearing
to do entirely right lest something wrong should come of it;
fearing to give the black man an equal chance with us in the
race of life lest we might have to grapple with the vast, vague

afrite of amalgamation; and in all this hundred years, with the
enemies of slavery getting from us such names as Negrophiles,
Negro-worshipers, and miscegenationists; and while we were
claiming to hold ourselves rigidly separate from the lower race
in obedience to a natal instinct which excommunicated them
both socially and civilly; just in proportion to the rigor, the
fierceness, and the injustice with which this excommunication
from the common rights of man has fallen upon the darker
race, has amalgamation taken place. Look—we say again—at
the West Indies. Then turn and look at those regions of our
common country that we have been used to call the nests of
fanaticism; Philadelphia, Boston, Plymouth Church, and the
like. Look at Oberlin, Ohio. For years this place was the grand
central depot, as one might say, of the "Underground Railway"; receiving and passing on toward Canada and freedom
thousands of fugitive slaves; weeping over them, praying over
them, feeding them, housing them, hiding them in her bosom,
defying the law for them, educating them, calling them sir
and madam, braving no end of public contumely, and showing them every exasperating consideration. Look at Berea,
Kentucky, where every kind thing contrivable that, according
to our old ideas, could destroy a white man's self-respect and
"spoil a nigger" has been practiced. What is the final fact?
Amalgamation? Miscegenation? Not at all. The letters of the
presidents of these two famous institutions lie before the present writer, stating that from neither of them throughout their
history has there resulted a single union of a white with a
black person either within their precincts or elsewhere within
the nation's wide boundaries. And of the two towns in which
they are situated, in only one have there been from first to last
three or four such unions. How have they been kept apart?
By law? By fierce conventionality? By instinct? No! It was because they *did not* follow instinct, but the better dictates of
reason and the ordinary natural preferences of like for like.
But, it is sometimes asked, admitting this much, will not undivided civil relations tend eventually—say after a few centu-

ries—to amalgamation? Idle question! Will it help the matter
to withhold men's manifest rights? What can we do better for
the remotest future than to be just in the present and leave
the rest to the Divine Rewarder of nations that walk uprightly?

XI. THE NATURAL-GROWTH POLICY

There is a school of thought in the South that stands mid-
way between the traditionists and us. Its disciples have reasoned away the old traditions and are now hampered only by
vague ideas of inexpediency. They pray everybody not to
hurry. They have a most enormous capacity for pausing and
considering. "It is a matter," says one of them in a late peri-
odical, "of centuries rather than decades, of evolution rather
than revolution." The heartlessness of such speeches they are
totally unconscious of. Their prayer is not so much that our
steps may be logical as geological. They propose to wait the
slow growth of civilization as if it were the growth of rocks,
or as if this were the twelfth or thirteenth century. They contemplate progress as if it were a planetary movement to be
looked at through the telescope. Why, we are the motive
power of progress! Its speed depends on our courage, integrity,
and activity. It is an insult to a forbearing God and the civilized world for us to sit in full view of moral and civil wrongs
manifestly bad and curable, saying we must expect this or
that, and that, geologically considered, we are getting along
quite rapidly. Such talk never won a battle or a race, and the
hundred years past is long enough for us of the South to have
been content with a speed that the rest of the civilized world
has left behind. The tortoise won in the race with the hare,
the race didn't win itself. We have listened far too much already to those who teach the safety of being slow. "*Make haste
slowly*," is the true emphasis. Cannot these lovers of maxims
appreciate that "Delays are dangerous"? For we have a case
before us wherein there is all danger and no safety in floating
with the tide.

Our fathers had such a case when African slavery was first fastening its roots about the foundations of our order of society. They were warned by their own statesmen to make haste and get rid of it. "You must approach the subject," cried the great Jefferson. "You must adopt some plan of emancipation or worse will follow"; and all the way down to Henry Clay that warning was with more or less definiteness repeated. But our fathers were bitten with the delusion of postponement, and the practice of slavery became an Institution. It grew, until every element of force in our civilization—the political arena, the sacred desk, the legislative hall, the academical chair—all —were wrapped in its dark shadow. Where might not our beloved South be today, far on in front, but for that sad mistake? At length, suddenly, rudely, slavery was brought to an end. What that cost we all know; yet let us hope there are many of us who can say with our sainted Lee, not merely "I am rejoiced that slavery is abolished"; but "I would cheerfully have lost all I have lost by the war, and have suffered all I have suffered, to have this object attained."[9]

Such was our fathers' problem. The problem before us is the green, rank stump of that felled Institution. Slavery in particular—the slavery of the individual man to his one master, which rested upon the law, is by the law abolished. Slavery in general—the subordination of a fixed rule to a fixed ruling class—the slavery of *civil caste*, which can only in part, and largely cannot, be legislated away, remains. Sad will it be for our children if we leave it for their inheritance.

A Southern man traveling in the North and a Northern man just returned from a commercial tour of the South lately fell into conversation on a railway train. Said the Northerner, "What the South needs is to import capital, induce immigration, develop her enormous latent wealth, and let politics alone." "Sir," said the Southerner, "I know you by that sign

[9] See open letter in the *Century* for May 1885.

for a commercial man, as I might know a hard student by his glasses and peering eyes. With you all things else are subsidiary to commerce; hence, even commercially, you are near-sighted. It is true the South should seek those things you mention. They are for her better safety, comfort, and happiness. But what are politics? In this land, at least, simply questions concerning the maintenance or increase of our safety, comfort, and happiness; questions that cannot be let alone, but must be attended to as long as those things demand to be maintained or increased." —The train stopped in a depot. Men could be heard under the wheels, tapping them with their hammers to test their soundness.—"To ask us to let politics alone is to ask us to leave the wheels of our train untested, its engine unoiled, its hot boxes glowing, while we scurry on after more passengers and passengers' fares—which is just the way not to get them. Do not ask it of us. Our scantiness of capital, meagerness of population, and the undeveloped condition of our natural resources are largely owing, this day, to our blindly insisting that certain matters in our politics shall be let alone. It was our letting them alone that brought federal interference, and that interference has been withdrawn upon our pledge not to let them alone but to settle them."

About a year ago the present writer visited the thriving town of Birmingham, Alabama. Its smelting furnaces were viewed with special interest. It was fine to see the crude ore of the earth, so long trampled under foot, now being turned by great burnings and meltings into one of the prime factors of the world's wealth. But another thought came with this, at sight of the dark, brawny men standing or moving here and there with the wild glare of molten cinder and liquid metal falling upon their black faces and reeking forms. These were no longer simple husbandmen, companions of unfretted nature. If the subterranean wealth of the South is to be brought to the surface and to market all over the land, as now it is in this miniature of the great English Birmingham; if, as seems inevitable, the black man is to furnish the manual labor for this vast result, then how urgent is our necessity for removing from him all sense of grievance that we rightly may remove, and all impediment to his every proper aspiration, ere the bright, amiable influences of green fields and unsoiled streams, of leafy woods, clear sky, fragrant airs, and song of birds pass out of his life, and the sooty, hardening, dulling toils of the coalpit and the furnace, and the huddled life that goes with it, breed a new bad knowledge of the power of numbers and a thirst for ferocious excitements, and make him the dangerous and intractable animal that now he is not. For our own interests, one and all of them, we ought to lose no time.

Our task is one whose difficulties can never be less, its facilities never be greater. We have no wars to distract and preoccupy. Here is a kindly race of poor men unlearned in the evil charms of unions, leagues, secret orders, strikes and bread riots; looking not upon the capitalist as a natural enemy; stranger to all those hostilities against the richer and stronger world around them which drive apart the moneyed man and the laborer wherever living has become a hard struggle. What an opportunity is ours today that will never return when once it goes from us. Look at Ireland.

XII. "MOVE ON"

We occupy, moreover, a ground on which we cannot remain. It is not where we stood at the war's end. We approve the Freedman's ownership of himself. We see and feel there is no going back from universal suffrage. And its advocate may make a point of tremendous strength in the fact that this very universality of suffrage is what has bred in the South a new sense of the necessity of public education for all and of whatever else will enlighten and elevate the lower mass. Ignorance, penury, unintelligence, and the vices that go with them—the bonds that hold the Freedman down from beneath—we are helping them to cast off. But to cut these loose and still lay on the downward pressure of civil caste—is there any consistency in this? We cannot do it and respect our own intelligence. Socially we can do nothing for the Freedman or against him by rule or regulation. That is a matter, as we might say, of specific gravity. But as to his civil rights, we cannot stay where we are. Neither can we go backward.

To go forward we must cure one of our old-time habits—the habit of letting error go uncontradicted because it is ours. It grew out of our having an institution to defend, that made a united front our first necessity. We have none now. Slavery is gone. State rights are safer than ever before, because better defined; or, if unsafe, only because *we* have grown loose on the subject. We have nothing peculiar left save civil caste. Let us, neighbor with neighbor, and friend with friend, speak of it, think of it, write of it, get rid of it. Ruskin's words seem almost meant for our moment and region: "For now some ten or twelve years," he says, "I have been asking every good writer whom I know to write some part of what was exactly true, in the greatest of the sciences, that of Humanity." We speak for this when we speak truly against civil caste. It is caste that the immortal Heber calls "a system which tends . . . to destroy the feelings of general benevolence." As far, then, as civil rights are concerned, at least, let us be rid of it. This done, the words North and South shall mean no more than East or West, signifying only directions and regions, and not antipodal ideas of right and government; and though each of us shall love his own state with ardor, the finest word to our ear as citizens shall be America.

To America we see irreversibly assigned the latest, greatest task in the "science of Humanity": to burst the last chrysalis of the national relation and consummate its last grand metamorphosis. Once it knew no wider bound than the tribal relation. But the day is on us at length, the problem is ours, and its great weight and responsibility and the honor of it when achieved rest and will rest on our Southern states. It is to make

national harmony and unity broader than race; to crystallize
into fact the truth that national unity need not demand unifica-
tion of race; to band together—without one single class disa-
bility or privilege diminishing or enhancing any individual's
intrinsic value—in that one common, undistinguished enjoyment of every human civil right which only can insure national
harmony and unity, two antipodal races; two races that have
no wish to, and for all we know never will, mingle their two
bloods in one stream.

Nationalization *by* fusion of bloods is the maxim of barba-
rous times and peoples. Nationalization *without* racial confusion is ours to profess and to procure. It is not a task of our
choosing. But our fathers, unawares, entailed it upon us, and
we cannot but perform it. We cannot hold American principles
in perfect faith and not do it. The good doctrine of liberty to
all and license to none thrusts it inevitably into our hands. To
make national unity without hybridity—the world has never
seen it done as we have got to do it; but it is the business
of every generation that comes into the world to bring into it
better things than it has ever seen. We have got to build a
nationality as free from all civil estrangement as from social
confusion, yet wider than the greatest divergence of human
races. This is the meaning of the great revolution upon us today. Daily the number increases of those who grasp it. A little
while ago the whole nation rejected it. To reject it today is to
be left behind the nation's best thought. How fast that thought
is spreading in the South few know. Like the light of kindling
watch fires it is catching from mind to mind. The best men of
the South are coming daily into convictions that condemn their
own beliefs of yesterday as the antiquated artillery of an outgrown past; and to the present writer, as one who himself
found this not easy, but hard, to do, it seems no improbability
that our traditionist friends, even before this reply can reach
them, may be found ranging themselves among that number,
for the promotion of this revolution that everybody knows

must come. To say what must, is to say what will be; and so
shall the reproach of slavery, the greatest moral mistake made
by the whole American nation, be swallowed up in the honor
of this noble gain for the cause of humanity and universal
peace.

The Negro Question

[Cable saw cumulative evidence that the Silent South did actually exist. Marion A. Baker, brother of Page Baker and literary editor of the *Times-Democrat,* held opinions in no significant way different from Cable's but kept them secret. He considered leaving the paper, he said, when Page Baker launched it into the attack on Cable. Though he kept quiet and held his position, he remained Cable's closest friend in New Orleans until his death. Cable had dozens of correspondents over the South who collected information for him, reported the tenor of opinion around them, or stated objections to his views, as was often the case, and asked for help in reaching their own conclusions. Booker T. Washington, engaged in his heroic work at Tuskegee Institute, supplied information but asked that his name not be associated with it, for he must keep the friendship of Southern whites. Washington wrote once to another of his correspondents, "There are many in the South who *think* as Mr. Cable does but have not the moral courage to express their sentiments."

In May and June 1887, Cable traveled through the South for the first time since the publication of "The Freedman's Case in Equity," more than two years earlier. He found the people at first wary or unfriendly, as the journalists and politicians had taught them to be; but as they talked together they showed themselves willing to believe him sincere and reasonable at least in his goals. From Richmond he wrote his wife, "The gentle negatives are obvious." From Spartanburg, South Carolina, "The light is breaking." At Macon, Georgia, people came to him to discuss "the great sore question" and "debated in a very commendable spirit," he said. "It is a noble sign of the change that is beginning to work in the public mind." At Fayetteville, Tennessee, and at Nashville he delivered an address which had grown from his observations on his tour. He had seen prosperity but he had seen also Bourbonism of the worst kind. There must be a reliance on the will of the majority, he concluded, as the only assurance that natural private inequality will not grow into public inequality. In the functioning of a free electorate the unqualified segment will always be represented by the qualified minority. Acceptance of these assumptions would be returning, in the phrase he made the title of his address, to "The Faith of Our Fathers."

This address was made later into the magazine essay "The Negro Question in the United States." It was published in the London *Contemporary Review,* March 1888, and in *The Negro Question,* 1890, with the title shortened. It was published also in the Chicago *Inter-Ocean* and the New York *Tribune,* March 4, 1888, and as a pamphlet by the American Missionary Association, New York, 1888.]

The Negro Question

THE QUESTION

I

The matter that is made the subject of these pages is not to-day the most prominent, but it is the gravest, in American affairs. It is one upon which, of late years, as we might say, much inattention has been carefully bestowed. It has become a dreaded question. We are not politically indolent. We are dealing courageously with many serious problems. We admit that no nation has yet so shaken wrong and oppression from its skirts that it may safely and honorably sit down in a state of mercantile and aesthetical preoccupation. And yet the mat-

ter that gives us daily the profoundest unrest goes daily by
default. The nation's bitter experiences with it in years past,
the baffling complications that men more cunning than wise
have woven around it, its proneness to swallow up all other
questions, and the eruptions of rancor and strife that attend
every least sign of its spontaneous re-opening have made it
such a weariness and offense to the great majority, and especially to our commercial impatience, that the public mind
in large part eagerly accepts the dangerous comfort of postponement.

What is this question? Superficially, it is whether a certain
seven millions of the people, one ninth of the whole, dwelling
in and natives to the Southern states of the Union, and by
law an undifferentiated part of the nation, have or have not
the same full measure of the American citizen's rights that
they would have were they entirely of European instead of
wholly or partly African descent. The seven millions, concerning whom the question is asked, answer as with one voice,
that they have not. Millions in the Northern states, and thousands in the Southern, of whites, make the same reply. While
other millions of whites, in North and South, respond not so
often with a flat contradiction as with a declaration far more
disconcerting. For the "Southerner" speaks truly when he re-
torts that nowhere in the entire Union, either North or South,
are the disadvantages of being a black, or partly black, man
confined entirely to the relations of domestic life and private
society; but that in every part there is a portion, at least, of
the community that does not claim for, or even willingly yield
to, the Negro the whole calendar of American rights in the
same far-reaching amplitude and sacredness that they do for,
or to, the white man. The Southern white man points to thousands of Northern and Western factories, counting rooms,
schools, hotels, churches, and guilds, and these attest the
truth of his countercharge. Nowhere in the United States is
there a whole community from which the black man, after
his physical, mental, and moral character have been duly

weighed, if they be weighed at all, is not liable to suffer an
unexplained discount for mere color and race, which he would
have to suffer publicly in no other country of the enlightened
world. This being the fact, then, in varying degrees according
to locality, what does it prove? Only that this cannot be the
real point of issue between North and South, and that this
superficial definition is not the true one.

Putting aside mere differences of degree, the question is
not, Are these things so? but, Ought they so to be? To this a
large majority in the Northern states from all classes, with a
small minority of the Southern whites, also from all ranks of
life, and the whole seven million blacks, irrespective of party
leanings, answer "No." On the other hand, a large majority of
the whites in the Southern states—large as to the white population of those states, but a very small minority in the nation
at large—answer a vehement "Yes; these things should and
shall be so."

But how does this small minority maintain itself? It does
so owing to the familiar fact that, although by our scheme of
government there is a constant appeal to the majority of the
whole people, the same scheme provides, also, for the defense
of local interests against rash actions of national majorities by
a parallel counterappeal (constantly through its Senate and
at times in other ways) to the majority, not of the people *en
masse,* but of the states in their corporate capacity. Now a
very large minority in the Northern states, whose own private
declaration would be against a difference between white
men's rights and other men's rights, nevertheless refuse now,
as they refused before the Civil War, to answer with a plain
yes or no, but maintain, with the Southern white-rule party,
that *whether these things ought so to be or not is a question
that every state must be allowed to answer for, and to, itself
alone;* thus so altering the voice of the nation, when it speaks
by states, as virtually to nullify that negative answer which
would be given by a majority of the whole people. In the
Civil Rights bill the verdict of the states was once given

against all race discrimination in all matters of public rights
whatsoever, and for confining it within that true domain—of
private choice—to which the judgment of other Christian nations consigns it. But the Civil Rights bill, never practically
effective in the communities whose upper ranks were hostile
to it, has at last perished in the inner citadel of our government's strong conservatism, the national Supreme Court, and
the Senate majority that passed the bill was long ago lost by
revolutions in the Southern states. Thus, by a fundamental
provision in the national government, intended for the very
purpose of protecting the weak from the strong, a small
national minority has for twenty-five years been enabled to
withstand the pressure of an immense majority.

Whether this is by a right or wrong use of the provision
is part of the open question. The weak are protected from the
strong, but the still weaker are delivered into the hands of
the strong. Seven millions of the nation, mostly poor, ignorant,
and degraded, are left for the definition and enjoyment of
rights, worth more than safety or property, to the judgment
of some ten other millions of unquestioned intelligence and
virtue, but whose intelligence and virtue were not materially
less when, with a courage and prowess never surpassed, they
drenched their own land with their own blood to keep these
darker millions in slavery. However, be it a use or an abuse of
the nation's scheme of order; be it right or wrong; this is politically the stronghold of the conservative party in the Southern
states; and it is made stronger still, steel-clad and turreted, as
it were, with the tremendous advantage of the *status quo*—
that established order of things which, good or bad, until it
becomes intolerable to themselves, men will never attack with
an energy equal to that with which it is defended.

But political strength is little by itself. The military maxim,
that no defenses are strong without force enough in them to
occupy their line, is true of civil affairs. Entrenchment in the
letter of a constitution avails little with the people at large
on either side of a question, unless the line of that entrench-

ment is occupied by a living conviction of being in the right. The most ultra-Southern position on the Negro question has an element of strength close akin to this. To be right is the only real necessity; but where is the community that will not make and defend with treasure and blood the assumption that what is necessary is right? "Southerners," in the political sense of the term, may sometimes lack a clear, firm-founded belief that they are right; they may have no more than a restless confidence that others are as wrong as they; but they have at least a profound conviction that they are moved by an imminent, unremitting, imperative necessity. Not that this is all; hundreds of thousands of them, incapacitated by this very conviction from falling into sympathy with the best modern thought, have been taught, and are learning and teaching, not only on the hustings, but in school, in college, at the fireside, through the daily press, in the social circle, and in church, that in their attitude on the Negro question they are legally, morally, and entirely right.

II

Now, specifically, what are these things that the majority of a free nation says ought not to be, while a sectional majority triumphantly maintains they must, will, ought to and shall be? Give an example of an actual grievance. One commonly esteemed the very least on the list is this: Suppose a man, his wife and their child, decent in person, dress, and deportment, but visibly of African or mixed blood, to take passage on a railway train from some city of the Eastern states, as Boston, or of the Western, as Chicago. They will be thrown publicly into company with many others, for an ordinary American railway passenger coach seats fifty persons, and a sleeping car accommodates twenty-five; and they will receive the same treatment from railway employees and passengers as if, being otherwise just what they are, they were of pure European descent. Only they will be much less likely than white per-

sons to seek, or be offered, new acquaintanceships. Arriving in
New York, Philadelphia, or any other Northern city, they will
easily find accommodations in some hotel of such grade as
they would be likely to choose if, exactly as they are, they
were white. They may chance upon a house that will refuse,
on account of their color, to receive them; but such action, if
made known, will be likely to receive a wide public reproba-
tion, and scant applause even from the press of the Southern
states. If the travelers choose to continue their journey through
the night, they will be free to hire and occupy berths in a
sleeping car, and to use all its accessories—basins, towels, pil-
lows, etc.—without the least chance of molestation in act or
speech from any one of the passengers or employees, let such
passengers or employees be from any state of the Union,
Northern or Southern.

But, on reaching the Southern states, the three travelers
will find themselves at every turn under special and offensive
restrictions, laid upon them not for any demerit of person,
dress, or manners, but solely and avowedly on account of the
African tincture in their blood, however slight that may be.
They may still be enjoying the comforts of the sleeping car,
by virtue of the ticket bought in a Northern state and not yet
fully redeemed. But they will find that while in one Southern
state they may still ride in an ordinary first-class railway coach
without hindrance, in another they will find themselves turned
away from the door of one coach and required to limit themselves to another, equal, it may be, to the first in appointments,
and inferior only in the social rank of its occupants. They may
protest that in America there are no public distinctions of
social rank; but this will avail them nothing. They may object
that the passengers in the car from which they are excluded
are not of one, but palpably of many and widely different
social ranks, and that in the car to which they are assigned
are people not of their grade only but of all sorts; they will
be told with great plainness that there is but one kind of Negro. They will be told that they are assigned equal but sepa-

rate accommodation because the presence of a person of
wholly, or partly, African blood in the same railway car on
terms of social equality with the white passengers is to those
white passengers an intolerable offense; and if the husband
and father replies that it is itself the height of vulgarity to
raise the question of private social rank among strangers in
railway cars, he will be fortunate if he is only thrust without
more ado into the "colored car," and not kicked and beaten by
two or three white men whose superior gentility has been in-
sulted, and he and his wife and child put off at the next
station to appeal in vain to the courts. For in court he will
find that railway companies are even required by the laws of
the state to maintain this ignominious separation of all who
betray an African tincture, refined or unrefined, clean or unclean, from the presence of the white passengers in the first-
class cars, be those passengers ever so promiscuous a throng.

Such is an example of one of the least grievances of the
colored man under the present regime in the Southern states;
and so dull is the common perception of wrongs committed at
a distance, that hundreds of thousands of intelligent, generous,
sensitive people in the Northern states are daily confessing
their inability to see any serious hardship in such a case, if
only the "colored car" be really equal in its appointments to
the one in which only white people of every sort are admitted;
as if a permanent ignominious distinction on account of an-
cestry, made in public, by strangers and in the enjoyment of
common public rights were not an insult or an injury unless
joined to some bodily discomfort.

Let it be plainly understood that though at least scores of
thousands are intelligent and genteel, yet the vast majority of
colored people in the United States are neither refined in mind
nor very decent in person. Their race has never had "a white
man's chance." In America it has been under the iron yoke of a
slavery that allowed no distinction of worth to cross race lines;
and in Africa it has had to contend for the mastery of wild
nature on a continent so unconquerable that for thousands of

years the white race has striven in vain to subdue it, and is only now at last strong enough to pierce it, enriched, enlightened and equipped by the long conquest of two others less impregnable. For all that is known the black is "an inferior race," though how, or how permanently inferior, remains unproved. But the core of the colored man's grievance is that the individual, in matters of right that do not justly go by race, is treated, whether man or child, without regard to person, dress, behavior, character, or aspirations, in public and by law, as though the African tincture, much or little, were itself stupidity, squalor, and vice. But let us see whether the grievance grows.

On passing into a third Southern state, the three travelers, though still holders of first-class tickets, will be required to confine themselves to the so-called second-class car, a place never much better than a dramshop. When the train stops for meals, and the passengers, men, women, and children, the rough, the polished, all throng into one common eating room to receive a common fare and attention, those three must eat in the kitchen or go hungry. Nor can they even await the coming of the train, in some railway stations, except in a separate "colored room." If they tarry in some Southern city they will encounter the most harassing and whimsical treatment of their most ordinary public rights as American citizens. They may ride in any streetcar, however crowded, seated beside, or even crammed in among, white men or women of any, or every station of life; but at the platform of the railway train, or at the threshold of any theater, or concert, or lecture hall, they will be directed to the most undesirable part of the house, and compelled to take that or nothing. They will find that the word "public" rarely means public to them; that they may not even draw books from the public libraries or use their reading rooms.

Should the harried and exasperated man be so fierce or indiscreet as to quarrel with, and strike, some white man, he will stand several chances to a white man's one of being killed on the spot. If neither killed nor half killed, but brought into court, he will have ninety-nine chances in a hundred of confronting a jury from which, either by, or else in spite of, legal provision, men of African tincture have been wholly or almost wholly excluded. If sent to prison he must come under a penal system which the report of the National Commissioner of Prisons officially pronounces "a blot upon civilization." He will find the population of the state prisons often nine tenths colored, divided into chain gangs, farmed out to private hands, even subleased, and worked in the mines, quarries, in railway construction and on turnpikes, under cordons of Winchester rifles; veritable quarry slaves. He will find most of the few white convicts under this system suffering the same outrages; but he will also find that the system itself disappears wherever this general attitude toward the black race disappears, and that where it and its outrages continue, the race line in prison is obliterated only when the criminal becomes a negotiable commodity and it costs the lessee money to maintain the absurd distinction. He would find the number of colored men within those deadly cordons out of all proportion to the colored population outside, as compared with the percentages of blacks in and out of prison in states not under this regime. There are state prisons in which he would find the colored convicts serving sentences whose average is nearly twice that of the white convicts in the same places for the same crimes. In the same or other prisons he would find colored youths and boys by scores, almost by hundreds, consorting with older criminals, and under sentences of seven, ten, twenty years, while the state legislatures vote down year after year the efforts of a few courageous and humane men either to establish reformatories for colored youth, or to introduce the element of reform into their so-called penitentiaries.

But suppose he commits no offense against person or property; he will make another list of discoveries. He will find that no select school, under "Southern" auspices, will receive his child. That if he sends the child to a public school, it must be, as required by law, to a school exclusively for colored children, even if his child is seven times more white than colored. Though his child be gentle, well behaved, cleanly, and decorously dressed, and the colored school so situated as to be naturally and properly the choice of the veriest riff-raff of the school population, he will have no more liberty than before; he will be told again, "We know but one kind of Negro." The child's father and mother may themselves be professional instructors; but however highly trained; of whatever reputation for moral and religious character; however talented as teachers or disciplinarians; holding the diploma of whatever college or university, Wellesley, Vassar, Yale, Cornell; and of whatever age or experience; they will find themselves shut out by law from becoming teachers in any public school for white children, whether belonging to, and filled from, the "best neighborhood," or in, and for, the lowest quarter of alleys and shanties. They will presently learn that in many hundreds of Southern school districts where the populations are too sparse and poor to admit of separate schools for the two races, the children of both are being brought up in ignorance of the very alphabet rather than let them enjoy a common public right under a common roof. They will find that this separation is not really based on any incapacity of children to distinguish between public and private social relations; but that the same separation is enforced among adults; and that while every Southern state is lamenting its inability to make anything like an adequate outlay for public education, and hundreds of thousands of colored children are growing up in absolute illiteracy largely for lack of teachers and schoolhouses, an expensive isolation of race from race is kept up even in the normal schools and teachers' institutes. Even in the house of worship and the divinity school they would find themselves pursued by the same invidious distinctions and separations that had followed them at every step, and would follow and attend them still to, and in, the very almshouse and insane asylum.

III

And then they would make one more discovery. They would
find that not only were they victims of bolder infractions of
the most obvious common rights of humanity than are offered
to any people elsewhere in Christendom, save only the Chinaman in the Far West, but that to make the oppression more
exasperating still, there is not a single feature of it in any one
state, though justifiable on the plea of stern necessity, that does
not stand condemned by its absence, under the same or yet
more pronounced conditions, in some other state. Sometimes
even one part of a state will utterly stultify the attitude held in
another part. In Virginia or South Carolina a colored person of
decent appearance or behavior may sit in any first-class railway car, but in Georgia the law forbids it, and in Kentucky
the law leaves him to the caprice of railway managements,
some of which accord and others withhold the right. In some
states he is allowed in the jury box, in some he is kept out by
the letter of statutes, and in some by evasion of them; while in
Tennessee some counties admit him to jury duty and others
exclude him from it. In one or two Southern cities, the teachers
in colored public schools must be white. In certain others they
must be colored; and in still others they may be either. In
Louisiana certain railway trains and steamboats run side by
side, within a mile of one another, where in the trains a Negro
or mulatto may sit where he will, and on the boats he must
confine himself to a separate quarter called the "Freedman's
bureau."

The Civil Rights bill was fought for years and finally destroyed, with the plea that it infringed the right of common
carriers and entertainers to use their own best judgment in dis-
tributing their passengers and guests with an equitable consideration for the comfort of all. In fact, it only forbade distributions that, so far from consulting the common comfort,
humor the demand of one crudely self-assorted private social

class for an invariable, ignominious isolation or exclusion of another. Yet the same states and persons who so effectually made this plea either allow and encourage its use as a cover for this tyrannous inequity, or else themselves ignore their own plea, usurp the judgment of common carriers and entertainers, and force them by law to make this race distribution, whether they deem it best or not.

And yet again, all over the South there are scattered colleges, academies, and tributary grammar schools, established and maintained at the expense of individuals and societies in the Northern states, for the education, at low rates of tuition and living, of the aspiring poor, without hindrance as to race or sex. For more than twenty years these establishments have flourished and been a boon to the African-American, as well as to the almost equally noted "poor whites" of the Southern mountain regions, sand hills, and "pauper counties," and through both these classes to the ultra-Southern white man of the towns and plantations—a boon the national value of which neither he nor one in a thousand of its hundreds of thousands of Northern supporters has an adequate conception, else these establishments would receive seven times their present pecuniary support. These institutions have graduated some hundreds of colored students as physicians and lawyers. At one time lately they had more than eight hundred divinity students, nearly all of them colored. Their pupils of all grades aggregate over seventeen thousand, and the sixteen thousand colored teachers in the public schools of the South have come almost entirely from them. But now in these institutions there is a complete ignoring of those race distinctions in the enjoyment of common public rights so religiously enforced on every side beyond their borders; and yet none of those unnamable disasters have come to or from them which the advocates of these onerous public distinctions and separations predict and dread. On scores of Southern hilltops these schools stand out almost totally without companions or competitors in their peculiar field, so many refutations, visible and complete, of the

idea that any interest requires the colored American citizen to
be limited in any of the civil rights that would be his without
question if the same man were white. Virtually the whole
guild of educators in the Southern states, from once regarding
these institutions with unqualified condemnation and enmity,
are now becoming their friends and, in some notable cases,
their converts. So widely have the larger colleges demonstrated their unique beneficence that in some cases Southern
state governments, actively hostile to the privileges of civil liberty they teach and apply, are making small annual appropriations in contribution toward their support.

So bristling with inconsistencies, good and bad, would our
three travelers find this tyrannous and utterly unrepublican
regime. Nowhere else in enlightened lands and in this day do
so many millions see their own fellow citizens so play football
with their simplest public rights; for the larger part of the
Southern white people do with these laws of their own making what they please, keeping or breaking them as convenient.

But their discoveries would still go on. They would hear
these oppressions justified by Southern white people of the
highest standing, and—more's the shame—by Northern tourists
in the South, on the ground that the people upon whom they
are laid are a dull, vicious, unclean race, contact with which
would be physically, intellectually, and morally offensive and
mischievous to a higher race. And when they might ask why
the lines of limited rights are not drawn around the conspicuously dull, vicious, and unclean of both races for the protection
of the opposite sort in both, they would come face to face
upon the amazing assumption that the lowest white man is
somehow a little too good for even so much contact with the
highest black as may be necessary for a common enjoyment of
public rights; and, therefore, that no excellence, moral, mental,
or physical, inborn or attained, can buy for a "man of color"
from these separationists any distinction between the restrictions of his civil liberty and those of the stupidest and
squalidest of his race, or bring him one step nearer to the en-

joyment of the rights of a white man; or, if at all, then only as a
matter of the white man's voluntary condescension and with
the right disguised as a personal privilege. They would find
that the race line is not a line of physical, moral, or intellectual
excellence at all. Stranger yet, they would learn that no proportion of white men's blood in their own veins, unless it washes
out the very memory of their African tincture, can get them
abatement of those deprivations decreed for a dull, vicious, and
unclean race, but that—men, women, and children alike—hundreds and thousands of mixed race are thus daily and publicly
punished by their brothers for the sins of their fathers. They
would find the race line not a race line at all.

They would find that the mere contact of race with race is
not the matter objected to, but only any and every sort of contact on an equal footing. They would find that what no money,
no fame, no personal excellence, and no fractional preponderance of European blood can buy can nevertheless be bought
instantly and without one of these things by the simple surrender of the attitude of public equality. They would find that
the entire essence of the offense, any and everywhere where
the race line is insisted on, is the apparition of the colored man
or woman as his or her own master; that masterhood is all
that all this tyranny is intended to preserve, and that the moment the relation of master and servant is visibly established
between race and race there is the hush of peace.

"What is that Negro—what is that mulattress—doing in
here?" asks one private individual of another in some public
place, and the other replies:

"That's nothing; he is the servant of that white man just
behind him; she is the nurse of those children in front of her."

"Oh, all right." And the "cordial relation" is restored. Such
conversation, or equivalent soliloquy, occurs in the South a
hundred times a day.

The surrender of this one point by the colored man or
woman buys more than peace—it buys amity; an amity
clouded only by a slight but distinct and constant air and tone

of command on the one part, a very gross and imperfect attitude of deference on the other, and the perpetual unrest that always accompanies forcible possession of anything. But since no people ever compelled another to pay too much for peace without somehow paying too much for it themselves, the master caste tolerates, with unsurpassed supineness and unconsciousness, a more indolent, inefficient, slovenly, unclean, untrustworthy, ill-mannered, noisy, disrespectful, disputatious, and yet servile domestic and public menial service than is tolerated by any other enlightened people. Such is but one of the smallest of many payments which an intelligent and refined community has to make for maintaining the lines of master and servanthood on caste instead of on individual ambition and capacity, and for the forcible equalization of millions of unequal individuals under one common public disdain. Other and greater payments and losses there are, moral, political, industrial, commercial, as we shall see when we turn, as now we must, to the other half of this task and answer the two impatient questions that jostle each other for precedence as they spring from this still incomplete statement of the condition of affairs.

The two questions are these: If the case is so plain, then, in the first place, how can the millions of intelligent and virtuous white people of the South make such a political, not to say such a moral, mistake? And, in the second place, how can the overwhelming millions of the North, after spending the frightful costs they spent in the war of '61–'65, tolerate this emasculation of the American freedom which that war is supposed to have secured to all alike?

THE ANSWER

I

As to the Southern people the answer is that, although the Southern master class now cordially and unanimously admit the folly of slaveholding, yet the fundamental article of political faith on which slavery rested has not been displaced. As to the people of the North the answer is simpler still: the Union is saved.

The Northern cause in our Civil War was not primarily the abolition of slavery, although many a Northern soldier and captain fought mainly for this and cared for no other issue while this remained. The Southern cause was not merely for disunion, though many a Southern soldier and captain would never have taken up the sword to defend slaveholding stripped of the disguise of state sovereignty. The Northern cause was pre-eminently the national unity. Emancipation—the emancipation of the Negroes—was not what the North fought for, but only what it fought with. The right to secede was not what the South fought for, but only what it fought with. The great majority of the Southern white people loved the Union, and consented to its destruction only when there seemed to be no other way to save slavery; the great bulk of the North consented to destroy slavery only when there seemed no other way to save the Union. To put in peril the Union on one side and slavery on the other was enough, when nothing else was enough, to drench one of the greatest and happiest lands on earth with the blood of hundreds of thousands of her own children. Now, what thing of supreme value rested on this Union, and what on this slavery, that they should have been defended at such cost? There rested on, or more truly there underlay, each a fundamental principle, conceived to be absolutely essential to

the safety, order, peace, fortune, and honor of society; and
these two principles were antagonistic.

They were more than antagonistic; they were antipodal and
irreconcilable. No people that hold either of these ideas as cardinal in their political creed will ever allow the other to be
forced upon them from without so long as blood and lives will
buy deliverance. Both were brought from the mother country
when America was originally colonized, and both have their
advocates in greater or less number in the Northern states, in
the Southern, and wherever there is any freedom of thought
and speech.

The common subject of the two is the great lower mass of
society. The leading thought of the one is that mass's elevation, of the other its subjugation. The one declares the only
permanent safety of public society, and its highest development, to require the constant elevation of the lower, and thus
of the whole mass, by the free self-government of all under
one common code of equal civil rights. It came from England,
but it was practically, successfully, beneficently applied on a
national scale first in the United States, and Americans claim
the right to call it, and it pre-eminently, the American idea,
promulgated and established, not by Northerners or Southerners, one greatly more than another, but by the unsectional
majority of a whole new nation born of the idea. The other
principle declares public safety and highest development to
require the subjugation of the lower mass under the arbitrary
protective supremacy of an untitled but hereditary privileged
class, a civil caste. Not, as it is commonly miscalled, an aristocracy, for within one race it takes in all ranks of society; not
an aristocracy, for an aristocracy exists, presumably, at least,
with the wide consent of all classes, and men in any rank of
life may have some hope to attain to it by extraordinary merit
and service; but a caste; not the embodiment of a modern
European idea, but the resuscitation of an ancient Asiatic one.

That one of these irreconcilable ideas should by-and-by become all-dominant in the formation of public society in one

region, and its opposite in the other region, is due to original differences in the conditions under which the colonies were settled. In the South, the cornerstone of the social structure was made the plantation idea—wide lands, an accomplished few, and their rapid aggrandizement by the fostering oversight and employment of an unskilled many. In the North, it was the village and town idea—the notion of farm and factory, skilled labor, an intelligent many, and ultimate wealth through an assured public tranquillity. Nothing could be more natural than for African slavery, once introduced, to flourish and spread under the one idea, and languish and die under the other. It is high time to be done saying that the South retained slavery and the North renounced it merely because to the one it was, and to the other it was not, lucrative. It was inevitable that the most conspicuous feature of one civilization should become the public schoolhouse, and of the other the slave yard. Who could wish to raise the equally idle and offensive question of praise and blame? When Northerners came South by thousands and made their dwelling there, ninety-nine hundredths of them fell into our Southern error up to the eyes, and there is nothing to prove that, had the plantation idea, to the exclusion of the village idea, been planted in all the colonies, we should not by this time have had a West Indian civilization from Florida to Oregon. But it was not to be so. Wherever the farm village became the germinal unit of social organization, there was developed in its most comprehensive integrity that American idea of our Northern and Southern fathers, the representative self-government of the whole people by the constant free consent of all to the frequently reconsidered choice of the majority.

Such a scheme can be safe only when it includes inherently the continual and diligent elevation of that lower mass which human society everywhere is constantly precipitating. But slaveholding on any large scale could not make even a show of public safety without the continual and diligent debasement of its enslaved lower millions. Wherever it prevailed it was bound

by the natural necessities of its own existence to undermine
and corrode the national scheme. It mistaught the new generations of the white South that the slaveholding fathers of the
republic were approvers and advocates of that sad practice,
which by their true histories we know they would gladly have
destroyed. It mistaught us to construe the right of a uniform
government of all by all, not as a common and inalienable right
of man, but as a privilege that became a right only by a people's merit, and which our forefathers bought with the blood
of the Revolution in 1776–83, and which our slaves did not
and should not be allowed to acquire. It mistaught us to seek
prosperity in the concentration instead of the diffusion of
wealth, to seek public safety in a state of siege rather than in
a state of peace; it gave us subjects instead of fellow citizens,
and falsely threatened us with the utter shipwreck of public
and private society if we dared accord civil power to the degraded millions to whom we had forbidden patriotism. Thus,
it could not help but misteach us also to subordinate to its
preservation the maintenance of a national union with those
Northern communities to whose whole scheme of order slaveholding was intolerable, and to rise at length against the will
of the majority and dissolve the Union when that majority refused to give slaveholding the national sanction.

The other system taught the inherent right of all human
society to self-government. It taught the impersonal civil
equality of all. It admitted that the private, personal inequality of individuals is inevitable, necessary, right, and good; but
condemned its misuse to set up arbitrary public inequalities.
It declared public equality to be, on the one hand, the only
true and adequate counterpoise against private inequalities,
and, on the other, the best protector and promoter of just private inequalities against unjust. It held that virtue, intelligence,
and wealth are their own sufficient advantage, and need for
self-protection no arbitrary civil preponderance; that their
powers of self-protection are never inadequate save when by
forgetting equity they mass and exasperate ignorance, vice, and

poverty against them. It insisted that there is no safe protection but self-protection; that poverty needs at least as much civil equipment for self-protection as property needs; that the right and liberty to acquire intelligence, virtue, and wealth are just as precious as the right and liberty to maintain them, and need quite as much self-protection; that the secret of public order and highest prosperity is the common and equal right of all lawfully to acquire as well as retain every equitable means of self-aggrandizement, and that this right is assured to all only through the consent of all to the choice of the majority frequently appealed to without respect to persons. And last, it truly taught that a government founded on these principles and holding them essential to public peace and safety might comfortably bear the proximity of alien neighbors, whose ideas of right and order were not implacably hostile; but that it had no power to abide unless it could put down any internal mutiny against that choice of the majority which was, as it were, the nation's first commandment.

The war was fought and the Union saved. Fought as it was, on the issue of the consent of all to the choice of the majority, the conviction forced its way that the strife would never end in peace until the liberty of self-government was guaranteed to the entire people, and slavery, as standing for the doctrine of public safety by subjugation, destroyed. Hence, first, emancipation, and, then, enfranchisement. And now even the Union saved is not the full measure of the nation's triumphs; but, saved once by arms, it seems at length to have achieved a better and fuller salvation still; for the people of the once seceded states, with a sincerity that no generous mind can question, have returned to their old love of this saved Union, and the great North, from East to utmost West, full of elation, and feeling what one may call the onus of the winning side, cries "Enough!" and asks no more.

II

Thus stands the matter today. Old foes are clasping hands on fields where once they met in battle, and touching glasses across the banqueting board, pledging long life to the Union and prosperity to the South, but at every feast there is one empty seat.

Why should one seat be ever empty, and every guest afraid to look that way? Because the Southern white man swears upon his father's sword that none but a ghost shall ever sit there. And a ghost is there; the ghost of that old heresy of public safety by the mass's subjugation. This is what the Northern people cannot understand. This is what makes the Southern white man an enigma to all the world beside, if not also to himself. Today the pride with which he boasts himself a citizen of the United States and the sincerity with which he declares for free government as the only safe government cannot be doubted; tomorrow comes an explosion, followed by such a misinterpretation of what free government requires and forbids that it is hard to identify him with the nineteenth century. Emancipation destroyed domestic bondage; enfranchisement, as nearly as its mere decree can, has abolished public servitude; how, then, does this old un-American, undemocratic idea of subjugation, which our British mother country and Europe as well are so fast repudiating—how does it remain? Was it not founded in these two forms of slavery? The mistake lies just there: They were founded in it, and removing them has not removed it.

It has always been hard for the North to understand the alacrity with which the ex-slaveholder learned to condemn as a moral and economic error that slavery in defense of which he endured four years of desolating war. But it was genuine, and here is the explanation: He believed personal enslavement essential to subjugation. Emancipation at one stroke proved it was not. But it proved no more. Unfortunately for the whole

nation there was already, before emancipation came, a defined status, a peculiar niche, waiting for freed Negroes. They
were nothing new. Nor was it new to lose personal ownership
in one's slave. When, under emancipation, no one else could
own him, we quickly saw he was not lost at all. There he
stood, beggar to us for room for the sole of his foot, the land
and all its appliances ours, and he, by the stress of his daily
needs, captive to the land. The moment he fell to work of his
own free will, we saw that emancipation was even more ours
than his; public order stood fast, our homes were safe, our
firesides uninvaded; he still served, we still ruled; all need of
holding him in private bondage was disproved, and when the
notion of necessity vanished the notion of right vanished with
it. Emancipation had destroyed private, but it had not disturbed public, subjugation. The ex-slave was not a free man;
he was only a free Negro.

Then the winners of the war saw that the great issue which
had jeopardized the Union was not settled. The government's
foundation principle was not re-established, and could not be
while millions of the country's population were without a voice
as to who should rule, who should judge, and what should be
law. But, as we have seen, the absolute civil equality of privately and socially unequal men was not the whole American
idea. It was counterbalanced by an enlarged application of the
same principle in the absolute equality of unequal states in the
federal Union, one of the greatest willing concessions ever
made by stronger political bodies to weaker ones in the history
of government. Now manifestly this great concession of equality among the unequal states becomes inordinate, unjust, and
dangerous when millions of the people in one geographical
section, native to the soil, of native parentage, having ties of
interest and sympathy with no other land, are arbitrarily denied that political equality within the states which obtains
elsewhere throughout the Union. This would make us two
countries. But we cannot be two merely federated countries
without changing our whole plan of government; and we can-

not be one without a common foundation. Hence the Freedman's enfranchisement. It was given him not only because
enfranchisement was his only true emancipation, but also because it was, and is, impossible to withhold it and carry on
American government on American ground principles. Neither
the nation's honor nor its safety could allow the restoration of
revolted states to their autonomy with their populations divided by lines of status abhorrent to the whole national
structure.

Northern men often ask perplexedly if the Freedman's enfranchisement was not, as to the South, premature and inex-
pedient; while Southern men as often call it the one vindictive
act of the conqueror, as foolish as it was cruel. It was cruel.
Not by intention and, it may be, unavoidably, but certainly
it was not cruel for its haste, but for its tardiness. Had enfranchisement come into effect, as emancipation did, while the
smoke of the war's last shot was still in the air, when force
still ruled unquestioned, and civil order and system had not
yet superseded martial law, the agonies, the shame, and the
incalculable losses of the Reconstruction period that followed
might have been spared the South and the nation. Instead
there came two unlucky postponements, the slow doling out of
re-enfranchisement to the best intelligence of Southern white
society and the delay of the Freedman's enfranchisement—his
civil emancipation—until the "Old South," instead of reorganiz-
ing public society in harmony with the national idea, largely
returned to its entrenchments in the notion of exclusive white
rule. Then, too late to avert a new strife, and as little more
than a defensive offset, the Freedman was invested with citizenship and the experiment begun of trying to establish a form
of public order wherein, under a political equality accorded
by all citizens, to all citizens, new and old, intelligence and
virtue would be so free to combine, and ignorance and vice
feel so free to divide, as to insure the majority's free choice
of rulers of at least enough intelligence and virtue to secure
safety, order, and progress. This experience, the North be-

lieved, would succeed, and since this was the organic embodiment of the American idea for which it had just shed seas of
blood, it stands to reason the North would not have allowed
it to fail. But the Old South, still bleeding from her thousand
wounds, but as brave as when she fired her first gun, believed
not only that the experiment would fail, but also that it was
dangerous and dishonorable. And today, both in North and
South, a widespread impression prevails that this is the experiment which was made and did in fact fail. Whereas it is just
what the Old South never allowed to be tried.

This is the whole secret of the Negro question's vital force
today. And yet the struggle in the Southern states has never
been by the blacks for and by the whites against a black supremacy, but only for and against an arbitrary pure white supremacy. From the very first until this day, in all the Freedman's intellectual crudity, he has held fast to the one true,
national doctrine of the absence of privilege and the rule of
all by all, through the common and steadfast consent of all to
the free and frequent choice of the majority. He has never rejected white men's political fellowship or leadership because
it was white, but only and always when it was unsound in
this doctrine. His party has never been a purely black party
in fact or principle. The "solid black vote" is only by outside
pressure solidified about a principle of American liberty, which
is itself against solidity and destroys the political solidity of
classes wherever it has free play. But the "solid white vote"—
which is not solid by including all whites, but because no colored man can truly enter its ranks, much less its councils, without accepting an emasculated emancipation—the solid white
vote is solid, not by outside pressure but by inherent principle.
Solid twice over; first, in each state, from sincere motives of
self-preservation, solid in keeping the old servile class, by arbitrary classification, servile; and then solid again by a tacit
league of Southern states around the assumed right of each
state separately to postpone a true and complete emancipation
as long as the fear remains that, with full American liberty—

this and no more—to all alike, the Freedman would himself usurp the arbitrary domination now held over him and plunder and destroy society.

So, then, the Southern question at its root is simply whether there is any real ground sufficient to justify this fear and the attitude taken against it. Only remove this fear, which rests on a majority of the whole white South despite all its splendid, well-proved courage, and the question of right, in law and in morals, will vanish along with the notion of necessity.

Whoever attempts to remove this apprehension must meet it in two forms: First, fear of a hopeless wreck of public government by a complete supremacy of the lower mass; and second, fear of a yet more dreadful wreck of private society in a deluge of social equality.

III

Now, as to public government, the Freedman, whatever may be said of his mistakes, has never shown an intentional preference for anarchy. Had he such a bent he would have betrayed something of it when our Civil War offered as wide an opportunity for its indulgence as any millions in bondage ever had. He has shown at least as prompt a choice for peace and order as any "lower million" ever showed. The vices said to be his in inordinate degree are only such as always go with degradation, and especially with a degraded status; and when, in Reconstruction years, he held power to make and unmake laws, amid all his degradation, all the efforts to confine him still to an arbitrary servile status, and all his vicious special legislation, he never removed the penalties from anything that the world at large calls a crime. Neither did he ever show any serious disposition to establish race rule. The whole spirit of his emancipation and enfranchisement, and his whole struggle, was, and is, to put race rule of all sorts under foot, and set up the common rule of all. The fear of anarchy in the Southern states, then, is only that perfectly natural and largely excusable fear that besets the upper ranks of society everywhere, and often successfully tempts them to commit inequitable usurpations; and yet a fear of which no amount of power or privilege ever relieves them—the fear that the stupid, the destitute, and the vicious will combine against them and rule by sheer weight of numbers.

Majority rule is an unfortunate term, in that it falsely implies this very thing; whereas its mission in human affairs is to remove precisely this danger. In fact a minority always rules. At least it always can. All the great majority ever strives for is the power to choose by what, and what kind of, a minority it shall be ruled. What that choosing majority shall consist of, and hence the wisdom and public safety of its choice, will depend mainly upon the attitude of those who hold, against the power of mere numbers, the far greater powers of intelligence, of virtue, and of wealth. If these claim, by virtue of their own self-estimate, an arbitrary right to rule and say who shall rule, the lower elements of society will be bound together by a just sense of grievance and a well-grounded reciprocation of distrust; the forced rule will continue only till it can be overturned, and while it lasts will be attended by largely uncounted but enormous losses, moral and material, to all ranks of society. But if the wise, the upright, the wealthy command the courage of our American fathers to claim for all men a common political equality, without rank, station, or privilege, and give their full and free adherence to government by the consent of all to the rule of a minority empowered by the choice of the majority frequently appealed to without respect of persons, then ignorance, destitution, and vice will not combine to make the choosing majority. They cannot. They carry in themselves the very principle of disintegration. Without the outside pressure of common and sore grievance, they have no lasting powers of cohesion. The minority always may rule. It need never rule by force if it will rule by equity. This is the faith of our fathers of the Revolution, and no community in America that has built squarely and only upon it has found it unwise or unsafe.

This is asserted with all the terrible misrule of Reconstruction days in full remembrance. For, first be it said again, that sad history came not by a reign of equal rights and majority rule, but through an attempt to establish them while the greater part of the wealth and intelligence of the region involved held out sincerely, steadfastly, and desperately against them, and for the preservation of unequal privileges and class domination. The Reconstruction party, even with all its taxing, stealing, and defrauding, and with the upper ranks of society at war as fiercely against its best principles as against its bad practices, planted the whole South with public schools for the poor and illiterate of both races, welcomed and cherished the missionaries of higher education, and, when it fell, left them still both systems, with the master class converted to a belief in their use and necessity. The history of Reconstruction dispassionately viewed is a final, triumphant proof that all our American scheme needs to make it safe and good, in the South as elsewhere, is consent to it and participation in it by the law-abiding, intelligent portions of the people, with one common freedom, in and between high life and low, to combine, in civil matters, against ignorance and vice, in high life and low, across, yet without disturbing, the lines of race or any other line of private rank or predilection.

There are hundreds of thousands in the Southern states who, denying this, would promptly concede it all in theory and in practice, but for the second form of their fear: the belief that there would result a confusion of the races in private society, followed by intellectual and moral debasement and by a mongrel posterity. Unless this can be shown to be an empty fear, our Southern problem cannot be solved.

IV

The mere ambiguity of a term here has cost much loss. The double meaning of the words "social" and "society" seems to have been a real drawback on the progress of political ideas among the white people of the South. The clear and definite term, civil equality, they have made synonymous with the very vague and indefinite term, social equality, and then turned and totally misapplied it to the sacred domains of private society. If the idea of civil equality had rightly any such application, their horror would certainly be just. To a forced private social equality the rest of the world has the same aversion, but it knows and feels that such a thing is as impossible in fact as it is monstrous in thought. Americans, in general, know by a century's experience that civil equality makes no such proposal, bears no such results. They know that public society—civil society—comprises one distinct group of mutual relations, and private society entirely another, and that it is simply and only evil to confuse the two. They see that public society comprises all those relations that are impersonal, unselective, and in which all men, of whatever personal inequality, should stand equal. They recognize that private society is its opposite hemisphere; that it is personal, selective, assortive, ignores civil equality without violating it, and forms itself entirely upon mutual private preferences and affinities. They agree that civil status has of right no special value in private society, and that their private social status has rightly no special value in their public social—i.e., their merely civil—relations. Even the Southern Freedman is perfectly clear on these points; and Northern minds are often puzzled to know why the whites of our Southern states, almost alone, should be beset by a confusion of ideas that costs them all the tremendous differences, spiritual and material, between a state of truce and a state of peace.

But the matter has a very natural explanation. Slavery was

both public and private, domestic as well as civil. By the plantation system the members of the master class were almost constantly brought into closer contact with slaves than with their social equals. The defensive line of private society in its upper ranks was an attenuated one; hence there was a constant, well-grounded fear that social confusion—for we may cast aside the term "social equality" as preposterous—that social confusion would be wrought by the powerful temptation of close and continual contact between two classes—the upper powerful and bold, the under helpless and sensual, and neither one socially responsible to the other, either publicly or privately. It had already brought about the utter confusion of race and corruption of society in the West Indies and in Mexico, and the only escape from a similar fate seemed to our Southern master class to be to annihilate and forget the boundaries between public right and private choice, and treat the appearance anywhere of any one visibly of African tincture and not visibly a servant, as an assault upon the purity of private society, to be repelled on the instant, without question of law or authority, as one would fight fire. Now, under slavery, though confessedly inadequate, this was after all the only way; and all that the whites in the Southern states have overlooked is that the conditions are changed, and that this policy has become unspeakably worse than useless. Dissimilar races are not inclined to mix spontaneously. The common enjoyment of equal civil rights never mixed two such races; it has always been some oppressive distinction between them that, by holding out temptations to vice instead of rewards to virtue, has done it; and because slavery is the foulest of oppressions it makes the mixture of races in morally foulest form. Race fusion is not essential to national unity; such unity requires only civil and political, not private social, homogeneity. The contact of superior and inferior is not of necessity degrading; it is the *kind* of contact that degrades or elevates; and public equality—equal public rights, common public liberty, equal mutual responsibility—this is the great essential to beneficent

contact across the lines of physical, intellectual, and moral difference, and the greatest safeguard of private society that human law or custom can provide.

v

Thus we see that, so far from a complete emancipation of
the Freedman bringing those results in the Southern states
which the white people there so justly abhor, but so need-
lessly fear, it is the only safe and effectual preventive of those
results, and final cure of a state of inflammation which nothing but the remaining vestiges of an incompletely abolished
slavery perpetuates. The abolition of the present stage of siege
rests with the Southern white man. He can abolish it, if he
will, with safety and at once. The results will not be the return
of Reconstruction days, nor the incoming of any sort of black
rule, nor the supremacy of the lower mass—either white, black,
or mixed; nor the confusion of ranks and races in private society; nor the thronging of black children into white public
schools, which never happened even in the worse Reconstruction days; nor any attendance at all of colored children in
white schools or of white in colored, save where exclusion
would work needless hardship; nor any new necessity to teach
children—what they already know so well—that the public
school relation is not a private social relation; nor any greater
or less necessity for parents to oversee their children's choice
of companions in school or out; nor a tenth as much or as
mischievous playmating of white and colored children as there
was in the days of slavery; nor any new obstruction of civil or
criminal justice; nor any need of submitting to any sort of
offensive contact from a colored person that it would be right
to resent if he were white. But seven dark American-born
millions would find themselves freed from their constant lia-
bility to public, legalized indignity. They would find themselves, for the first time in their history, holding a patent, with
the seal of public approval, for all the aspirations of citizen-

ship and all the public rewards of virtue and intelligence. Not merely would their million voters find themselves admitted to, and faithfully counted at, the polls—whether they are already or not is not here discussed—but they would find themselves, as never before, at liberty to choose between political parties. These are some of the good—and there need be no ill—changes that will come whenever a majority of the Southern whites are willing to vote for them.

There is a vague hope, much commoner in the North than in the South, that somehow, if everybody will sit still, "time" will bring these changes. A large mercantile element, especially, would have the South "let politics alone." It is too busy to understand that whatever people lets politics alone is doomed. There are things that mere time can do, but only vigorous agitation can be trusted to change the fundamental convictions on which a people has built society. Time may do it at last, but it is likely to make bloody work of it. For either foundation idea on which society may build must, if let alone, multiply upon itself. The elevation idea brings safety, and safety constantly commends and intensifies itself and the elevation idea. The subjugation idea brings danger, and the sense of danger constantly intensifies the subjugation idea. Time may be counted on for such lighter things as the removal of animosities and suspicions, and this in our nation's case it has done. Neither North nor South now holds, or suspects the other of holding, any grudge for the late war. But trusting time to do more than this is but trusting to luck, and trusting to luck is a crime.

What is luck doing? Here is the exclusive white party in the Southern states calling itself, and itself only, "The South," praying the nation to hold off, not merely its interference, but its counsel—even its notice—while it, not removes, but refines, polishes, decorates, and disguises to its own and the nation's eyes this cornerstone of all its own and the South's, the whole South's woes; pleading the inability of any but itself to "understand the Negro," when, in fact, itself has had to correct more, and more radical mistakes about the Negro since the war than all the nation beside; failing still, more than twenty years since Reconstruction began and more than ten since its era closed, to offer any definition of the Freedman's needs and desires which he can accept; making daily statements of his preferences which the one hundred newspapers published for his patronage, and by himself, daily and unanimously repudiate; trying to settle affairs on the one only false principle of public social order that keeps them unsettled; proposing to settle upon a *sine qua non* that shuts out of its councils the whole opposite side of the only matter in question; and holding out for a settlement which, whether effected or not, can but perpetrate a disturbance of interstate equality fatal to the nation's peace—a settlement which is no more than a refusal to settle at all.

Meanwhile, over a million American citizens, with their wives and children, suffer a suspension of their full citizenship, and are virtually subjects and not citizens, peasants instead of free men. They cannot seize their rights by force, and the nation would never allow it if they could. But they are learning one of the worst lessons class rule can teach them—exclusive, even morbid, preoccupation in their rights as a class, and inattention to the general affairs of their communities, their states, and the nation. Meanwhile, too, the present one-sided effort at settlement by subjugation is not only debasing to the under mass, but corrupting to the upper. For it teaches these to set aside questions of right and wrong for questions of expediency; to wink at and at times to defend and turn at account evasions, even bold infractions, of their own laws, when done to preserve arbitrary class domination; to vote confessedly for bad men and measures as against the better, rather than jeopardize the white man's solid party and exclusive power; to regard virtue and intelligence, vice and ignorance, as going by race, and to extenuate and let go unprosecuted the most frightful crimes against the under class, lest that class, being avenged, should gather a boldness inconsistent with its arbitrarily fixed status. Such results as these are contrary to our own and to all good government.

There is now going on in several parts of the South a remarkable development of material wealth. Mills, mines, furnaces, quarries, railways are multiplying rapidly. The eye that cannot see the value of this aggrandizement must be dull indeed. But many an eye, in North and South, and to the South's loss, is crediting it with values that it has not. To many the "New South" we long for means only this industrial and commercial expansion, and our eager mercantile spirit forgets that even for making a people rich in goods a civil order on sound foundations is of greater value than coal or metals, or spindles and looms. May the South grow rich! But every wise friend of the South will wish, besides, to see wealth built upon public provisions for securing through it that general beneficence, without which it is not really wealth. He would not wish those American states a wealth like that which once was Spain's. He would not wish to see their society more diligent for those conditions that concentrate wealth than for those that disseminate it. Yet he must see it. That is the situation, despite the assurances of a host of well-meaning flatterers that a New South is laying the foundations of a permanent prosperity. They cannot be laid on the old plantation idea, and much of that which is loosely called the New South today is farthest from it—it is only the Old South readapting the old plantation idea to a peasant labor and mineral products. Said a mineowner of the far North lately: "We shall never fear their competition till they get rid of that idea." A lasting prosperity cannot be hoped for without a disseminated wealth and public social conditions to keep it from congestion. But this dissemination cannot be got save by a disseminated intelligence, nor intelligence be disseminated without a disseminated education, nor this be brought to any high value without liberty, responsibility, private inequality, public equality, self-regard, virtue, aspirations, and their rewards.

Many ask if this new material development of the South will not naturally be followed by adequate public provisions for this dissemination by-and-by. There is but one safe answer: that it has never so happened in America. From our furthest East to our furthest West, whenever a community has established social order in the idea of the elevation of the masses, it has planned, not for education and liberty to follow from wealth and intelligence, but for wealth and intelligence to follow from education and liberty; and the community whose intelligent few do not make the mass's elevation by public education and equal public liberty the cornerstone of a projected wealth is not more likely to provide it after wealth is achieved and mostly in their own hands.

Our American public-school idea—American at least in contrast with any dissimilar notion—is that a provision for public education adequate for the whole people is not a benevolent concession but a paying investment, constantly and absolutely essential to confirm the safety of a safe scheme of government. The maintenance and growth of public education in the Southern states, as first established principally under Reconstruction rule, sadly insufficient as it still is, is mainly due to the partial triumph of this idea in the minds of the Southern whites, and its eager acceptance, with or without discordant conditions, by the intelligent blacks, and in no region is rightly attributable to an exceptionable increase of wealth. Much less is it attributable, as is often conjectured, to the influx of Northern capital and capitalists, bringing Northern ideas with them. It ought to go without saying that immigration, with or without capital, will always try to assimilate itself to the state of society into which it comes. Every impulse of commerce is not to disturb any vexed issue until such issue throws itself immediately across the path. It never purposely molests a question of social order. So it is in the South.

Certain public men in both North and South have of late

years made, with the kindest intentions, an unfortunate misuse of statistical facts to make it appear that public society
in the South is doing, not all that should be done, but all it
can do for the establishment of permanent safety and harmony
through the elevation of the lower masses especially, in the
matter of public education. In truth, these facts do not prove
the statement they are called upon to prove, and do the Southern states no kindness in lulling them to a belief in it.[1] It is
said, for instance, that certain Southern states are now spending more annually for public education, in proportion to their
taxable wealth, than certain Northern states noted for the com-
pleteness of their public-school systems. Mississippi may thus
be compared with Massachusetts. But really the comparison
is a sad injustice to the Southern state, for a century of public
education has helped to make Massachusetts so rich that she
is able to spend annually twenty dollars per head upon the
children in her public schools, while Mississippi, laying a
heavier tax, spends upon hers but two dollars per head. Manifestly it is unfair to a state whose public-school system is new
to compare it with any whose system is old. The public-
school property of Ohio, whose population is one million, is
over twice as great as that of ten states of the New South,
whose population is three and a half times as large.[2] And
yet one does not need to go as far as the "New West" to find
states whose taxpayers spend far more for public education
than Southern communities thus far see the wisdom or need
of investing. With one third more wealth than Virginia, and
but one tenth the percentage of illiteracy, Iowa spends over
four times as much per year for public instruction. With one
fourth less wealth than Alabama, and but one fourteenth the
percentage of illiteracy, Nebraska spends three and a half
times as much per year for public instruction. With about the

[1] For a treatment of the question of national aid to Southern
education, see the short article printed [later in this volume].
[2] See Report of United States Commissioner of Education,
1883–84, page 21, last column of table.

same wealth as North Carolina and less than one eighth the percentage of illiteracy, Kansas spends over five times as much per year for public education. If the comparison be moved westward again into new regions, the Territory of Dakota is seen making an "expenditure in the year per capita on average attendance in the public schools" of $25.77, being more than the sum of the like per capita expenditures by Mississippi, South Carolina, Tennessee, North Carolina, Alabama, and Georgia combined. In Colorado it is about the same as in Dakota, while in Nevada it is much greater and in Arizona twice as large. As to comparative wealth, the taxable wealth of Dakota in 1880, at least, was but one two thousandth part of that of the six states with which it is compared.

Now what is the real truth in these facts? That the full establishment of this American public-school idea and of that elevation idea of which it is an exponent, and which has had so much to do toward making the people of the Northern states the wealthiest people in the world, waits in the South not mainly an increase of wealth, but rather the simple consent of the Southern white man to see society's best and earliest safety, the quickest, greatest, and most lasting aggrandizement, in that public equality of all men, that national citizenship, wider than race and far wider than the lines of private society, which makes the elevation of the masses, by everything that tends to moral, aesthetical and intellectual education, in school and out of school, the most urgent and fruitful investment of public wealth and trust. Just this sincere confession. All the rest will follow. The black man will not merely be tolerated in his civil and political rights as now sometimes he is and sometimes he is not; but he will be welcomed into, and encouraged and urged to, a true understanding, valuation, and acceptance of every public duty and responsibility of citizenship, according to his actual personal ability to respond.

To effect this is not the herculean and dangerous task it is sometimes said to be. The North has twenty million foreign

immigrants to Americanize, and only this way to do it. The
South, for all her drawbacks, has this comparative advantage;
that her lower mass, however ignorant and debased, is as yet
wholly American in its notions of order and government. All
that is wanting is to more completely Americanize her upper
class, a class that is already ruling and will still rule when the
change is made; that wants to rule wisely and prosperously,
and that has no conscious intention of being un-American.
Only this: To bring the men of best blood and best brain in
the South today, not to a new and strange doctrine, but back
to the faith of their fathers. Let but this be done, and there
may be far less cry of Peace, Peace, than now, but there will
be a peace and a union between the nation's two great his-
toric sections such as they have not seen since Virginia's Washington laid down his sword, and her Jefferson his pen.

What Shall the Negro Do?

[An address delivered before a Negro audience in Boston, April 13, 1888.

At Meriden, Connecticut, October 29, 1885, Cable addressed the Lincoln Club, which was dedicated primarily to Negro rights. There he assumed a tone and an attitude to which he was to return in the future when he spoke to audiences mainly Negro. He said little of the Freedmen's grievances and dealt mainly with their needs and duties. They must never draw the color line but must strive always for the benefit of both races. In education, tolerance, and work lay their hope. They must develop their own leaders. Even when addressing such audiences, however, Cable gave no quarter to the idea of race superiority. Before the Sumner League of Hartford on January 12, 1887, he took occasion to protest against the views on race Henry W. Grady had been expounding. Cable insisted on becoming not an honorary member but a regular member of the Sumner League and was proud, he said, to be its first member from the former slave states. He assisted in drafting the constitution of the League.

"What Shall the Negro Do?" was the only one of Cable's addresses to Negro audiences which he published. It appeared in the *Forum*, August 1888, and in *The Negro Question*.]

What Shall the Negro Do?

1. This paper is addressed directly to the colored people of the United States. A large mass of them, of course, will not see it; yet others of them will. Nothing more forcibly illustrates the great progress of our times than the fact that already one may safely count on reaching a considerable body of readers, wholly or partly of Negro blood, through the pages of a monthly publication adapted to the highest popular intelligence of the Anglo-Saxon race. The explanation of this is that, although the colored man in America enters the second quarter-century of his emancipation without yet having attained the full measure of American freedom decreed to him, he has, nevertheless, enjoyed, for at least twenty years, a larger share of private, public, religious, and political liberty than falls to the lot of any but a few peoples—the freest in the world.

It would be far from the truth to say that other men everywhere, or even that all white men, are freer than he. No subject of the Czar, be he peasant or prince, however rich in *privileges,* dares claim the *rights* actually enjoyed by an American Freedman. The Negro's grievance is not that his liberties are few; it is that, in a land and nation whose measure of every man's freedom is all the freedom any one can attain without infringing upon a like freedom in others, and where all the competitions of life are keyed on this idea, his tenure of almost every public right is somehow mutilated by arbitrary discriminations against him. Not that he is in slave's shackles and between prison walls, or in a Russian's danger of them, but that, being entered in the race for the prize of American citizenship, in accordance with all the rules of the course, and being eager to run, he is first declared an inferior competitor and then, without gain to any but with only loss to all, is handicapped and hobbled.

Without gain to any and with loss to all. For in this contest no one truly wins by another's loss; no one need lose by another's gain; the prize is for every one that reaches the goal, and the more winners there are the better for each and all. The better public citizen the Negro can be the better it will be for the white man. But the Negro's grievance is that the discriminations made against him are more and more unbearable the better public citizen he is or tries to be; that they are impediments, not to the grovelings of his lower nature, but to the aspirations of his higher; that as long as he is content to travel and lodge as a ragamuffin, frequent the vilest places of amusement, laze about the streets, shun the public library and the best churches and colleges, and neglect every political duty of his citizenship, no white man could be much freer than he finds himself; but that the farther he rises above such life as this the more he is galled and tormented with ignominious discriminations made against him as a public citizen, both by custom and by law; and finally, that as to his mother, his wife, his sister, his daughter, these encouragements to ignoble, and discouragements to nobler, life are only crueler in their case than in his own.

2. What large enjoyment of rights, with what strange suffering of wrongs! Yet to explain the incongruity is easy; the large enjoyment of rights belongs to a new order of things, which has only partly driven out the old order, of which these wrongs are, by comparison, but a slender remnant. To explain is easy, but to remove, to remove these sad and profitless wrongs, what shall the nation do?

There are many answers. We are reminded of what the nation has done, and the record is a great one. For forty years of this nineteenth century, one of whose years counts for a score of any other century's, it made the condition of the Negro the absorbing national question, to which it sacrificed its peace and repose. Admitting much intermixture of motives of selfish power and of self-preservation, yet the fundamental matter was a moral conviction that moved the majority of the nation to refuse to hold slaves or countenance slaveholding by state legislation. To have waived this conviction would have avoided a frightful civil war. The freedom of the Negro was bought at a higher price, in white men's blood and treasure, than any people ever paid, of their own blood and treasure, for their own liberty. Since the close of the war, many millions of dollars have been spent by private benevolence in the North to qualify the Southern Negro, morally and intellectually, for his new freedom, and the outlay continues still undiminished. No equal number of people elsewhere on earth receives so great an amount of missionary educational aid. In the South itself a great change has taken—is taking—place in popular sentiment concerning certain aspects of the Negro's case. In 1885–86 over 58 per cent of the colored school population in seven great Southern states were enrolled in state public schools, in recognition of the necessity and advantage of the Negro's elevation.

These things are not enumerated to remind the Negro of his obligations. His property, as far as it goes, is taxed equally with the white man's for public education and the maintenance of the state; and all the benefactions he has received, added to all the peculations of which he stood accused in the days of his own misrule, are not yet equal to the just dues of a darker past still remaining, and that must ever remain, unpaid to him. They are enumerated not to exhaust the record, but merely to indicate the range of what has been done in the past, and is being done in the present, by white men concerning the Negro's rights and wrongs. The great national political party that first rose to power, and for almost a quarter of a century held governmental control, by its espousal and maintenance of the Negro's cause, still declares that cause a living issue in the national interest. The great party now in power,[1] with one or more disaffected wings from the opposition, though it does not propose to do anything as to the Negro that has thus far been left undone, at least consents not to

[1] The Democratic Party, 1887.

undo anything that has been done. Yet other important issues
have been pushed to the front by both parties, and the "Negro
question," however pre-eminent in the nation's true interest,
is not paramount in the public attention.

But what has the Negro done? What is he doing? The trite
answer is that he has increased from four millions to seven,
and is still multiplying faster by natural increase than any
other race on the continent. But, also, he has accepted his
freedom in the spirit of those who bestowed it; that is, limited
by, and only by, the civil and political rights and duties of
American citizenship equally devoid of special privileges and
special restrictions. He fought in no mean numbers in the great
army that achieved his liberation, and he has laid down, since
then, many a life rather than waive the rights guaranteed to
him by the American Constitution. In the infancy of his citizenship, steeped in moral and intellectual ignorance, with
some of his former masters disfranchised and the rest opposed
to almost the whole list of his civil rights, he fell into the arms
of unscrupulous leaders and covered not a few pages of history
with a record of atrociously corrupt government; yet, as the
present writer has lately asserted elsewhere, the Freedman
never by legislation removed the penalties from anything that
the world at large calls a crime, and here it may be added
that he never put upon the statute book a law hostile to the
universal enjoyment of American liberty. In the darkest day
of his power he established the public-school system. He has
exceeded expectation in his display of industry, his purchase
of land, his accumulation of wealth, his eagerness and capa-
bility for education, and even in his political intelligence and
parliamentary skill. Even under the artificial and undiscrimi-
nating pressure of public caste he is developing social ranks
with wide moral and intellectual differences, from the stupid,
idle, criminal, and painfully numerous minority at the bottom to a wealth-holding, educated minority at the top; each
emerging, or half emerging, from a huge middle majority of
peace-keeping, but uneducated and unskilled farmers, me-

chanics, and laborers, yet a majority unestranged from the more cultured and prosperous minority of their own race by any differences of religion, conflict of traditions, or rivalry of capital and labor, and hearkening to their counsels more tractably than the mass listens to the few among any other people on the continent. He is not open to the charges urged against the Indian or the Chinaman; he does not choose to be a savage, as the one, nor a civil alien and a heathen, as the other, is supposed to choose. He accepts education, sometimes under offensive, and sometimes under expensive, conditions. He proposes to stay in this country, and is eager to be in all things a citizen. His religion is Christianity; and if it is often glaringly emotional and superficial, so, confessedly, is the Christianity of his betters the world over. He only shares the fault, after all, in large and gross degree, amply explained by his past and present conditions; and in many leading features a description of his faith and practice, worship and works, would differ but little from the history of religion among our white settlers of the Mississippi Valley scarcely seventy-five years ago.

3. Thus far has the nation come, and in view of these developments the old but still anxious question, What shall be done with the Negro? makes room beside it for this: What shall the Negro do? For, as matters stand, it seems only too probable that until the Negro does something further, nothing further will be done. And, indeed, are not the times and the question saying, themselves, by mute signs, that the day has come when the Negro, not the rice-field savage, but you, the educated, the law-abiding, taxpaying Negro, must push more strenuously to the front in his—in your—own behalf, and thus in the behalf of all your race in the land? In particular, then, What can—what shall—the Negro do?

You can make the most of the liberty you have. You have large liberty of speech, much freedom of the press, of petition, of organization, of public meeting, liberty to hold property, to prosecute civil and criminal lawsuits, a perfect freedom to use

the mails, and a certain—or must we say an uncertain—freedom
of the ballot. All these are inestimable liberties, and have been,
and are being, used by you. But are they being used faithfully
to their utmost extent?

Freedom of public organization, for instance. From the earliest days of his emancipation the Negro has shown a zest and
gift for organization, and today his private, public, and secret
societies, which cost him money to maintain, have thousands
of members. Yet only here and there among them is there a
club or league for the advocacy and promotion of his civil
rights. There is probably no other great national question so
nearly destitute of the championship of an active national
organization, with officers, treasury, and legal counsel. The
causes of this are plain enough. As long as it was the supreme
political issue it was left, after our American fashion, entirely
to the heated treatment of the daily press, the stump, and the
national and state legislatures. From them a large part of the
question passed into a long period of suspense in the Supreme
Court. Only the matter of casting and counting votes kept, and
keeps, the attention of parties, and this with a constant loss of
power, showing that partisan treatment is no longer the question's only or chief need.

In the politics of a great nation even the greatest questions
must take their turns, according as now one and now another
gains the lead in the public attention, and the more sagaciously
and diligently any worthy question is pressed to the front by
the forces that dictate to the daily press, the stump, and the
national and state legislatures, the sooner and oftener will its
turn come round to lay uppermost hold upon the national conscience and policy. There always was good reason, but now
there is the greatest need, that you give and get this kind of
backing for the question of your civil and political rights. We
say give and get, because every endeavor should be used to
secure by personal solicitation, not the condescension—there
has been enough of that—but the friendly countenance and active co-operation of white men well known in their communi-

ties for intelligence and integrity. A certain local civil-rights club of colored men that had thought this impracticable at length tried it, and soon numbered among its active members some of the best white citizens of its town. And naturally, for it declared only such aims as any good citizen ought gladly to encourage and aid any other to seek by all lawful means.[2]

You can as urgently claim the liberty to perform all your civil duties as the liberty to enjoy all your civil rights. The two must be sought at the same time and by the same methods. They should never be divided. You must feel and declare yourself no longer the nation's, much less any political party's, still less your old master's, mere nursling; but one bound by the duties of citizenship to study, and actively to seek, all men's rights, and the public welfare of the nation, and of every lesser community—state, county, city, village—to which he belongs. Nothing else can so hasten the acquisition of all your rights as for you to make it plain that your own rights and welfare are not all you are striving for, but that you are, at least equally with the white man, the student of your individual duty toward every public question in the light of the general good.

Holding this attitude, you can make many things clear, concerning the cause of civil rights, that greatly need to be made so. For instance, that this cause is not merely yours, but is a

[2] After stating that any adult male citizen of the United States may become a member, it declares its object to be "to foster and promote, by every lawful use of the pen, the press, the mails, the laws, and the courts, by public assemblage and petition, and by all proper stimulation of public sentiment: 1. Both the legal and the conventional recognition, establishment, and protection of all men in the common rights of humanity and of all citizens of the United States in the full enjoyment of every civil right, without distinction on account of birth, race, or private social status. 2. The like recognition of every man's inviolable right to select and reject his social companions and acquaintances according to his own private pleasure and conscience, limited in the family relationship only by laws made under the full enjoyment of equal civil rights throughout the whole community coming under such laws; and in the social circle only by the same inviolable right in others."

great fundamental necessity of all free government, in which every American citizen is interested, knowing that they who neglect to defend any principle of liberty may well expect to lose its substance.

Or, for another instance, that the demand for equal civil, including political, rights is by no means a demand for supremacy, much less for the supremacy of one race over another.

Or, again, that this demand is not for a share in the popular power by a mass knowing and caring nothing about the popular welfare.

Or, yet again, that it is not the demand of an irresponsible herd deaf to the counsels of its own intelligent few and of any other.

Or, that the demand for equal unpolitical civil rights is not a demand that public indecency and unrespectability shall enjoy all the rights of decency and respectability, but that mere color be not made the standard of public decency and respectability.

Or, that equality in these unpolitical civil rights is urged, not for the difference in comfort, but for the effect upon the inward character of those qualified to enjoy it, and for its power to awaken, even in those yet without them, aspirations that should not be lacking in the mind of any citizen.

Or, lastly, you can make it clear that the Negro is not the morally and mentally nerveless infant he was fifteen years ago.

But there is a negative side to what the Negro may do.

4. You can proclaim what you do not want. We have already implied this in what goes just before. There are tens of thousands of intelligent people who today unwittingly exaggerate the demands made by and in behalf of the Negro into a vast and shapeless terror. Neither he, his advocates, nor his opponents have generally realized how widely his claims have been, sometimes by and sometimes without intention, misconstrued. He needs still to make innumerable reiterations of facts that seem to him too plain for repetition; as, for example, that he does not want "Negro supremacy," or any supremacy save

that of an intelligent and upright minority, be it white, black, or both, ruling, out of office, by the sagacity of their counsels and their loyalty to the common good, and, in office, by the choice of the majority of the whole people; that, as to private society, he does not want any man's company who does not want his; or that, as to suffrage, he does not want to vote solidly, unless he must in order to maintain precious rights and duties denied to, and only to, him and all his.

There is another thing which the Negro must learn to say, and feel, that he does not want. It is hard for a white man to name it, for it is principally the fault of white men that it is hard for the Negro to say it. It is our—the white man's—fault that the only even partial outlet for the colored man from a menial public status, in the eyes of the white man, is political office. Even when he attains a learned profession he attains no such consideration as he gains in political office, superficial and tawdry though it be. Yet, self-regard has grown; scholarly callings win for him more and more regard from both whites and blacks; in the whole national mind the idea has wonderfully grown—scarcely current at all when the Negro began his political life—that public office is not the legitimate spoils of party and the legitimate reward of mere partisan loyalty and activity, to be apportioned, *pro rata*, to each and every race, class, and clique among the partisan victors; and the time has come when the Negro, for his own interest, must learn to say: "My full measure of citizenship I must and will have; but I yield no right of public office or emolument to any man because he is white, nor claim any because I am black; and I do not want any office that does not want me." Such an attitude will win better rewards than the keeping of doors and sweeping of corridors.

But it is equally important to say that there are other things for the Negro to do that must by no means be either negative or passive.

5. You must keep your vote alive. This means several things. It means that, without venality or servility, you must

hold your vote up for the honorable competitive bid of political parties. A vote which one party can count on, as a matter of course, and the opposite party cannot hope to win at any price, need expect nothing from either. In no campaign ought the Negro to know *certainly* how he will vote before he has seen both platforms and weighed the chances of their words being made good. You will never get your rights until the white man does not know how you are going to vote. You must let him see that the "Negro vote" can divide whenever it may, and come together solidly again whenever it must.

Keeping your vote alive means, also, that while to be grateful is right and to be ungrateful is base, you must nevertheless stop voting for gratitude. The debts of gratitude are sacred, but no unwise vote can lighten them. A vote is not a free-will offering to the past; it is a debt to the present.

Again, keeping your vote alive means voting on all questions. What makes great parties if it be not the combination of men of various political interests consenting to concern themselves in one another's aims and claims for the better promotion of those designs in the order of their urgency and practicability? Now, here is the Negro charged, at least, with rarely—almost never—making himself seen or heard in any widespread interest except his own. Small wonder if other men do not more hotly insist upon his vote being cast and counted. The Negro may be not the first or principal one to blame in this matter, but he is largely the largest loser.

Last, keeping the vote alive means casting it. You must vote. You must practically recognize two facts, which if white men had not recognized in their own case long ago, you would be in slavery still today: that there is an enormous value in having votes cast; first, even though they cannot win; and, secondly, even though they are not going to be counted. A good cause and a stubborn fight are a combination almost as good as victory itself; better than victory without them; the seed of certain victory at last. Even if you have to cope with fraud, make it play its infamous part so boldly and so fast that it shall work its own disgrace and destruction, as many a time it has done before Negroes ever voted. Vote! Cast your vote though taxed for it. Cast your vote though defrauded of it, as many a white man is today. Cast your vote though you die for it. Let no man cry, "Liberty or blood"; leave that for Socialists and Parisian mobs; but when liberty means duty, and death means one's own extinction, then the cry of "Liberty or death" is a holy cry, and the man who will not make it his own, even in freedom is not free. Seek not to buy liberty with the blood either of friends or of enemies; it is only men's own blood at last that counts in the purchase of liberty. Whatever may have been the true philosophy for more ferocious times, this is the true philosophy for ours. Cast your votes, then, even though many of you die for it. Some of you have died, but in comparison how few; three hundred thousand white men poured out their blood to keep you bound, other three hundred thousand died to set you free, and still the full measure of American freedom is not yours. A fiftieth as much of your own blood shed in the inoffensive activities of public duty will buy it. Keep your vote alive; better nine free men than ten half free. In most of the Southern states the Negro vote has been diminishing steadily for years, to the profound satisfaction of those white men whose suicidal policy is to keep you in alienism. In the name of the dead, black and white, of the living, and of your children yet unborn, not as of one party or another, but as American free men, vote! For in this free land the people that do not vote do not get and do not deserve their rights.

6. And you must spend your own money. No full use of the liberties you now have can be made without co-operation, however loose that co-operation may have to be; and no co-operation can be very wide, active, or effective without the use of money. This tax cannot be laid anywhere upon a few purses. Falling upon many, it will rest too lightly to be counted a burden. White men may and should help to bear it; but if so, then all the more the Negro must spend his own money.

Half the amount now idled away on comparatively useless societies and secret orders will work wonders.

Money is essential, especially for two matters. First, for the stimulation, publication, and wide distribution of a literature of the facts, equities, and exigencies of the Negro question in all its practical phases. This would naturally include a constant and diligent keeping of the whole question pruned clear of its dead matter. From nothing else has the question suffered so much, at the hands both of friends and of foes, as from lack of this kind of attention. And, secondly, money is essential for the unofficial, unpartisan, prompt, and thorough investigation and exposure of crimes against civil and political rights.

You must press the contest for equal civil rights and duties in your separate states. The claim need by no means be abated that the national government has rights and duties in the matter that have not yet been fully established; but for all that you can urge the question's recognition in state political platforms, and, having made your vote truly and honorably valuable to all parties, can bestow it where there is largest prospect of such recognition being carried into legislation and such legislation being carried into effect.

There is a strong line of cleavage already running through the white part of the population in every Southern state. On one side of this line the trend of conviction is toward the establishment of the common happiness and security through the uplifting of the whole people by the widest possible distribution of moral effects and wealth-producing powers. It favors, for example, the expansion of the public-school system, and is strongest among men of professional callings and within sweep of the influence of colleges and universities. It antagonizes such peculiar institutions as the infamous convict lease system, with that system's enormous political powers. It condemns corrupt elections at home or abroad. It revolts against the absolutism of political parties. In a word, it stands distinctively for the New South of American ideas, including the idea of material development, as against a New South with no ideas except that of material development for the aggrandizement of the few, and the holding of the whole Negro race in the South to a servile public status, cost what it may to justice, wealth, or morals. Let the Negro, in every state and local issue, strive with a dauntless perseverance intelligently, justly, and honorably to make his vote at once too cheap and too valuable for the friends of justice and a common freedom to despise it or allow their enemies to suppress it. Remember, your power in the nation at large must always be measured almost entirely by your power in your own state.

And, finally, you must see the power and necessity of individual thought and action. It is perfectly natural that the Negro, his history being what it is, should magnify the necessity of co-operating in multitudinous numbers to effect any public result. He has not only been treated, but has treated himself too much, as a mere mass. While he has too often lacked in his organized efforts that disinterested zeal, or even that semblance of it which farsighted shrewdness puts on, to insure wide and harmonious co-operation, he has, on the other hand, overlooked the power of the individual and the necessity of individual power to give power to numbers.

You rightly think it atrocious that you should lose your vote by its fraudulent suppression. But what can your vote when counted procure you? Legislation? Probably. But what can legislation procure you if it is contrary to public sentiment? And how are public sentiment and action, in the main, shaped? By the supremacy of individual minds; by the powers of intellect, will, argument, and persuasion vested by nature in a few individuals here and there, holding no other commission but these powers, and every such individual worth from a hundred to a hundred thousand votes. Without this element and without its recognition there is little effective power even in organized masses. Do not wait for the mass to move. The mass waits for the movement of that individual who cannot and will not wait for the mass. You may believe your powers to be, or they may actually be, humble; but even so, there are all degrees of leadership and need of all degrees. There is work to be done which it is not in the nature of violence or votes or any mere mass power, organized or unorganized, to accomplish.

An attempt has been made here to enumerate a few of its prominent features. They are things that the Negro can do so profitably and honorably to all, of whatever race, class, or region, that no white citizen can justly refuse his public, active co-operation. The times demand these things. The changes already going on in the South are just what call for promptness and vigor in this work, for they mark the supreme opportunity that lies in a formative stage of public affairs. What will the Negro do?

A Simpler
Southern Question

[Invited by the editor of the *Forum* to write on the Southern question, Cable took the occasion to reply to several authors who had written in the same magazine during recent months. Chief among them were Governor Alfred H. Colquitt of Georgia ("Is the Negro Vote Suppressed?" November 1887), Henry Watterson of the Louisville *Courier-Journal* ("The Hysteria of Sectional Agitation," April 1888), Senator Wade Hampton of South Carolina ("What Negro Supremacy Means," June 1888), Senator William E. Chandler of New Hampshire ("Our Southern Masters," July 1888), and Senator J. B. Eustis of Louisiana ("Race Antagonism in the South," October 1888).

Cable's essay was published in the *Forum* of December 1888, and in *The Negro Question*.]

A Simpler Southern Question

I

To bring any public question fairly into the open field of literary debate is always a long step toward its final adjustment. It is across that field that the question must go to be so purged of its irrelevancies, misinterpretations, and misuses, personal, partisan, or illogical, and so clarified and simplified as to make it easy for the popular mind to take practical and final action on it and settle it once for all by settling it right.

It is in this field that the Negro problem still forces itself to the front as a living and urgent national question. Such distinguished and honored men as Messrs. Hampton, Chandler, Colquitt, Foraker, Halstead, Edmunds, and Watterson are engaged in its debate, and in the October (1888) number of the *Forum*, Senator Eustis writes that "this Negro question is still a running sore in our body politic," and that among the problems of this country it "promises to be the most serious of all," and "is still far from being solved."

Now, it is only fair to assume that each and all the writers who have turned aside from the more effective partisan media of the daily newspaper, legislative halls, the public platform, and the "stump," to the pages of the magazines and reviews, have done so in the desire to help the question along toward its final solution by aiding to make it in each case clearer and simpler than it was before. If so, then we may assume also that writers, editors, and readers will not repel an effort, if it be intelligent and sincere, to gather from several of these writers' utterances some conclusive replies to questions whose answer and removal from the debate will greatly reduce the intricacies of the problem.

II

Can the Southern question be solved? There are men in the North and South who say no, and, without being at all able to tell what they mean by the phrase, think it must be "left to solve itself." But careful thinkers, on either side of the question, never so reply. Their admission, whether tacit or expressed, is that "can be" is out of the debate; it *must be* solved. It is a running, not a self-healing, sore; one of those great problems "whose solution," as Mr. Eustis says, "strains the bonds of society and taxes the wisest statesmanship"; that kind of

problems with some one of which "every nation must deal."
We must solve it.

Is it being solved? We look in vain for any one's direct yes
or no. Governor Colquitt seems to come nearest to the distinct
affirmation when he says: "A sense of moral and religious responsibility is restraining and directing us in our state polity
and practice; and . . . I think we have had more than an
average success in discharging the obligations imposed upon
us." Among these he includes pointedly the assuring of the
Negro in the full enjoyment of his political rights. But setting
out to speak for the South, he speaks in fact only for Georgia,
and makes no plain claim that, even so, the Negro question
in Georgia is really being pushed toward its settlement. On the
other hand, when Senator Chandler says: "The political control of the United States is now in the hands of a Southern
oligarchy as persistent and relentless as was that which
plunged the nation into the slaveholders' rebellion"; and when
Senator Eustis falls short only by a slender "if" of the blunt
assertion that "the Negro problem still exists in its original relations," these gentlemen surely are not to be understood as
implying that the question has made or is making no advance
toward solution. Both of them yield a recognition of facts
which make it unreasonable so to construe their meaning. In
truth, it is indisputable facts that we need from which to draw
our final answer to this important query, rather than any person's or any multitude of persons' general assurances or ever
so profound beliefs. And for some such facts we are indebted
to these gentlemen as well as to others.

III

The Negro question is three quarters of a century old.
Within that period a vast majority of the nation have totally
changed their convictions as to what are the Negro's public
rights. Within that period the sentiment of every community
and the laws of every state in the Union, as well as the federal

government, have been radically altered concerning him. In
their dimensions, in their scope, in their character, the problem's original relations have passed through a great and often
radical change. So far from the problem still existing in its
original relations, only two or three of those original relations
any longer exist. Within the memory of men still in active life
there was not a foot of soil under the American flag where a
Negro detected fleeing from slavery was safe from violence.
Now, it is several months since it was asserted in the *Forum*[1]
that the Negro in the United States "has enjoyed for at least
twenty years a larger share of private, public, religious, and
political liberty than falls to the lot of any but a few people—
the freest in the world," and thus far no writer, black or white,
has challenged the statement. And the vast changes that have
been effected—not by time, mark it, but by men, sometimes at
peril, sometimes at cost, of their lives, in Northern states as
well as in Southern—have been very uniformly in the direction
of the great problem's simplification and solution. The problem is being solved; slowly, through the years, it is true; in
pain, in sweat, in blood, with many a mistake, many a dis-
couragement, many an enemy, and, saddest of all, many a neu-
tral friend in North and South; yet it is being solved, and it is
only by misconceiving the motive of those who have effected
these changes that Mr. Eustis, for instance, can call the long,
fruitful, and still persistent and determined effort an "unsuc-
cessful experiment." For it is not, and never has been, an effort
"to balance or equalize the condition of the white and Negro
races in this country," but only to balance or equalize their
enjoyment of their public and political rights, to establish a
common and uniform public justice and equity, and trust the
untrammeled selections of private society and "the laws of nature and nature's God" still to maintain all proper equalities
and inequalities of race and condition. The fact must be admitted by all fair minds to be established and removed from
debate that in some aspects, at least, the Negro problem's

[1] See "What Shall the Negro Do?"

"original" relations are altered, when men like Governor Colquitt, men in the front ranks of political life, their political
fortunes largely dependent on what they say, eagerly choose
to deny with indignation that either they or their constituents,
in states where once it was against the law to teach a colored
child to read, now either practice or believe in the entire or
partial suppression of the Negro vote, and as eagerly boast—
with statistical figures to back them—that their public schools
are educating twice as many thousands of colored youth now
as they were educating hundreds fifteen years ago. True, there
are men in the South who talk very differently. Aye, and in
the North, too. When there are none such left in the Southern
states they will be far ahead, at least of where the Northern
are now, toward the whole question's final solution.

IV

One of the most conclusive proofs that the changes that have
been made in the Negro's *status* have been generally in the
direction of true progress is that wherever and whenever these
changes have been made complete and operative, opposition
to them has disappeared and they have dropped out of the
main problem, leaving it by so much the lighter and simpler.
The most notable instance, of course, is the abolition of slavery; but there are many lesser examples in the history of both
Northern and Southern states: the teaching of Negroes in private schools; their admission into public schools; their sitting
on juries; their acceptance as court witnesses; their riding in
streetcars; their enlistment in the militia; their appointment on
the police, etc. It is a fact worthy of more consideration than
it gets from the debaters on either side of the Negro question
that such changes as these, which nobody finds any reason for
undoing in any place where they have been fully established,
were, until they were made, as fiercely opposed and esteemed
as dishonorable, humiliating, unjust, and unsafe to white men
and women as those changes which, in many regions of our

country, not all of them Southern, still remain to be made before the Negro question will let itself be dismissed. This fact no one will dispute. Yet thousands shut their eyes and ears, or let others shut them, to the equal though not as salient truth of this fact's corollary, to wit: that every step toward the perfecting of one common public liberty for all American citizens is opposed and postponed only where it never has been fairly tried.

Even the various public liberties intended to be secured to all men alike by the Civil Rights bill have rarely, if ever, in any place, been actually secured and made operative and afterward withdrawn and lost. Only where they have been merely legalized and not practically established, but bitterly fought and successfully nullified throughout Reconstruction days, have they since been unlegalized, condemned, and falsely proclaimed to have been fairly tried and found wanting. The infamous Glenn bill, in the Georgia legislature, may be thrust before us by debaters of the passionate sort on either side as a glaring exception; but its fate, its final suffocation, makes it more an example than an exception, even though this was effected by a compromise which will hardly be brought forward as evidence of "a sensibility of honor that would 'feel a stain like a wound.' "[2]

V

But the Negro vote. Surely, many will say, that was abundantly tried, and earned its own condemnation in the corruptions and disasters of the Reconstruction period. Now this would be a fair statement only if the ultimate purpose of the Reconstruction scheme had been simply to secure the Negro in his right to vote. We shall see that it was not. Much less was it to establish, to use Senator Hampton's phrase, "the political supremacy of the Negro," or, as Mr. Watterson charges, to erect "a black oligarchy at the South," or, as Governor Col-

[2] Governor Colquitt, in the *Forum*, November 1887.

quitt puts it, "to Africanize the states of the South." These
definitions belong—to borrow again Mr. Watterson's thought—
to the hysterics of the question. That fervid writer more than
half refutes the charge when he follows it closely with the
assertion that "the scheme was preposterous in its failure to
recognize the simplest operation of human nature upon human affairs, and in its total lack of foresight." But surely, whatever may be said of Sumner, Stevens, and the men who gathered around them, they were not a herd of perfect fools with
a "total lack of foresight." Not the scheme was, but the charge
that this was the scheme is, "preposterous." The scheme included the establishment of the Negro in his right to vote; but
its greater design was, as we have stated in an earlier paper,[3]
"to put race rule of all sorts under foot, and set up the common
rule of all," or rather "the consent of all to the rule of a minority the choice of the majority, frequently appealed to without respect of persons." As to the Negro in particular, the design, even at its extreme, was to enable him—and here we are
indebted to Mr. Eustis for a phrase—"to share with the white
man the political responsibility of governing"; or, more exactly, the political responsibility of choosing governors. This
scheme was never allowed a fair trial in any of the once se-
ceding states. Every effort to give it such was powerfully opposed by one great national political party throughout the
whole Union, "while"—to quote again from the same earlier
paper—"the greater part of the wealth and intelligence of the
region directly involved held out sincerely, steadfastly, and
desperately against it and for the preservation of unequal public privileges and class domination." "We thought we saw,"
says Governor Colquitt, speaking for that Southern wealth and
intelligence for which he has so large a right to speak, "a determined effort so completely to Africanize," etc. But Senator
Eustis, who also has his right to speak for them, treats that
thought as an absurdity worthy only the utterance of "that
foul bird of prey, the carpetbagger," who, he writes, "encour-

[3] "The Negro Question."

aged the *deluded Negro* to believe that the federal government
intended that he should govern the white race in the South."
The thought *was* an absurdity; an absurdity so palpable that
an intelligent people must have rejected it but for the conviction behind it that, whatever might be the experiment's
design, "Negro supremacy" would be the result. And here
Messrs. Eustis, Colquitt, Hampton, and the rest seem to agree.
This seems to be the potential conviction of all who speak or
write on that side of the debate; and we dwell upon the fact
because it furnishes such weighty evidence of the entire truth
of our earlier statement that this conviction, this fear, is the
whole taproot of the Negro question today. Man elsewhere
may hold some conjectural belief in "race antagonisms," or
even in their divine appointment. Nowhere in the world do the
laws forbid a man this belief. In every land, be it Massachusetts, Martinique, or Sierra Leone, he may indulge it to his
heart's content in every private relation. It is only where a people are moved by the fear of "Negro supremacy" that the simple *belief* in a divinely ordered race antagonism is used to
justify the withholding of impersonal public rights which belong to every man because he is a man, and with which race
and its real or imagined antagonisms have nothing whatever
to do. It is only under that fear that men stand up before the
intelligent and moral world, saying, "If this instinct does not
exist it is necessary to invent it."[4] There is a Negro question
which belongs to private society and morals and to the individual conscience: the question what to do to and with the
Negro within that realm of our own private choice where public law does not and dare not come. But the Negro question
which appeals to the nation, to the laws, and to legislation is
only, and is bound to be only, the question of public—civil
and political—rights. Mr. Eustis says truly, "Our plain duty
should be not to make its solution more difficult"; but when
he occupies eleven pages of the *Forum* with a recriminative

[4] See *Century Magazine,* April 1885, page 911, "In Plain
Black and White," by H. W. Grady.

entanglement of these two matters, one entirely within, the other entirely beyond, the province of legislation, he is wasting his own and his readers' time and impeding the solution of the *public* question; and we here challenge him, or any writer of his way of thinking, to show from the pen of any Negro of national reputation, Douglass, Lynch, Bruce, Downing, Williams, Grimké, Matthews, Fortune, or any other, anything but their repudiation of this—blind, let us believe, rather than willful—attempt to make a "Siamese union," as Mr. Gladstone would say, between these two distinct issues. As far as it is or of right can be a municipal, state, interstate, or national problem at all, the question today, pruned of all its dead wood, is this: Shall the Negro, individually, enjoy equally, and only equally, with the white man individually, that full measure of an American citizen's public rights, civil and political, decreed to him both as his and as an essential to the preservation of equal rights between the states; or shall he be compelled to abandon these inalienable human rights to the custody of Mr. Eustis's exclusively "white man's government," and "rely implicitly upon the magnanimity of his white fellow citizens of the South to treat him with the justice and generosity due to his unfortunate condition?" Shall or shall not this second choice be forced upon him for fear that otherwise these seven (million) black and lean kine may, so to speak, devour the twelve (million) white, fat kine, and "the torches of Caucasian civilization be extinguished" in the South, despite the "race antagonism" of the most powerful fifty-three million whites on earth? Is it not almost time for a really intrepid people to be getting ashamed of such a fear?[5] But that this fear is the main root of the whole Southern problem is further proved by the fact that no speaker or writer on that side of the debate, North or South, ever denies it. And neither does any attempt to prove that it is well grounded. Like Senator Hampton, all these de-

[5] For a special consideration of the question of "race instinct," and the maintenance of the color line, see the short article ["What Makes the Color Line?"].

baters content themselves with the absurd assumption that the
peaceable enjoyment, by the white man and the Negro, of an
equal and common civil and political citizenship was fairly
tried in the Reconstruction period, and that "a large class at
the North" have believed in and still want "Negro supremacy"
wherever the Negro is in the majority. Challenged to actual
argument, they are silent, until some one asks some subordinate question: Is the Negro contented and prosperous? Is he
allowed to vote? Is his vote fairly counted? Has he all his civil
rights? Are outbreaks due to political causes? Then their answers are abundant again; and as final proof that, not these,
but the earlier question, is truly the main issue now, there are
scarcely any two who do not contradict themselves and one
another.

VI

The least discordance of statement on these minor points is
on that of "race antagonism." And for the obvious reason that,
attributed to the Negro, who always denies it, it excuses the
bald assumption that no matter what he says, he must want
to establish a "black oligarchy"; while, attributed to the white
race, it excuses the theory that the white man cannot even by
way of experiment give the black man white men's rights, because natural instinct will not let him. "But you must!" says
conscience. "But I can't!" says fear. Yet even on this point there
is not full concord. Mr. Eustis "believes"—he counts it quite
enough to "believe" and needless to prove—that this instinctive
antagonism justifies the subjection of the Negro, forcible if
need be, to a "white man's government"; while, as far back as
1867, General Hampton "recognized that in a republic such
as ours no citizen ought to be excluded from any of the rights
of citizenship because of his color or of any other arbitrary
distinction." Where was and where is the gentleman's instinctive race antagonism? It is not in his list of necessities. He
believed "a large class" was bent on establishing "race suprem-

acy," and if there was to be "race supremacy," then, of course, and naturally enough, it must be the supremacy of the white race, instinct or no instinct; while Mr. Eustis regarded the race-supremacy scheme as a carpetbagger's lie, and could justify the subjugation of the Negro mainly on the *belief* that to protest against it is "an insolent demand for the revision of the laws of nature." But under neither philosophy does the Negro get a white man's public rights.

We find still wider variances on some other points. "Is the Negro vote suppressed?" Messrs. Foraker, Edmunds, Chandler, and Halstead still roundly make the charge. But they are all of one party and are human; what is the reply of the other side? Human, too, of course; but it is also what Mr. Silas Wegg might call "human warious." Says Governor Colquitt: "We therefore will not suffer the charge . . . of defrauding the Negro out of his vote to go unchallenged. We deny, as roundly as our enemies make the charge, that the Negro is denied a right to vote."

He speaks for the whole South. He addresses himself to the "alleged suppression of the Negro vote in the South," just as Mr. Watterson addresses himself to "a claim . . . that the Negro vote is suppressed . . . by the white people of the South." True, Governor Colquitt speaks especially for Georgia, but he distinctly offers Georgia as a fair sample of all the Southern states, and claims for the men on "the roll of members elect from Georgia to the next Congress, and in fact that from any other Southern state," "a love of truth and honesty that would cause them to refuse the presidency if it had to be won by fraud on any one, black or white." And Governor Colquitt ought to know. But who ought to know better than Mr. Watterson? And Mr. Watterson, not some time before, but six months later, writes: "I should be entitled to no respect or credit if I pretended that there is either a fair poll or count of the vast overflow of black votes in states where there is a Negro majority, or that in the nature of things present there can be." Now, the worst about these flat contradictions, in a matter confessedly involving the right to the nation's "respect and credit," and to a reputation for "love of truth and honesty," is that they will remain amicably unsettled. Each respondent will sincerely believe what he has stated, and the whole circle of party managers on their side of the issue will go on playing "thimble, thimble," with the tormented question.

Other secondary questions fare no better. Are outbreaks between the two races in the South frequently due to political causes? For twenty years we have heard that they are and that they are not. What says Senator Eustis? He has a divinely ordered race antagonism to assert, and so tells us that, this being the cause, almost anything may be the occasion. "Some sudden unforeseen incident, political, religious, educational, social, or what not, may at any moment arouse the passions of race hatred and convulse society by the outbreak of race conflicts." To him the real cause of amazement is "that these conflicts are not more frequent and more bloody." Exactly; the race antagonism theory does not half work. What says Governor Colquitt? "Friendly relations habitually exist between our white and black citizens, and are never disturbed except on those occasions when the exigencies of party politics call for an agitation of race prejudices."

VII

Such discrepancies are broad; but they shrink to narrowness when compared with Senator Eustis's contradictions of himself. Is the Negro contented and prospering? There are actually millions of citizens wanting to know. Let Mr. Eustis answer: 1. "His [the Negro's] craving for federal tutorship is still unsatisfied. The white man's patience is today taxed as ever by the unending complaints of the Negro and his friends. . . . He still yearns for this fruitless agitation touching his right and his *status*." 2. "This total want of possible assimilation produces antipathy, *quasi* hostility, between the two races, North as well as South," whose manifestations "both races regard as the incidents of a struggle for supremacy and domination." 3. "If this [race antagonism] were not the case the Negro would have the right to appeal to the enlightened judgment and to the sense of justice of the American people, to protect him against the unfeeling arrogance and relentless proscription which he has so long endured as the result of the white man's intolerance." 4. "In the South today he is happy, contented, and satisfied!" Mr. Eustis is almost as violently out of tune with himself as to the Negro's acceptance of his private social *status,* but we shall not quote; the question of the Negro's entrance into private white society, we again protest, is entirely outside the circle of his civil rights. No intelligent advocate of a common enjoyment of all civil rights by both races has argued to the contrary, and the present writer has never written a line in favor of it. As a moral and personal question it admits, no doubt, of public discussion, but as to its connection with any problem of political or civil rights between the two races, all that needs recognition is that it is completely out of that question.

Such is the conflict of testimony from the choicest witnesses on one side of the case. It is a common saying on that side that communities at a distance cannot understand this Negro problem. The fact is quite overlooked that a large majority of these communities no great while back held the very same views about it that are still held so largely in the South; and the very feminine argument that opposing debaters "cannot understand" because of "profound ignorance," etc., is only an unconscious way of admitting that one's own side cannot agree upon one full and clear explanation.

Fortunately we need not insist upon uniform answers to these questions. They are secondary. Let us only push on to the problem's main citadel. Whenever it falls all really dependent questions must surrender. And many others; as for instance, Must the average mental and moral caliber of the whole Negro race in America equal that of the white race, before *any* Negro in a Southern state is entitled to the civil

and political standing decreed to all citizens of the United
States except the criminal and insane? Or this: Does the Negro
throughout the domain of civil rights enjoy impersonal but individual consideration, or is he subjected to a merely class
treatment? The nation is tired of contradictory answers to
these questions. We can waive them, if only such chosen witnesses as these Southern writers in the *Forum* will answer this:
Do you, or your state party, recognize as civil rights whatever
rights belong to any and every person simply as a unit in the
civil community or in any public part of it; and do you advocate the Negro's enjoyment of each and every one of these
rights under only and exactly the same protections and limitations he would be under if, just as he is in everything else, he
were white? This is not a national party question. The Democratic party is answering both yea and nay to this in various
parts of the Union. The national party question is whether the
federal government may compel the people of a state to answer contrary to their will. We waive that question. Will you,
gentlemen, answer the question we ask?

If your answer is that you favor a separated but equivalent
enjoyment of civil rights by the two races, consider this: that
equal civil rights inhere in the *individual* and by virtue of individual conditions and conduct. *Equivalent* civil rights are
fictitiously vested in *classes* and without regard to individual
conditions or conduct. They cannot be even truly equivalent
when substituted for equal civil rights on the ground of the
offensiveness of one class to the other and without regard to
the conditions and conduct of the individual. Do you not see
that such pretended equivalence establishes unequal civil liberties, and do you favor or do you condemn it? Or answer a
yet simpler question: If a free ballot and a fair count should
seem about to decide in your state that *equivalent* civil rights
must give place to *equal* civil rights as the two are above defined, would you or your state party protect that free ballot
and fair count and stand by its decision?

Look at this question closely. It is not one upon which American political parties can honestly divide. It is the question whether the American government shall or shall not be a government "of the people, by the people, for the people," according to the Constitution's definition of who the people are. We beg to be believed that every word here written is uttered in a spirit of kindness and civil fraternity. We believe that to these two questions a true American loyalty can in calm reflection give but one answer. But we as sincerely believe that these gentlemen on the other side are as honorable and loyal in their intentions and are as sincere lovers of their state's and the nation's common welfare as they certainly are courteous in debate. We trust that loyalty and courtesy for an answer.

The Open Letter Club

[By the year 1888 Cable had concluded that his own voice
was having little effect; it was drowned out much of the time
by reiterations that no true Southerner would have such opinions as his. He had lost none of his faith in the Silent South,
and he knew that there were prominent Southerners who
might speak out if they were encouraged. He had been collecting the names of people, chiefly in the South, who would
read discussions of Southern topics, and he had distributed to
seven hundred of them pamphlet copies of his essay "The Negro Question," provided by the American Missionary Association. How much more would be gained, he thought, if such a
pamphlet carried the opinions of several thoughtful citizens
—and better still if it showed them joined in a debate which
would present varying opinions.

With the assistance of William M. Baskervill, a professor
at Vanderbilt University, Cable formed a loose organization of
some two dozen men who would write on selected topics important in the South, exchange papers for criticism and revision, and then publish them together. The members were in
widely varied activities and most of them were distinguished:
college presidents, university professors, ministers, lawyers,
judges, doctors, and businessmen.

The first symposium had as its subject "Shall the Negro Be
Educated or Suppressed?" Essays by eight members of the
club, including Cable, were published together in the *Independent* of February 21, 1889; with three other pieces
added, a pamphlet was printed for free distribution to the
readers on Cable's list, which now numbered nearly three

thousand. The second topic was to be "The Economics of the Southern Question," and Cable was enthusiastic about the possibilities. "We want both sides in this debate strong as they can be," he wrote one contributor, "and then God save the Right! So hurry up your reinforcements; no matter which side you're on, gallop up, unlimber, and begin firing! This is going to be a great paper." Along with Cable arguing for greater education and fuller rights for the Negroes was Charles Waddell Chesnutt, a Negro who had grown up in North Carolina, and Judge John Clegg of Louisiana. Daniel H. Chamberlain, formerly a carpetbagger governor of South Carolina, Baskervill, and John H. Boyd, a minister in Durant, Mississippi, took the conservative position.

But the second symposium was not completed and the club was abandoned in the spring of 1890. For one thing, no adequate means had been found to finance publication and distribution. But more important, several members decided that they could not afford to continue writing on the inflammatory topics; they were in danger of losing status in their communities and possibly their means of livelihood as well. To one of them Cable wrote, "Men of the South must speak out. How on earth is deliverance from error and misrule ever to come if the men who hold places of trust and influence cannot or do not give their counsel to the people?" Baskervill observed that the South had grown more conservative and more sensitive to criticism. For another thing, when the club was first organized the assumption was general that the Negro would be guaranteed normal constitutional rights, and thoughtful citizens such as those joining with Cable and Baskervill believed that the sooner those rights were extended in full the better it would be for the South. By 1890, however, the belief was growing that it might be possible to provide legally for segregation and ballot restrictions. Even Baskervill came before long to espouse segregation and exclusive white suffrage.

"New South Clubs" was the name first considered, but soon the choice was the "Open Letter Club."]

The Open Letter Club

I. STATEMENTS OF PURPOSE

[From manuscripts in the Tulane University Library.]

We must establish the "New South Clubs" all over the country for the development and promotion of the *New South of Ideas,* fundamental and practical. They shall be for information, discussion, dissemination, etc., etc. They shall reach over and around both sides of the merely partisan press. They shall give practical recognition to the fact that the Southern question is once more committed to the crucible of literary discussion and public debate. The idea is to open the arena of free speech in the South and join Northern and Southern and black and white intelligence and honesty in open debate, irrespective of party. The result of my effort, now less than two years old, to establish personal correspondence in the South is that I have just succeeded in putting my late essay into the hands of seven hundred picked men. It might as easily be seven thousand. What say you to the "New South Clubs"?

The "Open Letter Club" is a group, rather than an organization, of citizens mainly resident in the South operating, not by meetings, but through the mails, and designed to supply the widely felt need of some well-known medium through which information of every sort and from every direction, bearing upon the South, can be interchanged in order to the promotion of the South's best interests, moral, intellectual, and material.

The necessity of such co-operation is felt both by men of commerce and the industries, and by those whose pursuits draw their attention to problems of public policy on the right solution of which all permanent material prosperity must rest.

The "Open Letter Club" is intended to establish such a circuit of communications, throughout which information may pass freely and fully and which naturally will become high authority.

It is desired to secure the co-operation of individuals occupying every point of view, and of those who have any earnest desire for information, as well as those who are presumably able to furnish it.

The club is composed of men selected for their integrity, intelligence, and patriotism; and the better to preserve to the movement its public, and to exclude all private character, those qualities are made the only requisite of membership, except that, to remove all risk of the movement being drawn into the service of one or another political party, or of asserting political power for itself, persons holding political office, or distinctly of the political profession, may be admitted only in pairs from opposite parties.

No expense is involved in membership and there are no obligatory duties.

II. SHALL THE NEGRO BE EDUCATED OR SUPPRESSED?

[From a symposium with the same title, published first in the *Independent*, February 21, 1889, and later as a separate booklet, Nashville and New York, 1889.]

Editor of the *Independent*:

I have already discussed Senator Eustis's paper in the *Forum* of last December. I do not think any utterance of mine varies in principle from any made by Dr. Haygood in his criticism. Yet I gladly accept the invitation to comment on Dr. Haygood's paper. I give my heartiest applause to his main statement, that it is folly for the South and shame for the North to call the Negro question less than national.

He seems to me quite as clearly right when he welcomes writers of Senator Eustis's kind into the arena of literary de-

bate. I count it an incalculable misfortune that for twenty
years the nation has left the discussion of this great question almost totally to the floors of Congress, where in the nature of the
case it is bound to suffer fatally from heat, and to the columns
of the daily press, where it is inevitably bound to suffer fatally
from haste. The difficulties of the problem demand that it be
subjected to the most careful, dispassionate, studious discussion, a discussion purged of personalities, partisan rallying
cries, and unauthenticated conjectures and recriminations, especially a *progressive* discussion, where each particular division of the question, once settled—once fairly taken prisoner
and paroled, so to speak—shall not have to be fought over
again. Such discussion it is reasonable to hope for only, or at
least mainly, through the medium of the nation's more distinctively literary utterance, as it comes to us in the dispassionate columns of our magazines, reviews, and periodicals not
devoted primarily to news.

It may be said in reply that that is all very well for educated
people, people of studious tastes. But, in fact it is just the
educated people that first have got to settle this great question.
That done, there is no other question on our continent that
will be so nearly settled altogether.

Let us rejoice in the New South of material development,
and even read in our daily newspapers statistics without signa-
ture or official sanction and too often palpably padded; but
neither official nor conjectural figures can tell the value it will
be to the South and the nation to bring into the clear light and
air of a calm, friendly, and faithful national literary debate the
principles of law and order on which a New South must be
founded if it is to endure.

III. A LETTER IN THE OPEN
LETTER CLUB

[The copy of this letter which Cable kept is in the Tulane University Library.]

Dec. 30, '89

My dear Mr. Boyd:

I have not been able to answer yours of 4 Nov. until now. Thank you for it, heartily. Let me answer it.

You say, "It is a curious fact that all of those who hold views similar to Mr. Chesnutt's live in the land where this terrible question is not vital." But really this is not a fact at all. As you know, in Virginia, North Carolina and Tennessee there are so many thousands of white Southern property-holding native residents—over and above office-seekers, immigrants and protectionists—who are of Mr. Chesnutt's way of thinking that those states are almost classable as "doubtful" in national elections. As to Mr. Chesnutt and myself, I have not changed a single one of my views since I moved from the South five years ago after having been born and brought up in Louisiana, served in the Confederate Army, and seen the whole agony of Reconstruction and subsequent revolution at elbow's touch. Mr. Chesnutt is a North Carolinian who has not lived north so long as I have and has not acquired any new view of the Southern problem since moving. He saw the Reconstruction period, the revolutions that ended it, in North Carolina, as closely as I did, in Louisiana, and is himself one of the men to whom you deny the right of human brotherhood and American citizenship. He is "colored."

Now, see: You admit Mr. Chesnutt's "reasoning is faultless" and that his "premises"—for his and mine are identical—"are unassailable." You must allow, also, that thousands of Southern white men of family and property are in favor of acting and legislating in their own states, counties, and towns on the basis of this "faultless reasoning" from "unassailable premises."

Yet you say you dare not act in recognition of them but must act in defiance of them. Is not that saying you are afraid to do right? And yet you dare not say that. It is the test of our Christianity.

You say we are theoretical. But you overlook the fact that you are just as theoretical as we are. The main difference is that our theory, you admit, is demonstrable; while yours is not; indeed is not a theory at all but only a fear.

You say, "Prove to us that it isn't death to do otherwise"—than suppress the Negro. But your faith in God ought to be proof enough. The Bible bristles with promises that a righteous people guiltless of oppression shall prosper. And if men must have proofs instead of promises, shall Christians demand them? What did Christ come to earth for; to excuse us from doing right, or to teach us to do right at all hazards? You think it easy for me to say these hard things in Massachusetts; but I said and wrote and printed them for years, first, in Louisiana. Do they cease to be true because I say them now from a distance? What right—what room—has a Christian to say he dare not do right because of this or that—"my property, my peace, my life"? Dare a *soldier* say such things?

You say, "Prove to us"—so and so. The burden of proof is on those who plead necessity for wrongdoing. You say it would bring back the scenes of '68-'76. Prove it. You offer not the slightest proof of it. There is none. The single, simple, reasonable proposition that for twenty-five years has been before the party calling itself exclusively "the South" is that certain restrictions upon other men's rights and liberties be removed. Negro rule was never intended, expected, or reasonably feared to be the result. The refusal to allow consent to this removal divided the Southern white vote, consolidated the black, and opened the double doors of opportunity to thieves and robbers. But for that refusal the Negro could never have wielded the power of misrule. The division of the whites was no calamity; there can never be a safe, free government with less than two political parties equal in freedom and rights. The one-party idea is today the curse of the South. The division of the whites was no calamity: the calamity was that they divided on the only question that could ever make the Negro vote a solid vote, and could never make the white vote solid. The white man's consent to the removal of these restrictions has always been sufficient to make the Negro his political ally. And yet we have the plea—but always without argument—that an opposite cause will produce an identical effect; that to remove the potential cause of the Reconstruction chaos would produce that same chaos over again. Among white men in the Southern states who favor these concessions there are probably not more than here and there an abandoned scamp or two who favor Negro rule. They only, and rightly, have no intentions or fear that it will ever result. They may be depended on, the great mass of them, never to suffer it to be. The nation will never suffer it. The party that would advocate it—even in Maine or Oregon—could never elect another candidate to any important office. See enclosed pages torn from one of my essays.

Moreover: You want to avoid the risks of corrupt government. Are you avoiding them? Your whole plan for the tenure of power is corrupt & is corrupting the whole mass of the people. It is just as distinctly corrupting the whole national mind as ever slavery and its apologists did. In Reconstruction days the political economy of the dominant party was good and its financial managements were execrable. In these Negro-suppression days the financial managements of the dominant party are generally good, but its political economy is execrable, and the last end is worse than the first—only you don't see it. The losses of material wealth are greater, though unrealized. Edward Atkinson writes me under date of Dec. 11, "I am afraid that our Southern friends must pass through a period of rather bitter experiences in many lines. It is not by way of speculation, booms, or the sudden enhancement of the value of real estate, or the sudden acquirement of wealth by a few sagacious men, that the general progress and welfare of states can be established or secured. This is but a passing phase. It is by the slow, persistent development of individual effort and capacity *throughout* the community . . . that the true establishment of Southern industry on a solid foundation will be secured."

Let me recapitulate. I maintain:

1. The men who favor a cessation of Negro suppression are not all ignorant of, or distant from, the facts.

2. The suppression policy is untenable ground for a Christian.

3. The burden of proof (on the question whether or not non-suppression would be fatal to peace and order) lies with the advocates of suppression.

4. The disorder & corruption of Reconstruction days was primarily & ultimately owing to the policy of suppression, uniting the blacks, dividing the whites, and giving opportunity to rogues and robbers. To abandon suppression is to remove the cause.

5. To avoid the policy of non-suppression does not give pure or free government or open up the true fountains of public wealth. It gives corrupt & oppressive government and a political economy only something better than that which was based upon slaveholding. . . .

What Makes
the Color Line?

[In an essay entitled "Centralization in North Carolina," 1890, Cable dealt with the enactments which in that state permitted state officials to appoint county and other local officers and thus to insure that no office would slip from the control of the Democratic party.

This essay was published in the Chicago *America,* June 13, 1889, and in *The Negro Question.*]

What Makes the Color Line?

The popular assumption that a certain antagonism between the white and black races is natural, inborn, ineradicable has never been scientifically proved or disproved. Even if it were, that would not necessarily fix a complete and sufficient rule of conduct. To be governed merely by instincts is pure savagery. All civilization is the result of the subordination of instinct to reason, and to the necessities of peace, amity, and righteousness. To surrender to instinct would destroy all civilization in three days. If, then, the color line is the result of natural instincts, the commonest daily needs of the merest civilization require that we should ask ourselves, is it better or worse to repress or cherish this instinct and this color line? Wherein and how far is its repression, or its maintenance, the better? If we decide that in civil and political matters the color line is bad, the next question must be, who makes the color line in politics, and what will break it? The fact is, certain men are continually swinging between two statements: first, that the color line in everything else but politics is an imperative necessity; and, second, that the color line in politics is the source of all their trouble, and is drawn by the black man, against the white man's choice. But politics is not and cannot be a thing by itself; without the other provinces of life, politics is no more than the ciphers of an arithmetical number. Politics is what we do or propose to do in and for the various relations of public society. So, then, no progress can be made in the solution of Southern troubles until we settle the question, not *who* makes, but *what* makes the color line in politics. For, obviously, one set of people may be compelled to draw a line in politics for which another set of people is morally responsible. But when we settle *what* draws the color line in politics, we are preparing ourselves to say whether the line need be drawn or not. However, to inquire carefully who draws the color line may be the easiest way to demonstrate *what* draws it. Let us point out the strictly artificial character of certain things, now existing and active, which would compel the drawing of race lines by any race under heaven that might be subjected to them.

Some of these, says a recent Southern writer, are just as strictly of white men's own making as they are artificial. To deny, abridge, or jeopardize a Negro's right to vote, to hold office, to sit on jury, or to enjoy any of the public advantages around him on the same terms as others, without any consideration of his own individual values—good, bad, or indifferent —except that he is an individual of a certain *race,* is making an entirely artificial and irrelevant use of a limited natural distinction. But, says this writer, the Negroes obtained all these "cardinal and essential rights in spite of our [Southern white men's] most determined and bitter opposition." Speaking as an old citizen of Virginia, he says that the poll tax as a qualification for voting was a measure aimed solely at the Negro, and was finally abolished because it was found to keep more whites than blacks from the polls. In North Carolina, by laws expressly and avowedly enacted for that purpose, the form of government is centralized, the county officers are appointed by the governor, and the Negroes are deprived of the local self-government which county majorities of their race might give them. In South Carolina, the system of electoral machinery is especially and confessedly designed, and effectually operated, to deprive the Negroes of a voice in politics. He quotes from a leading Southern newspaper, that "as long as a white man capable of holding office can be found, no Negro, however worthy and capable, shall be appointed."

The Negroes never did and do not now draw a strict color line in politics. Even in Reconstruction days, when everything favored Negro supremacy, the Negroes generally entrusted the public offices of county and state to white men. And speaking for Virginia, even as late as 1878–82, when the party of which the Negroes were the main strength had absolute control of the state, almost every office, from United States senator to clerks in the state capitol, were given to white men, and white men were elected to Congress, and to the state legislature, by unquestioned Negro majorities. Even to this day, in the so-called "Black Counties," the Negroes generally yield to the whites all but the smallest and least desirable offices. "Whatever their other defects," says the writer quoted, "the Negroes, as a rule, have sense enough to select for officeholders the best whites they can find in their own party, and in default of them they select the best Democrats obtainable." If the Negroes are too ignorant to fill the offices themselves, surely no better testimony than this to their wisdom and public spirit could be asked for. And if they do this because of their own incompetency to govern, all the more from this example, Southern white people "should dismiss, as unmanly and unwarrantable, the fear that ruin and disaster will follow in the train of the free suffrage of the blacks."

The adherence of the Negro to what the South calls the "Radical" party is the only result that could be expected, in view of the attitude of the two parties in the South toward him. The one gave him freedom and citizenship, and *promises*, at least, to do what it can to secure him in the exercise of his rights. The other still says to him not only that he belongs to a degraded and inferior race, but that in all his public relations he must be judged and treated according to his *race's* merits and demerits, while his white fellow citizen monopolizes the ennobling liberty of being judged and treated according to what he is himself. "With these facts before us, how can we expect the Negroes to be anything but our political opponents and the adherents of our political adversaries?"

"To break this dark and ominous color line rests with us; but we can only obliterate it by treating the Negroes with equity and impartiality, and by according them cheerfully all the rights that we ourselves enjoy."

The sum is this:

1. That where the color line is drawn arbitrarily and artificially in any merely civil relation in the South, it is drawn by the white man.

2. That even by the white man the black man is not charged with drawing the color line contrary to the white man's wish, save only in politics.

3. That even in politics the black man draws the color line only where any man would draw it if he were colored; that is, only against those white men who draw the color line inexorably in every other public relation.

Why, then, in strictly public relations should not this incalculably expensive color line be removed?

National Aid
to Southern Schools

[In its initial version, this essay was introduced by a specific plea for the Blair bill then before Congress, which would provide federal assistance to public schools.

Published in the *Independent*, August 29, 1889, as "The Nation and the Illiteracy of the South," in the Minneapolis *Northwestern Congregationalist*, September 6, 1889, as "A National Debt," and in *The Negro Question* with the title "National Aid to Southern Schools."]

National Aid to Southern Schools

Should the national government make appropriations for public schools? This seems to be the right form of the question; not may it? but should it? If it may, it may; but if it should, it must. The Civil War taught us what it can cost to answer "we should" with "we may not."

We ought to recognize that the constitutionality of one or another congressional bill is but a small part of the question. A bill, however fine its intention may be, will never become operative if burdened with conditions which state majorities consider imperious and inquisitorial. Moreover, to base the plea for national aid upon the presence of a surplus in the national treasury strikes me as in principle extremely mischievous, and in policy fatal to the measure. As long as this is made the reason why, it seems to me the scheme will fail.

And yet I certainly think the national government should make appropriations for public schools in destitute parts of the country, at least in the South. On the general principle I have made in my own mind these points: first, that the constitutionality of national aid to education is not the question that properly comes first in order. The nation should first ask itself, "Do we in this direction owe a national debt?"—for if so, there *must be*, and we are bound in honor and common honesty to find, some constitutional way to liquidate it. If we owed a debt to a foreign nation, we should cut a sorry figure pleading that we could not make it constitutional to pay it. Shall we not treat our citizens as well as we would have to treat the citizens of a foreign government?

I think we are confronted here with a distinctly national debt. The educational destitution in the South, so contrary to our American scheme of social order, is distinctly the result of gross defects in that social order inevitably accompanying the institutional establishment of African slavery. It was certainly the nation's crime.

It is not enough for the North to point to her bloody expiation in war, nor the South to her proportionately greater sacrifice. Expiations, however awful, are not restitutions. Expiations do not pay damages. Here is one of the vast evils resulting from the nation's error still unremoved. If it had not been for the political complicity of millions of Northern voters we never need have had a war, and slavery must have perished without one. I think, therefore, that, beyond question, the removal of our vast Southern illiteracy is an obligation resting upon the whole nation, yet one which the states of the North and West cannot meet effectively except through the action of the national government.

Let national aid to education be supplied, not as a national condescension or charity, but as the one final payment of a national obligation, so regarded by payer and payee, and no community will be pauperized. It is absurd to fear that the payment of a just debt, and its payment in *education*, is going to pauperize a community and make it content to bring up the next generation in ignorance. It is hardly convincing to draw large inferences from small examples in exceptional communities, as has been done too frequently in this debate. Our whole wide knowledge of human history and human nature makes it axiomatic that a free and educated generation under self-government will not fail to educate its children at its own cost.

We need to make one distinction very plain here—between adults and children. To bestow a professional education gratuitously upon an adult certainly does have some tendency to pauperize him, for it puts advantages of life into his hands at a lower price than *manhood* ought to pay. But the case of a child in school is just the reverse. Under gratuitous aid he still gets education at no abatement of price to *him,* but finds himself, instead, filled with needs which call forth his finest manhood to supply. Let the nation pay its debt of public education to Southern illiteracy in one generation of school children. It is true that the Southern states could do more for public education if they would, and he is no friend of the South who flatters her people into the delusion that they are doing all they can. To show this, one need only compare these states with the new states and territories of the West, where the people invest not only much more *per capita* of school population, but a very much larger proportion of their taxable wealth, even when they are poorer and more preoccupied in establishing the preliminary framework of society, and are burdened with a constant inflow of alien immigrants. In short, they treat public education as the very first of preferred claims. But the supreme fact is not that the South is or is not doing all it can for education. It is that hundreds and thousands of children, white and black, as the result of the nation's crime, of which they are only the innocent victims, are growing up in an ignorance more pauperizing than education, however paid for. To those who rest their argument against national aid upon isolated examples in an exceptional state here and there, we might ask one question: Which are the paupers, the tens of thousands who have received Northern aid and even remote individual aid, the most hazardous of all aids, or those who have grown up in ignorance without it? Is it not the fact that most parts of the South have learned the value and applied the lesson of public education from the aid, gratuitous as to them, of Northern missionary societies? I do not consider the education of the lower masses in the South a cure for all the ills of Southern society, but I fail to see how they can be cured without it, and I fail to see any excellence in the policy that is content to withhold it.

But, again, our national scheme, in recognizing the right of every man to vote as a necessary part of the universal right of self-government, forces upon us, as a correspondingly imperative public necessity, to see that no part of the public mass is left without the means to vote intelligently. The one idea stands for freedom, the other for safety.

I am not of those who consider that when the nation enfranchised the Negro it created a new danger. The range of history, even within our own times, gives proof enough that the illiterate Negro is neither as dangerous nor as much feared enfranchised as he was enslaved. But I do insist that enfranchisement—which my mind emphatically approves—was only half the essential national provision for permanent safety. In other words, I recognize civil freedom as an element of public safety, not danger, yet an inadequate element demanding the establishment and maintenance of intelligence to complete the provision.

To pay the world what it had borrowed was one part of the nation's obligation. To liberate bodily, politically and civilly, the slave, was and is another. There are others. But to loose the bonds of the Negro's ignorance is still another. To banquet, toast, and embrace the men who conscientiously fought for the destruction of the Union and the perpetuation of slavery is generous, inspiring, and largely admirable; but it pays no part of the national debt to either side; and I sincerely believe that North and South would think more of one another if one common, noble sentiment would recognize the fact that feasting and embracing cannot of themselves pay the debts of either party. Let us have the banquet, by all means; but let us have the wedding first and the banquet afterward.

Whatever we say with regard to illiteracy of blacks in the South applies to the illiteracy of whites also, since they are both the fruit of the same tree, whose root drew its nourishment from a moral error as wide as the nation. Let us be constitutional; but I think no reasonable mind will doubt that when the nation recognizes this matter as a national debt, it will find or will make a constitutional way to mend it.

We are told by the opponents of national aid to education that it would incur the risk of pauperizing the communities aided; but surely we cannot run a more glaring risk than to go on leaving the reduction of an enormous mass of illiteracy to communities that believe themselves, and are widely believed, to be doing all they can, while they are hardly performing half the entire bulk of the task. There is not in the range of our choice any condition or possible attitude free from risks, and the maxim is as true in politics and government as in commerce and finance—"Nothing venture, nothing have." Another maxim is to the point, that "Forewarned is forearmed." And certainly all hazards in national aid would be reduced to trivial proportions when made conditional upon at least the full maintenance of the present degree of self-help supplied by the states themselves.

[Believing education to be crucial in the solution of the Southern problem and disappointed in the provisions made to educate the Freedman, Cable gave more and more attention to education. He wrote out a long manuscript on the subject from which he mined an address, "Northern Wine in Southern Bottles," to deliver before the Union League Club of Chicago, January 9, 1892, and two essays: "Does the Negro Pay for His Education?" in the *Forum*, July 1892, and "Education for the Common People in the South," in the *Cosmo-politan*, November 1892. In these papers his concern was for the entire subject of public education in the South, and he dealt most with the Negro, he said, simply because the Negro suffered greatest privation, being the "South's poor man and underling." Citing an abundance of specific facts taken from the reports of state superintendents and national commissioners of education and from the successive constitutional and legis-lative enactments since the Civil War, he stated his conclu-sions: Because of the heavy reliance on the poll tax and the statutory limitations some states had placed on property taxa-tion for schools, the Negro paid "a larger proportion of his whole school fund than any poor man out of the South in America"; a disproportionate amount of tax money went to in-stitutions of higher learning (restricted to whites) and to the city and town schools, leaving only the barest support for schools in rural areas, where most of the Negroes lived. "It is black illiteracy that fosters white illiteracy," and the poor whites suffered only slightly less than the Negroes from the meagerness of educational provisions.

As he had done in writing the newspaper letters in 1875, Cable argued that money spent for public education is an in-vestment which will yield returns many fold. More specifically, he urged that a democratic government has the obligation and the necessity to make sure it has an enlightened electorate.]

Congregational Unity
in Georgia

[Though Cable could tolerate segregation in the churches no more than elsewhere, he had hesitated to raise the issue, for he knew that the cause of the Negro was supported by many who would not accept integration in the church. In 1889 the Congregational churches of Georgia took a position which in effect nullified a policy of the national church, adopted at a meeting in Saratoga, encouraging the white and Negro churches to unite. Cable wrote on the subject in an issue of the *Congregationalist* given over mainly to the problem, September 26, 1889.]

Congregational Unity in Georgia

The hope expressed in the resolutions passed this summer at Saratoga, that the two state bodies of Congregational churches in Georgia, white and colored, would unite, clearly reflected the conviction that a difference of race should not, in any body of Christians, be accepted as in itself a sufficient occasion or excuse for disunion. The appointment by the two bodies in Georgia of a joint conference committee to consider the question of their union was at least a partial recognition of the same principle. The refusal of the Association (colored) to accept the plan of the joint conference committee implies that it did not seem to the Association to offer satisfactory terms

of union. And now, where is the wrong—and what will right
it?

Certainly the rejected plan seems to discard the very principle in which the duty of union is implied. It provides carefully for the preservation of the Conference (white) and Association (colored) as separate local bodies, yet with no local
boundary between them. Thus it really admits that being local
representative bodies is not the cause of separation.

The Saratoga resolutions contemplate the union of the two
bodies "on principles of equal recognition and fellowship *of all
the churches of each body.*" Now, to be genuine and complete,
such recognition and fellowship must radiate from all the
churches to all the churches, and from each church to each
church, of both bodies. But the joint committee's proposition
is to establish, by delegations from each, a third body, and
profess by proxy a fellowship denied by disunion. The Saratoga idea ignores caste in the church relation; the joint committee's plan accommodates caste. It is really a plan for putting
forth a maximum of profession with a minimum of per-
formance.

Is this right, or wrong? If right, is it so on permanent principles, or only on present necessities? Hardly on principle, for
the resolutions presenting the plan declare in plain words the
very principle which the plan itself sets aside. On present necessity, then. What is this necessity? Is it that a controlling
number of colored churches are holding out for something in
excess of a whole Christian recognition and fellowship, or does
a controlling number of white churches desire the colored
churches to be satisfied with something less than full measure? We have seen no evidence of any colored church demanding anything which would not have been granted it had it
been a white church; but we see in the official offer of the
white churches to the colored such a visible tendency to econo-
mize their recognitions and fellowships that any real union of
Association and Conference would be "awkward." The neces-

sity, then, for non-union, as far as any is supposable, lies in the attitude of the white churches.

On what plea is this attitude held? If we assume that these churches have done all they believe it is their duty to do, then we must infer that a controlling number of these churches, or controlling numbers of them, do not count it their duty to award the very same recognition and fellowship to colored churches as to white. Most probably, even in the churches believing, there are minorities who believe their debt of recognition and fellowship is exactly the same whether a church or person is white or colored. Which are right, these minorities, or those majorities? To which does the great Congregational Church at large owe its hearty commendation and support?

When the question of the Congregational Church's duty was as to slavery and slaveholders, it was met nobly. Any present temptation to be less courageously faithful comes from other churches' traditions, rather than her own, and the question is really simpler. Slaveholding was a civil and governmental institution. It belonged to the structure of public society, and therefore to those things the Church's relations to which are always a difficult problem. But in the present case the Church is not put at issue with government at all, but only with certain usages and sentiments of private society, where in all questions of right and wrong it is the Church's radical duty to be the teacher, not the pupil; to pronounce, and not to yield or compromise. Neither have we here a case in which the conscience of the Congregational Church is not educated. For fifty years it has held that the spirit of caste is unequivocally wicked, and a step backward is a step fifty years back.

Nevertheless, the wrong that lies in the state of affairs indicated by the proposition of the Georgia joint committee results from mistaken views; but views that lie somewhat remotely back of the immediate question. There is, in all our American Protestant churches, much confusing of the fraternal relations of church membership with the inevitably narrower relations of private society. The two relations, both of them

right and good, are not even ideally one. Church membership
should establish fraternal relationships across distances of personal dissimilarity which, even under ideal conditions, the companionships of private society cannot embrace in any one un-
broken span. Christian fraternity does take into one span the
utmost extremes of earthly conditions. But to insist upon a private companionship between each and every two members of
a church tends only to cramp Christian fraternity into the narrow boundaries practicable to private social affinities. It is
just and Christian that worshipers maintain the right to select
their private social companionships within a circumference far
smaller than the church relation has any right to contract itself to; and the proposition to make the two relations identical
will always be met with more or less revolt, even within the
Church, and will inevitably reduce the conception of church
fellowship to false limitations. All the wheels of a watch move
in one common harmony and with one common purpose; but
we cannot make any one of them as large as the whole watch,
or all of them the same size, or set them all on one center, or
have them all turn in one direction or at one speed. But we
have each wheel smaller than the whole watch, and all of
them of different sizes, hung on divers centers, turning this
way and that, at various speeds, and yet have them all in one
perfect watch.

The mischief of the error lies in its misteaching us that our
exchanges of recognition and fraternity may stop at the boundaries of mutual private social adaptability, and that those who
are not mutually qualified for private social fellowship ought
somehow to be excused from a practical and complete recognition of Christian equality and fraternity as members of one
church. It is with this confusion of relations in the minds of
their members that the Congregational churches of Georgia
find themselves handicapped as they confront the problem of
caste.

Let us see if we can define the true line of tolerance and
intolerance concerning this matter, on which the Church at

large may fulfill, without exceeding, the measure of a faithful righteousness and Christian charity. The spirit of race caste, too prevalent everywhere, but sweeping through all the relations of Southern life, has produced in American private society of all grades certain conventions which Christianity condemns. Yet he must be a bigot indeed who would insist that the Church *command* its individual members as to how far they may or must fly into the face of these unjust conventions in their own private selections of personal friends, companions, and guests of their homes. In other words, the individual church worshiper holds certain social prerogatives. Concerning the proper use of them, it is his duty to hearken to the Church as his teacher; while yet the Church has no right to take the attitude of a magistrate. But the moment he attempts to carry such private prerogatives out of their lawful province, and in the larger domain of the church relation to ask and offer to his fellow worshipers inequalities of church privilege and fellowship, it is the solemn duty of the Church magisterially to cry Halt.

Here is the true field of debate. The question of relative rights and duties settled here is settled in every larger church body. Nor need settlement on this line make serious confusion. The impulses, good and bad, of private social selection will live on, and even excessively dominate church congregations, as they now undoubtedly do. Worshipers will still sort themselves even too largely along the natural and artificial lines of social stratification. There will even still be white churches and colored churches, just as there will still be rich men's and poor men's, educated men's and uneducated men's churches. But the Church in her government and in her teaching will be found faithfully protesting, and no doubt prevailing, against that spirit of caste which is the subtlest enemy of Christianity that in all our land attacks the Church in her organic capacity.

Churches, in North or South, that see this matter clearly, are in duty bound to hold themselves firmly toward the ideals set by Christ, remembering that Southern churches especially are under the stress of peculiar and acute temptations. The disposition, on the part of any church, anywhere, to offer the slightest abridgment to the rights and privileges of any worshiper on account of his race or any other private social drawback not of a moral nature, should be discountenanced and rebuked.

This principle of treatment applies to individual churches exactly as it applies to individual church members. In any organized group of churches each church must be supposed to have its individual conscience, and its individual moral ignorances and oversights, just as it has its rights and duties. It is not merely a subject of government, but a pupil in school. Among its sister churches it must be under precept and suasion, and not merely under law and penalty. Only bigotry would set the larger ecclesiastical body in magisterial inquisition over its individual churches to dictate to the uttermost their treatment of their individual members. But the moment individual churches in any organized group begin to ask or offer toward other churches any inequality of recognition and fellowship not properly disciplinary, it is instantly the duty of the larger organization to withstand and condemn such encroachment, even meeting them, when it must, with law and penalty.

By close adherence to both sides of this principle we preserve both law and liberty. But the liberty is put under the salutary pressure of constant moral suasion in all its forms, and the law is confined within those boundaries of the general conscience which the individual choice has no right to overstep.

See the present case: Suppose colored members of a white church to demand the private social companionship of its white members. The Church will answer that while Christianity teaches us, and bids the Church teach, the noblest rules by which to choose the social companions of our private life, it does not authorize the Church to sit in official inquisition upon such choice. Christianity is a religion not of mere moral law, but of precepts over and above law; yet church members are not subject to compulsions and penalties in matters of precept, but only in matters of moral law.

Suppose, however, the same church confronted with another proposition: because colored people here or there are not generally received or receivable in the private social life of white people, that this shall somehow qualify and abridge the church's hospitality to them as public worshipers, or their fraternal recognition as church members. The Church will reply that scripture has exhausted the figures of speech to declare the absolute equality that runs throughout the church relation; "There is neither Jew nor Greek, bond nor free, male nor female"; and that a *church* has a conscience and a responsibility, answerable to Christ and not to caprices of individuals or in any mere conventions or private social circles. And if such a church does its whole duty it will admonish the consciences of its individual members with diligence, fearless of surrounding pressure.

But suppose, again, certain churches, as well as church members, so to have erred in this matter of caste as passively or otherwise to have allowed the color line to qualify church relations, and even their relations with other churches. Such an event might thrust upon the association or conference to which they belong some very delicate questions of liberty and discipline, demanding special consideration in each case; yet some points of duty would be quite plain and of general application. It would be, first of all, and clearly, the general body's duty to repel inflexibly any effort of such churches to impose their error upon it, or secure its approval or silent consent. It might be found on experiment that this alone would convey quite enough of rebuke to awaken those in error to the fact and character of their mistake.

As in all such cases, so in this, we shall doubtless be told that an unflinching adherence to principle will result in jeopardizing the efficiency, even the very existence, of a large number of churches. Our answer must be that in the scheme of

THE NEGRO QUESTION

the world's salvation, not the life, or numerical or financial prosperity of one or another church, but the maintenance and spread of the Divine Master's teachings *in their integrity* is the supreme necessity and command; and it is as true for a church as for the individual, "He that loveth his life loseth it."

What the
Negro Must Learn

[An address delivered at the annual meeting of the American
Missionary Association at Northampton, Massachusetts, Octo-
ber 22, 1890; adapted from an address entitled "The South's
First Needs," delivered at Washington the previous May 16
under the auspices of Howard University. Published in *The
American Missionary*, January 1891, and as a pamphlet by the
American Missionary Association (1891?).]

What the Negro Must Learn

To the Protestant church in these Northern states of our Union, the sister states of the South are the richest mission field
in the world. They are not foreign lands. They are here. They
are the most conveniently adjacent part of our national domain. Their whole people are by birth members of our own
political household. In our North and West there are vast areas
where one third of all the people are of alien birth. In almost
the whole South, the people of foreign birth are less than one
in a hundred. In religious traditions and affiliations, virtually
its entire population is Protestant. In the eleven states south of
Maryland, West Virginia, Kentucky, Missouri, and the Indian
Territory, there are—roughly speaking—fourteen million people. Now, consider the needs and opportunities of this field.
Not to quote their long familiar tables of absolute illiteracy,
millions—I fear it would not be far wrong to say five or six

millions—are without any real education or enlightened religious teaching. No other people in the world proposes to occupy for missionary work any notable part of this great field. The religious and educational work done by the Southern Protestant churches among the destitute millions of colored people of their states is positively too small to be counted. They are thrice disqualified for the work.

First, they owe their original separate existence to their former justification and support of the slavery out of which these millions have so lately escaped. Second, they owe their continued separation from churches of their own name elsewhere to the fact that they still cherish a civil, political, and ecclesiastical alienation from their ex-slaves. Third, they hold an antiquated underestimate of secular education as a means of spreading spiritual truths and graces, and see no great obligation to send to the intellectually and morally destitute any thing but preachers, tract distributers, and the catechism.

To such this great field is not open. To men who see in secular education no serious if even legitimate part of missionary work—as if because air is not food we need not provide for men to breathe—or, as if the city of Mansoul were not to be attacked or defended except in front—or, as if the gospel were vitiated or fatally diluted if run through the earthenware conduits of secular education—against such men this field is shut and double-locked. It is open only to Americans, because it is America. Of Americans it is really open only to those who believe in, and teach, the right of all men to civil and political, as well as bodily and religious, freedom. And of these it is widely open only to those who realize that without civilization religion cannot prosper. It is a field open to the subsoil plow of the belief that whatever makes for citizenship makes for Christianity. There never before were in one mass seven million ignorant people so eager for education and so willing to receive it saturated with the leaven of Christian truth. There never before were seven million people waiting for the Christian missionary with so little paganism to unlearn. There never

before was a field that promised so soon to liberate again the
outlay made in it, for reinvestment in other fields of slower
response. There never was a mission work of any such extent
where the financial, industrial, commercial, and civil reim-
bursements and rewards to its supporters lay so near the surface or promised such vast returns.

No other people but those of this field hold us so awfully
in their debt. The work done for the Indian owes much of its
vigor and extent to our sense—as a nation—of having grossly
wronged him in the past. The wrongs done the Negro—by the
slave trade carried on in Northern ships—by the laws and practices of Northern states and of the federal Congress and courts
for the protection of Southern slaveholders—by the postponement of the day of freedom until the alternative of national
destruction stared the whole nation in the face—and by the
further suspension of his right of citizenship until, three years
after the war's last gun was fired, it became plain that without
it his own and our own last state was worse than the first—
these wrongs have piled up an indebtedness that at least will
fairly match our "Century of Dishonor" concerning the red
man, who within our borders never numbered one entire half
million since white men began to oppress and defraud him.

There never was a missionary field of such extent, where the
claims of patriotic self-interest so mingled with the needs of
destitute souls. This country of ours is a giant with one arm
in a sling. That arm is the South. The whole country knows
that because of something wrong in the South, this whole
country, great, rich, free, and progressive as it is, is immeasurably less than it ought to be—immeasurably behind where it
ought to stand. Half the thought given to the betterment of
the economic and civic conditions of our country is taken up
with the problem how to establish a full share of our national
vigor, freedom, enlightenment, and wealth in this crippled,
bleeding, and aching arm. We know the South's natural advantages are unsurpassed if not unequalled. What has God not
given her? Natural beauty, military defensibility, harbors,

navigation, mineral treasures, forests, fertility of soil, water supply from spring and cloud, equable climate, abundant room. But natural resources are not all her endowment. She has a vast commerce, daily increasing mines and manufactures, banks, railways, public credit, courts, churches, schools, colleges, newspapers, and representative state governments. And still there is something wrong. Must we continue to assign its cause to the desolations and backsets of a war ended a quarter of a century ago, or the disorders of the seven or eight years that followed? But if these are only of the past they ought not still to count. In these days capital flows as freely and swiftly to any and every place where internal conditions do not exclude it as waters seek their level when set free. The same is true of immigration. To say the South lacks men and money is only to confess, not to explain, the hidden cause of her backwardness.

The South is the nearest Europe of all regions bidding for immigration and capital. There is not a spot in it east of Dallas, Texas, large enough to be shown on a census map, where artificial irrigation is required. Yet hundreds of thousands of acres of good farming lands lie mutely begging for the ax and the plow and find no occupants at from one to two dollars an acre. Emigration swarms hundreds and thousands of miles further on, and settles on rainless plains or in other hemispheres; and capital, four times out of five, looks but once upon the South's wounds and passes by on the other side. Why do they so?

Because they will not go to a land of plenty that is not also a land of promise. They seek a country where those who rule in public and private society are *going security* for the early establishment of all the safeguards and appliances of social order and political liberty.

I do not say that the South's great first need is tranquillity. Opium is not always the right medicine. Men and money are pouring into untranquil countries this very day. But there is one thing they keep away from. They keep away from coun-

tries whose prospect of future tranquillity is not proportionate
to the age of the community and the existence of the conventional institutions of social order. Capital and immigration
overlook in Chile or the Argentine, in the Dakotas, Wyoming,
or the Australasian colonies, untranquil conditions which they
will inflexibly refuse to encounter in countries, however rich
in natural resources, all the appointments of whose civil order
are already from fifty to one hundred years old. They tolerate
the untranquillity of formative, or even of reformative beginnings; but not of permanent strained relations. I may go into
a sod house or tent while my house is building; I will not
accept a tumble-down palace for a permanent residence.

Look at the South. What say the world's employment-
hunting capital and labor, when we ask them why they turn
aside from her? They reply, not in reproach; only in kindliest
explanation. But what say they? That she has legislatures a
hundred years old, but often no adequate popular reverence
for law; that she has judges and courts, but often no patience
to wait for their decrees or honor their mandates; that her
frightful prisons defend neither the criminal's rights nor those
of society; that her provisions for public education will not
bear comparison with that of any region bidding successfully
for immigration; that her agricultural system is characterized
by an ignorance and waste that keeps the husbandman degraded and poor on a soil that ought to make him rich; that
her factories and furnaces are short of skilled labor and her
millers and ironmasters wedded to the delusion of low pay and
long hours; that the curricula of her colleges are antiquated
and almost completely innocent of civics and economics; that
in whole states the laws so one-sidedly protect the landlord,
creditor, and mortgagee that they work intensely toward the
perpetuation of the landlessness, penury, unthrift, supineness,
and vice of the laboring masses. A greedy expansion of the
mortgage system to movable property, standing crops, and
even crops unplanted—nay, to the very household larder—has
strangled in its birth the personal credit of the liberated slave,

and persists in the ruinous effort to dispense with the necessity of his being honest. Remove these conditions, say capital and labor, and we will come in and wait not on the order of our coming. For the safety and prosperity of all society rests at last on the prosperity of its laboring masses.

And so Southern men have learned to say that public education is the South's first need and final deliverance. What helped them to this belief? The missionary schools and colleges of Northern churches in the South. These were their object lessons. Hampton, Atlanta, Fisk, Tougaloo, Straight, and the rest, they are the mothers of the whole public-school system of the Southern states as far as it embraces the colored race. They made the policy and system reasonable and practicable to Southern eyes and hands.

Instruction, now says the South, widens intelligence and evokes aspiration. From these come industry, skill, thrift, temperance, property, responsibility, and public spirit; and from these, public respect, esteem, confidence, and reward. And yet, mark! So saying she makes a half provision and then beckons and calls to the world's spare men and money to come on across the gulf that lies around her still with this bridge of public education built just halfway across it, and insisting on the fatal declaration that this half bridge is the most she can afford. O fellow citizens and brethren in the South, know you not that the piece of property that any people can most ill afford to own is a half-built bridge? And O Northern friends of educational missions in the South, is this truth true in the South and not in the North?

For a long time this declaration of the South that she is doing all she can was as widely believed in the North as it was sincerely uttered in the South. But the study of the question of national aid to education has brought out the fact that the Southern states are at best only spending more for public education in proportion to their wealth than older and richer regions which have long ago supplied themselves with an adequate school plant and have capital and emigrants to spare.

The Southern ratio of illiteracy demands an enlargement of the free school system more urgently than that of newer countries with which the South has to compete, and yet she is letting these newer countries, with less wealth, do proportionately more.

What is the cause of this? The friends of ample free schools in the South cannot elect legislative majorities that will vote for them. And why? Because such friends among educated whites dare not—or think they dare not—coalesce with the colored vote on a question on which the whites are divided and the colored vote is a unit. To do so seems to them too rash a step toward the final admission of the colored voter into the same complete civil and political fellowship that he would enjoy if he were white. Here, then, the cause of free schools in the South, half provided for and half denied, finds a deadlock. The nation refuses, whether wisely or unwisely, to supply the deficiency; the white Southerner will not league with the Negro on a Negroes' plank; and he cannot in his own exclusively white party command a majority willing to vote a sufficient school tax. For neither the Southern white people, nor any other people except a whole people, can ever furnish a majority that will vote a school tax ample for the whole people. Instead, we find the whole mass of three million colored people held under an incessant, galling, and tremendous pressure to abandon that claim. If they would but say: "All we want is education. All we want it for is to make ourselves better laborers and servants. Give us but ample free schools and we will waive all civil and political equality of rights, and consent to be, not Americans, but only Africans in America," there is no reasonable doubt that they could get it.

Christian fellow citizens, the day they do that—the day they speak thus—they abandon the whole end of which education is only the means—citizenship and Christian manhood. When men say to the Negro, Never mind your right to vote and belong freely to the party of your choice—get education even if you have to let these go to get it—I charge those men with

consummate folly! What is the elevation of books or the elevation of the workbench without that elevation, better than
either or both of these, which depends inseparably on civil and
political freedom? The education of the book and the bench
will always be as forlornly behind the age in quality as in
quantity until political bondage gives place to political liberty.
No people can ever catch step with the world's progressive
march, moral or material, by consenting to political bondage.
Our whole land, North and South, is glad slavery is dead. But
if ever the colored race in the South should become satisfied
with a debased civil and political status exclusively their own,
they would stand one great, dark, melancholy proof that they
never deserved to be anything but slaves. They will never do
it. But whence comes the exhortation to their children not to
do it? Where does white Christianity stand among them and
bid them quit themselves like men? Only in these missionary
colleges. Only they from the midst of the fray cry, "Don't do
it! Don't give up the ship." O friends, shall their cry, like the
cry of Lawrence, be the failing cry of a dying life? Or will
you in the name of God's fatherhood, man's brotherhood,
American freedom, and the world's salvation cry back across
the rivers and mountains, "Hold the fort."

If you will, there is but one honorable way to do: Open
your purses! rip them open! make your dollars tens, your tens
hundreds, your hundreds thousands. You've got the richest
missionary field in the world; let your provision for it be the
richest in the world. Multiply your colleges, endow them, enlarge them, enrich them. They are lighthouses, every one, and
on every beam of their radiance is written to all men of our
land, white, yellow, red, or black: Come and be American free
men and American citizens, with American rights, in a land
that is betrothed to Christ and must make haste for her ap-
proaching marriage.

If we do not do this, God will do it by some other hand.
If the church doesn't do it, the state at last must. "Evolution
or Revolution." But the church has no right to wait on the

state. Yet the state has no right to wait on the church. It is
not true that law cannot—that only truth can—make men free.
The truth can make no other man free half so quickly as it
can the man who is already free by law. Freedom by truth
first and by law afterward is the word of comfortable men,
not of a pitying Christ. If all law-abiding manhood has not an
inalienable right to a freedom to birth by law and to manhood
by truth, then our fathers never had a right to make the Declaration of Independence. Yet if free and comfortable Americans will let oppressed Americans remain oppressed and mock
their cries with this sad use of Christ's word, let us see to it as
we be Christians that when legal freedom comes at last, these
dark millions, made free by truth first and by law afterward,
come crowding into the church of Christ to subscribe themselves her children, saying: It was the church of Christ that
first brought us this deliverance.

The Southern Struggle
for Pure Government

[An address delivered before the Massachusetts Club in Boston on Washington's birthday, 1890.

For the first time Cable asked in this address for partial steps, hoping that thus the fears so often enunciated would be proved unreal and unwarranted. For the first time also he asked for federal intervention unless the states took effective steps themselves. As he saw it, the cause of equal rights had been virtually lost. The crop-lien laws and other enactments in the Southern states promised to hold the Freedman in an inferior economic status; segregation was becoming more firmly established by law; such schemes as the eight-box voting law of South Carolina and the centralization of county and community authority in the state officials of North Carolina were effectively restricting the Negro's political rights, and the talk of educational restrictions on the ballot promised further steps in the same direction. Most significant of all to Cable's mind, friends of the Negro in the North, such as Carl Schurz, were willing now to leave the solution of the matter in Southern hands, and in the South even Booker T. Washington was ready to see the Negro clamped into a segregated, non-voting station. To Cable's mind freedom without the rights necessary to protect that freedom would be finally worth little to the Negro.

The New York *Tribune*, in reporting Cable's speech in Boston, called it an answer to Henry W. Grady, who had died before the paper was delivered. Though Cable did not name Grady, he clearly had in mind the emotional pleas Grady had made in the preceding months for white supremacy and the sort of public restrictions which that doctrine would require.

This address was published for distribution as a pamphlet by the Massachusetts Club, Boston, 1890, and in *The Negro Question;* also in abridged form in the New York *Tribune,* February 23, 1890, the *American,* March 1, 1890, and *Our Day: A Record and Review of Current Reform,* April 1890. Matter from earlier unpublished addresses was incorporated in this one: "Some Very Old Politics" before the Yale University Y.M.C.A., November 12, 1888; "Can the Nation Afford a Suppressed Vote?" before the Chicago Union League Club, December 15, 1888, and "Moral Elements in Politics" before the Congregational Club of Cleveland, December 21, 1888.]

The Southern Struggle for Pure Government

I

The world has ceased to look to imperial rule for pure government. Men may at times still couple the two, but it is only in momentary resentment of the fact that nowhere yet is there a people under electoral rule whose government is entirely pure.

Yet, excepting Russia, there is hardly a people of European origin on earth that has not secured in some valuable degree the enjoyment of electoral representative government; and although the impurities remaining in such governments lie mainly in their defective electoral methods, yet the world refuses to look back to imperial rule for refuge or remedy. Not the suffocation, but the purification, of the ballot is recognized as the key to the purification of government.

But how shall we purify the ballot? We cannot say only the pure shall vote, and then decide, on crude generalizations, who, or what sorts, are pure. That would be as if instead of making a filter work thoroughly we should forbid that any but pure water be put into the filter. No class or party is so pure but its vote needs the filtration of effective electoral methods; methods so effective as to bear the whole strain of a genuinely popular vote. For any class to say, "The pure shall constitute the state, and we are the pure," is itself imperial tyranny. But we can say the vote shall be pure, and trust ultimately to see a purified ballot purify the balloters. Not the banishment of all impure masses from the polls, but the equal and complete emancipation of all balloters from all impure temptations or constraints, is the key to the purification of the ballot.

It stands to reason that most men want good government. If without constraints they choose bad government it is by mistake. Society disfranchises the felon, the idiot, the pauper, the lunatic, because it is fair to infer, as it is not of men in general, that they have no clear choice for good government. The only trouble is that though most men want good government, they want it, mostly, for themselves. From these two truths rise the wisdom and necessity of self-government. Men can never safely depend upon others to supply them benevolently with good government. "No man is good enough to govern another without his consent"; the only free government is self-government. But the only practicable self-government on any large scale being electoral and representative, the purity of the ballot becomes a vital necessity. For the only true end of self-government is free government, and of free government, pure government, as of pure government it is the purity, no less than the prosperity, of the whole people. No government or political party has ever yet attained complete purity, because ends must wait on means and pure government cannot be got except through free government, nor free government except by self-government.

Indeed, purity and freedom are so interwoven and identified with one another that to distinguish between them scarcely separates them in the mind. But a pure government is especially one where all the people are wholly and equally protected from the possible corruptness of officials; while a free government is one in which all civil classes, in office or out of office, and all political parties, in power or out of power, are fully and equally protected from each other. Obviously, there can be no united and effective effort for such pure government, while an insecurity of free government keeps classes or parties preoccupied with one another's actual or possible aggressions. Probity is the one absolute essential of society's happiness. An impure government makes an impure people, and pure government would be society's transcendent necessity were it not that to lose free government is to lose both. The end must wait on the means. Pure government is pure gold; but to get gold in continuous supply you must first have iron. Free government is iron—iron and steel. So first of all free government, and then pure government.

Yet we must confront the opposite truth. A government not free, nor trying to become free, must become corrupt—cannot become pure; but even a free government cannot remain corrupt and continue free. True freedom is liberty with equity; corruption is liberty without equity; and no man gets a freedom he ought not to have without paying for it some other freedom he cannot afford to lose. The Reconstruction state governments in the South after the Civil War were set up on very broad and commendable foundations of free government; but, not using free government as an end to pure government, they fell, owing their fall largely to the corruption of the ballot, and actually overthrown by a party whose opposing policy was the impracticable proposition of pure government first, free government afterward.

And now, as to these things, where do we, of America, stand? The answer is not inspiring. There is probably not a state in our Union whose good citizens do not confess and lament corruption in its elections. What the governor of New York writes of his own state is true of the whole Union. "Bribery and intimidation are not confined to any locality." How is this?

For one thing, overlooking the degree of freedom attained

by other countries since we declared ours, we have learned to lay upon our freedom the false charge of having produced our political corruption. Many countries have become almost or quite as free as we, even in the matter of suffrage, and are pressing forward, while among us voices are heard repenting our rashness, as though in manhood suffrage we had made a mistake which the rest of the world was condemning. Whether of the French, the Germans, the Italians, we admit or deny that they are as free as we, we have to confess that such freedom as they enjoy is not a gift bestowed upon them by the purity of "strong" governments. It is a prize snatched by them from corrupt governments, and such purification as they have wrought is the product of freedom. Even if they have, with less freedom than we, effected some larger purifications of government—this of the ballot, for instance—still they have done it on the plan of free government the means, pure government the end. They teach us not that we are too free, but only that we have been too well pleased with freedom as an ultimate end.

But our fathers had not only to establish free states and free institutions without models before them; they had other great tasks. For instance, they had to learn state and national banking and general public financiering; and they learned them in a series of gigantic blunders in comparison with whose devastating results those of the Southern Reconstruction governments of 1868–77 sink into insignificance. In other words, they had to learn how to vote wisely; and no people ever learned how to vote except by voting.

Moreover, while for over a hundred years we have had great freedom, for three fourths of that time we had also a great slavery, which constantly threatened the destruction of true freedom. Not that even the pro-slavery party, whatever its leaders may have been, wanted government to be bad, or free men to be less free; they even looked forward—though with more longing than hope—to some indefinite day when their own slaves might somehow enter into freedom. Beyond dis-

pute, then, as today, a vast majority of the whole people in
every state of the Union wanted both free and pure government; but we were divided into two opposing hosts; one for
pure government through free government, the other for pure
government before free government. Out of the resulting strife
has come the nation's declaration for all time, that pure government cannot come before free government, and that not
even in the name of pure government shall true freedom be
abridged.

Another obvious truth: pure and free governments advance
by alternating steps. Men will not help others to set up pure
government who refuse them free government. Nor will men
help those to advance free government who refuse them pure
government; and if each school holds out hostilely against the
other, ruin must follow; but if not, a patriotic and entirely
noble political commerce may spring up between the two. A
nation so doing may have to see itself outstripped for a moment in the direction of free government by others less pure,
or of pure government by others less free, or of material wealth
by others neither so pure nor so free; but it is, nevertheless,
on a broader, higher road to perfect freedom, purity, and prosperity at last, than any different sort can possibly be.

II

There is a part of our country, however, where conditions
are seemingly so peculiar and exceptional that to innumerable
minds both there and throughout the nation no theorizing on
the relations and necessities of pure and free government can
be made to appear practicably applicable. We must grapple
with the very facts in this specific case, or else our theorizings
are of no use to those who, in the North or South, stand dis-
traught between two seemingly antagonistic necessities, the
one for pure, the other for free, governments in our Southern
states.

Even the initial axiom, that most men want good govern-

ment, is denied. Most white men, yes; but here is the whole
lower mass made up of an inferior race which, we are assured,
neither knows nor cares anything about good government. So
ignorant, unintelligent, and base are they, it is said, that to give
them any larger freedom than they are now allowed would
only be to make them easily and certainly the tools of the
most vicious misleaders of popular cupidity, vanity, and passion. To offer by genuine proffers of fuller civil freedom to buy
their co-operation for measures looking to purer government,
it is maintained, would make them drunk with self-importance,
and would be a suicidal confession that the present ruling class
is not strong and pure enough to establish and maintain pure
government without the aid of the ruled. To give the Negro
the same full civil and political freedom that the white man
has would, they say, be fatal, because in that case white men
would never divide on questions of public policy, lest the
blacks, if not already united, should at once unite, and under
corrupt leaders seize the reins of power.

Now to these things what can we answer?

Let us take them seriatim. First, then, as to the statement
that virtually the whole mass of Negroes in the South care
nothing for good government, we say that to establish such a
vast exception to so general a truth requires exhaustive proofs.
Where are they? Reconstruction times do not furnish them.
They may show that the Reconstruction party, white and Negro, constantly and formidably opposed by a party exclusively
white and hostile to the equal civil liberties of whites and Negroes, did not achieve, maybe did not often earnestly try to
achieve, purity in government. But they do not prove that the
Negroes would not have been well pleased to join pure government with free. They only prove our premise that there can
be no effective effort for pure government, while an insecurity
of free government keeps classes or parties occupied with one
another's actual or possible aggressions. The great majority of
the Negroes are illiterate, improvident, reckless, and degraded.
But so is the Irish peasant. So is the Russian serf. The fact is

proof presumptive that Irish, Russian, or Negro—they are far more concerned for a better freedom, whether economic, civil, or political, than for pure government; but not that pure government is something they would rather not have.

How could it be? Tens of thousands of them own the land they till, the houses they live in. With scarcely a very rich man among them, they own today certainly not less than one hundred million dollars'—some say one hundred and sixty million dollars'—worth of taxable wealth. Over a million of their children, half their total school population, are enrolled in the public schools, where their average daily attendance is more than six hundred thousand. Their principal industry is agriculture, the most peaceable and peace-promoting labor of the hand known to mankind. Their crops in the year 1889, unless high journalistic authority is in error, aggregated the value of nine hundred million dollars. Is it to be believed that the whole mass, or any preponderating fraction of such a people as this, is so supinely indifferent to, or so abjectly ignorant of, the advantages of pure over corrupt government that they prefer the corrupt, other things being equal? And are we to credit this statement on the bare, emotional declaration of communities that a few years ago—claiming to be the only people who are in a position to understand the Negro—honestly believed he would not earn his bread in a state of freedom, and was mentally incapable of receiving an ordinary common school education? Must we go even further and believe that none of them, not even a moderate number, care enough for the purification of the governments over them to vote for pure measures and good rulers, even if these should boldly declare for a removal of unjust encroachments upon their public rights and liberties? Hundreds of thousands of them take pains—not a few take risks—to vote, voting far oftener for white men than for colored. Do these prefer corrupt rulers and measures, and for mere corruption's sake? The answer is familiar. Their leaders, it is said, do actually want corruption for its own sake, to fatten on it, and in vast solid masses the great black herd blindly follows

these leaders. But wherein lies the strange power of these leaders? In consanguinity? They are oftener white than colored.
In promises of official patronage? There are not places enough
to go half around among the leaders. How then? By the literal
buying of the ballots? Ballot buying may turn the fortune of a
close election, but it can never make whole vast masses of people vote all one way. How then do they lead them? They lead
them by means that prevail, not because these masses are of
Negro race, nor because they are ignorant and degraded, but
because they are human; by means of promises of deliverance
from oppressive or offensive public conditions, from which
they see other men profitably free and long themselves to be
delivered. That men should be willing to follow whoever is for
their introduction into all and only the full measure of American freedom, and count that their supreme necessity, is the
poorest proof in the world that they are all opposed to pure
government. It is rarely, if ever, said that the Negroes have
no patriotism. But patriotism inevitably implies some worthy
measure of desire for pure government. Can any one suppose
there is no patriotism anywhere among eight million people
who cannot be worried out of the country of their birth? The
assertation that the whole mass of Negroes in the South is in-
imical to pure government is emotional, not rational.

III

But we have next the assertion that they would become so
if the hand of suppression were withdrawn. This is a very ancient argument. A century ago it was believed and practically
applied against millions of white men, just as it is now urged
against millions of Negroes, and was based on the same spe-
cious assumption, that the ignorant, unintelligent, and unmoneyed man is virtually in all cases dangerous to society and
government, and most dangerous when invested with civil and
political liberty. Nor was its repudiation any rash leap taken
initially by our own country in the heat of revolution. Man-

hood suffrage, even for white citizens of the United States, is
barely seventy-five years old, and of all the earlier states of
the Union, is youngest in New England. Today, except only
Russia and one or two others less notable, every white man's
government in the world has either reached or is steadily moving toward manhood suffrage. The republics of South and
Central America, some of which are not purely white men's
governments at all, are well along on the same road, and, wherever they have also shaken off the slavery of slaveholding and
the fetters of ecclesiastical tyranny, are rising into commercial
and political greatness. Yet we must still meet the same argument, long overturned as to white men but readapted and
made special against Negroes as so far exceeding white men
in cupidity, vanity, and passion, that what political experiment
may have proved even as to ignorant, unintelligent, and unmoneyed white men, is not thereby made even supposably possible as to Negroes.

The loose assertions offered to support this assumption we
deny. We deny that this utter and manifest unfitness of the
Negro is believed by all respectable Southern white men. All
through the South there are worthy white men who deny that
the experiment need be futile or disastrous. We deny that
Southern white men by virtue of close daily contact with the
Negro in multitude are so exclusively able to decide this point
that their word ought to be final. Some men may be too far
off, but just as certainly others may be too near, to decide it
uncounseled; and in fact every great step thus far taken toward
the Negro's real betterment has been first proposed by those
remote from him, while it has been condemned as idle or dangerous by those nearest him. We deny that the experiment of
full civil and political liberty has ever been fairly tried on the
Negroes of the South. One thing has always been lacking, the
want of which has made the experiment a false and unfair
trial. It always lacked the consent—it had the constant vehement opposition—of almost the whole upper class of society in
the commonwealth where the Freedman's new and untried

citizenship rested. Without landownership, commerce, credit, learning, political or financial experience, the world's acquaintance and esteem, the habit of organization, or any other element of political power except the naked ballot and the ability to appeal at last resort to the federal authority, and with almost the whole upper class of society and well-nigh all these elements of power skillfully arrayed against them, the Negroes, accepting the party leadership and fellowship of any and every sort of white man who would only recognize their new tenure of rights, took up the task, abandoned to them in confident derision by their former masters, of establishing equal free government for all in the states whose governments had never before been free to other than white men. The resulting governments were lamentably corrupt. But it was the day of Tweed rings and Crédit Mobiliers, great and small, the climacteric hour of official corruption throughout a whole nation hitherto absorbed in the rougher work of establishing a complete freedom. Even so they began to rise on broader, truer foundations of political liberty and equity than had ever been laid in those states before: and certainly no people, even when not antagonized by the great bulk of a powerful class above them, ever set up both free and pure government in the first twelve years of their bodily emancipation or the first nine years of their enfranchisement. Another twelve years has passed, with the Negroes' political power nullified, and the white, intelligent, wealth-holding class in uninterrupted control; and still that class is longing and groping in vain for pure government, and is confessedly farther from it at the end of its twelfth year of recovered control than it was at the end of its first, while the principles of free government are crowded back to where they were twenty years ago. No, it is not the admission of, it is the refusal to admit, the Negro into political co-partnership—not monopoly—on the basis of a union of free and pure governments, that has produced the very conditions which it was argued such admission would precipitate.

It was this refusal that threw him, intoxicated with more

importance and power than either friend or foe intended him
to have, into the arms of political hypocrites and thieves. It is
this refusal that has demolished with ghastly clearness the
truth, counted suicidal to confess, that even the present ruling
class is not strong enough or pure enough to establish and
maintain pure government without the aid and consent of the
governed. I admit the Negro problem is not always and only
political. No problem can be. It is not in the nature of politics
for any question to be only political. The Negro question is
fundamentally a question of civil rights, including political
rights as the fortress of all the others. It is not always a peculiarly African proneness to anarchy; nor is it always race
instinct; it is often only the traditional pride of a master class
that remands the Negro to a separate and invidious tenure of
his civil rights; but it is to perpetuate this alienism that he is
excluded from the political co-partnership; and it is the struggle to maintain this exclusion that keeps the colored vote solid,
prevents its white antagonists from dividing where they differ
as to other measures, and holds them under a fatal one-party
idea that rules them with a rod of iron.

We see then how far the facts of history and present conditions are from proving the Southern states an exception to
the rule that pure government cannot be got by setting its
claims before and above free government. Rather, they present
these states as striking examples of free government itself falling into decay through the well-meant but fatal policy of seeking its purification by constricting the rights and liberties of
the weaker and inferior ranks of society.

IV

Washington, bidding a last farewell to public office, and
uttering his parental warnings to the people, pronounced, not
largeness or universality of freedom, nor illiteracy, nor unintelligence, but a rankness of party spirit the worst enemy of
popular government. If he could characterize "the alternate

domination of one faction over another" as "itself a frightful despotism," what would he have said of an arbitrarily *permanent* domination of one party over another and a culmination of party spirit into the one-party idea; the idea that a certain belief and policy are so entirely, surely, and exclusively right that men who do not assent to them are incendiary, vile, outrageous, and not morally entitled to an equal liberty and security under the laws with those from whom they dissent? A state ruled by such a sentiment is no longer under a free government. A people seeking pure government under that idea are trifling with destiny and hurrying toward disaster, and in simple humanity, if not in their own involved interest, those who see their error ought to stop them if there is a way to do it consistent with righteous law.

Is there any such way? Let us look at the situation. The Reconstruction governments in the South, while still holding, not for the Negro domination, which they never held for, but for equal free government for all, lost in large measure the nation's respect and good will by an acute moral and financial defalcation. They were allowed to be overturned by measures often severely revolutionary, on the assurance of their opponents to the nation and to the world that their only desire and design was pure government, and that they were more than willing and amply able to furnish it at once and follow it closely with the amplest measure of free government contemplated in the amendments to the Constitution. Some Southern men may deny that this was the understanding on which their party was allowed to retake the monopoly of its state governments. The question is not important, for it is not proposed here to mourn the extinction of the Reconstruction governments as one mourns the death of the righteous, nor to lay upon the men who destroyed them the whole blame of the error committed. Whatever one or another's understanding was, it cannot for a moment be denied that this was the hope and expectation of the great North and West. The blame—if blame were worthy to count—was on those—whether in North or South, in the Republican, or Democratic, or any third or fourth party—who comforted themselves with the delusion that a policy of pure government first, free government afterward, could produce either free or pure government. Seeing at last that this delusion is *what* was and is to blame, the question who was to blame—where no side was wrong by choice—is a question we may sink, with its answer, forever beneath the sea of oblivion.

Through twelve weary and distressful years this fallacy has been given as fair a trial as anything ever had, and today more manifestly then ever before it is weighed in the balances and found wanting. For years the show and promise of better things joined themselves with a faith in the all-healing power of time, peace, and material prosperity, to soothe the nation's solicitude and sustain its hope.

The Southern state governments had hardly changed hands when their financial credit began to rise with a buoyancy which proved—if such proof had been needed—that it was only the governments repudiated and antagonized by the wealth-holding portion of the people that were bankrupt, and, whether their action was justifiable or not, it was nearer the truth to say the people had bankrupted the governments than that the governments had bankrupted the people.

For a long time the sincerity and earnest diligence of the more intelligent and liberal wing of the Southern Conservatives bent itself to a most commendable progressive measure; one which had already been irrevocably begun under the Reconstruction governments as an indispensable adjunct to the extension of civil or political freedom. This measure was the expansion of the public-school system, a system which, wherever it has found large establishment—in America, England, or elsewhere—has always followed, not produced, the extension of the suffrage. This measure was, and is, practicable even under the rule of the one-party idea, because, while public education is the own child of the scheme of free government first, it is almost the only important factor of that scheme which does not obviously antagonize the opposite policy. And yet this opposite policy of pure government first is not, and by nature cannot be, the zealous promoter of the free school system that a free government policy is sure to be. A policy of freedom first inevitably precipitates and perpetuates an immediate and imperative exigency which can be met only by an entirely ample provision for the whole people's education. The policy of pure government first, assuming that ignorance and impurity are much the same thing, promises that ignorance shall therefore not participate in government, and casting about, now on the right hand and now on the left, for expedients to prevent it, accepts free schools as one, but with a divided credence and a tame enthusiasm. This is why the Southern states today have only schools enough for half their school population, and believe they are bearing as heavy a burden of school tax as any people of equal means can, while the states and territories of the West, under the ideas of free government first and of two parties of equal rights, are taxing themselves far heavier, even where they have less wealth. The example of some of these Western communities is complete proof that the only sense in which it can be said that the South is doing all it can for public education is that Southern state legislators may be levying as heavy a school tax as they can reasonably hope to collect from a people lulled by the assurances and methods of a policy of pure government first.[1] It has been much reiterated in the South and re-echoed in the North that the task of public education in the Southern states suffers a unique and unparalleled drawback in the fact that

[1] *The Donaldsonville (La.) Chief* of February —, 1890, says: "We have 38 public schools in this parish and 9855 scholars to educate in them, or about 260 pupils to the teacher!

"Taking the maximum number of pupils fixed by law, it would require no less than 250 teachers to do justice to the educational subjects of the parish. The 'vast improvement' is mere brain figment. The whole yearly school income for our parish is not much more than enough to conduct properly a sufficient number of schools presided over by competent instructors for thirty days. It is all that we can pay, however."

while the Negroes enjoy nearly half the outlay of the school funds, almost the entire amount of those funds is paid by white taxpayers. But assuming this to be quite true in every other regard, there are two points in which it is not so. First, the very alphabet of economics teaches us that all taxes do not rest entirely on those from whom they are collected, but that hundreds of thousands of men who are too poor to be found enumerated on the tax rolls are for all that reached by taxation through the medium of rents and similar indirections. And, second, that the fact quoted is far from being unique and unparalleled. The only thing peculiar about it is that this lower and unmoneyed mass, which, as a matter of good investment in the whole public interest, is in every state in the Union freely accorded an enjoyment of the school funds out of all proportion to its money contributions, happens in the South to be a distinct race which has been working for the last one hundred and fifty years, but has been drawing wages only for the last twenty-five.

v

Another great progressive measure which accompanied and still accompanies the policy of pure-government-first, though it, too, began under the opposite regime, was one which no policy save absolute anarchy can ever resent. This was the development of natural resources, the multiplication of industries, the increase of material wealth. The party that represented the bulk of society's landed and personal wealth, inspired by the only policy it could believe to be honorable or safe, entered into entirely new relations to the public credit of their towns, counties, and states, and gave the energy of a new hope to the making of private fortunes. The successes of this movement have been positively brilliant. The unadorned true stories of Anniston and Chattanooga and Birmingham, of Memphis and Nashville, and Atlanta and Richmond, are almost as romantic as they are inspiring, a theme lingered upon

by Northern tongues and a Northern press with a warmth that
indicates a proper recognition of the North's own great gain
in the South's prosperity. Nevertheless, the very fullness and
renown of this success has wrought two grave errors. A sagacious and enterprising few may get rich in any country blessed
with natural resources; but no *country* ever won or can win a
large and permanent prosperity save by the prosperity of its
poor. No country can ever build a sound prosperity while it
tolerates conditions that keep a large lower mass on low wages
and long hours. This is the word, not of politicians alone, but
of economists and financiers, and this is a fact which the sun-
burst of a sudden great material development in many regions
of the South has hidden in deep shadow. That Southern men,
still so largely under the stress of Southern traditions, should
overlook this is largely natural and excusable; but that the
North, too, with its so wide and fortunate experience of better
conditions, should not see and point out the oversight seems
strange. It may be doubted that there is a high school between
Boston and Denver whose pupils are not taught that the greatest source of the decay of nations is the congestion of wealth
and degradation of poverty. No sufficient offsets for it have
yet been found in any scheme of public society, but the search
for them is the great quest of the age, and the safety, peace,
and prosperity of Europe, the Americas, and the great Australasian colonies is mainly due to the adoption of such noble,
though incomplete, offsets as have been found. These are equal
rights and protection to opposing parties, free schools for the
whole people, manhood suffrage, and a pure, free ballot.

Such is one of the two great errors that have fastened themselves upon the otherwise entirely admirable material development of the "New South." The other is twin to it. It is that
this material development is not only economically sound, but
that it has also a political potentiality and can of itself solve,
and is solving, the Southern problem. Where is its solution?
The claim is absurd. It is simply fantastical to expect a mere
aggregation of private movements for the building of private

fortunes to unravel the snarled thread of civil and political en-
tanglements in a commonwealth. It may in self-defense rally
to the support of public financial credit; but farther it is not
in its nature to go. What has this one done? We are reminded
that "in the South there are Negro lawyers, teachers, editors,
dentists, doctors, and preachers working in peace and multiplying with the increasing ability of their race to support
them." But whence came they? Nine tenths of those teachers
and preachers and ninety-nine hundredths of those lawyers,
editors, dentists, and doctors have got their professions in colleges built and sustained by Northern money, and taught by
Northern missionary teachers whom the great bulk of this New
South rewards with social ostracism. They work in peace. But
what a peace! A peace bought by silent endurance of a
legalized system of arrogant incivilities that make them, in almost every public place, conspicuous objects of a public disdain which is not always even silent. What single one of those
tyrannous and vulgar intrusions of private social selection into
purely public places has this New South of iron and coal mines,
and new railways and cotton mills, and oil presses removed?
Not one! From the ennobling relaxations of the drama, the
opera, the oratorio, the orchestral symphony and sonata; from
the edifying diversions of the popular lecture, the picture gallery, and even the sacred service and sermon of the popular
preacher; from the refining comforts of the first-class railway
coach and the public restaurant; from the character-making
labors, disciplines, and rewards of every academy, college, and
even law, medical, and divinity school, supported by Southern
money and attended by white youth; and from the popular
respect paid to those who enjoy these things and withheld
from those to whom they are forbidden, these "Negro lawyers,
teachers, editors, dentists, doctors, and preachers, working in
peace and multiplying with the increasing ability of their race
to support them," are shut out by rules sustained by state
legislation, which refuses to share even the Decalogue on equal
terms with the Negro, but annexes to it an eleventh and "col-

ored" commandment—"Thou shalt try to become a gentleman." Where has this New South movement opened to col-
lored people, paying taxes or not, professionally educated or
not, the privileges of a single public library?

Our attention is challenged to nine hundred million dollars'
worth of crops raised in the South last year. We are not told
that the producers of this vast abundance enjoy in one full
and common measure all the public rights declared to be theirs
by the national Constitution. That falsehood, so long believed
by so many even of those who uttered it in North and South,
is utterly worn out. But we are asked if we can doubt that
such a product came from peaceful fields and contented and
duly remunerated labor. Yes, we can! Did the vast wheat crops
of ancient Egypt come from peaceful fields and a well-
contented husbandry? Are her pyramids the product of duly
remunerated labor? Did the great crop of 1860—raised when
the Negroes were half their present numbers—come from men
satisfied with their wages? From the eastern borders of Russia,
a huge wave of material development is at present rolling eastward across Siberia with an energy and speed until lately supposed by Americans to be found only in our own great, free
West. The commerce of the Volga rivals that of the Mississippi. The volume of trade of the city of Nizhni Novgorod rose
from some sixty million dollars in 1868 to about a hundred
and twenty million dollars in 1881. A great through Siberian
railway, to be completed in from three to six years, is now in
various stages of survey and construction, whose trunk line
alone will stretch eastward to the Japan Sea, about five thousand miles beyond Moscow. It runs already through millions
of acres of fruitful fields tilled by an industrious peasantry. But
is Siberia a free country? Spain is a land of harvest and song.
Have the laborers in her vineyards and olive yards a freedom
that ought to satisfy a citizen of the United States? Has America any class of society in which we can afford to cultivate
contentment with a Russian or Spanish measure of civil or political liberty? There is a contentment which is more intolera-

ble to the order and interest of a free country like ours than a discontent that leaves the ripened grain unharvested to guard the rights of free man. Which of the two has this industrial development, or any other outcome of the policy of pure government first, cherished and stimulated? For twelve years it has persuaded an apparent majority of the nation to leave to it the fitting of the Negro for citizenship, even refusing national aid to lift the burden of public education it counts insupportable; yet to this day it has made not the slightest provision for admitting any Negro to the full measure of any civil or political right by virtue of acquired fitness. The New Orleans *Times-Democrat* of Nov. 5th, says, "The race issue is a national antagonism . . . and has nothing whatever to do with education or the lack of education. To the Negro varnished with such learning as he is capable of acquiring, there is even a more pronounced antipathy than to the Negro of the cotton field and kitchen." "The schools," says the Atlanta *Constitution* barely six months ago, "have been in active operation for over twenty-five years, and it is estimated that several hundred thousand of the colored voters can now read and write. The difficulties, however, have increased with the progress of education, and are now more difficult than they ever were before. . . . Not the slightest advancement toward an adjustment of the two races on political grounds has been made anywhere, and even the direction of such advance is a matter of speculation." In plain words, after twelve years of wandering through a night of false political traditions, these largely sincere guides to pure government first and free government afterwards acknowledge at last that they are lost in the woods under a starless sky.

VI

The failure to get good government has been absolutely abject. Not only has no material advance been made toward free government, but the governments that started out twelve years ago full of honest intentions to be or become pure have grown confessedly corrupt, and are now avowing with hardihood or shame things that a few years ago they denied with indignation. Let it be gladly admitted that open personal bribery of officials is rare. And naturally; for where an upper and property-holding class holds secure and arbitrary power over an illiterate and destitute laboring class, and really desires pure government, personal official integrity will still be demanded after equity has been overlooked in legislation; and whereas in the struggle of an under class for better freedom against great odds the personal impurities of leaders may be for some time overlooked, in an effort of an upper class for pure government the personal dishonesty of officials will be the last symptom of hopeless and corrupt failure. The fact still stands that the Southern party, which really started in quest of the higher grounds of pure government, is moving in a mass of corrupt measures. In the late Prohibition movement in Georgia its wholesale bribery of ignorant Negro voters was open and boastful.

In Alabama, Mississippi, and other cotton states, under a domination which more and more tends to become merely a taxpayers' government, there has sprung up a system of crop-lien laws, mainly if not wholly devoted to the protection of landholders and storekeepers against farm tenants, so barren of counter protections for the tenant that they have fairly earned the name given them by a United States judge in Arkansas, of "anaconda mortgages." Said this gentleman in an address before the Arkansas State Bar Association, in 1886, "as a result of these defective and bad laws, the state is afflicted with a type of moneylenders, traders, and methods of doing business the like of which was never seen before." Quoting from a parliament report the statement that a certain creditor in Ireland had charged a Connaught peasant a rate of interest aggregating 43½ per cent per annum, he asked, "What is 43½ per cent compared to the profits charged by the holders of anaconda mortgages on tenants in Arkansas? They would scorn

43½ per cent." And another member of the Association had already said of a signer of one of these mortgages, "a place where he could borrow money at usury would be an asylum to him. . . . I have known men—laboring men, farmers, and renters—to pay 20 and 25 per cent interest for money and secure its payment, rather than mortgage their property and buy supplies on credit." If in the face of these facts Negroes are moving by tens of thousands from North and South Carolina to Mississippi and Arkansas, that surely is something, not for us, but for North and South Carolina to explain. Probably the best explanation, beyond the eager enterprise of railroad companies, is that these ignorant laborers, like thousands of other immigrants, do not know what they are going to.

It will be said that the burdens of this system fall as heavily on a white man as if he were black. That may be, but it is a system unknown in our free land except in states where the tenant class is mostly Negroes, and just as far as white debtors fall under it, it illustrates a fact of which it is far from being the only proof; that this whole policy of the black man's repression under a taxpayer's government is constantly escaping from its intended bounds and running into a fierce and general oppression of the laboring classes, white or black. Yet the wealth-holding, taxpaying citizens of these same states, still really and untiringly bent upon a large and noble renaissance in commerce, industry, and government, hold conventions and subscribe money to promote immigration. Can no one make them understand that a desirable immigration will never come to a land of long hours, low wages, and "anaconda mortgages." The only way to make the South a good place for white men to come to is to make it a good place for black men to stay in.

It belongs to the imperfections of human society even at its best that, as yet, even under the purest, freest conditions, the poor suffer many times more chances than the rich of being legally punished for criminal errors. Moreover, the poor man's home and neighborhood become the cesspool and garbage heap of the prisons' discharges, pardons, and escapes. The penal system of a country is therefore supremely the very poor man's concern, if not even his supreme concern. Hence it can never be stripped of a political value. If there were no other reason why the poor and ignorant should enjoy the scant self-protection of manhood suffrage, this would be enough. And with what clearness has the Southern party of one-party-and-pure-government proved this? For twelve years it has retained the convict lease system, a prison system entirely peculiar to the Southern states, and baffling comparison for corrupt and mortal cruelty with any system of prisons between here and St. Petersburg. It has not merely retained the system. Legislatures and governors have, sometimes officially, sometimes unofficially, allowed "penitentiary rings" to become financial and political factors in the fortunes of their parties and their states, while all the better elements of the party and press, burning with righteous shame and resentment, and crying out against them, nevertheless endure the outrage clamped and riveted upon them by the exigencies of a one-party policy and the alienation of the great bulk of the poor man's vote. Nowhere this side of Russia and Turkey is there a region or country, of such ratio of wealth or population, so recklessly, suicidally barren of reformatories for destitute and wayward boys and girls.

But there are other fruits of this well-meant but vain policy. In 1868 the Reconstruction party in North Carolina adopted, by a new constitution, the township system so well and favorably known in the states of the North and West. When in 1875 the party of pure-government-first gained power, however much personal corruption in office it may have found, it found also as perfect a form of republican state government as there was in the Union. Every provision which any state enjoyed for the protection of public society from its bad members and bad impulses was either provided or easily procurable under the constitution of the state. Yet within a year this party, for the avowed purpose of nullifying the power of their opponents in every county where those opponents were still in the majority, so amended the state constitution as to take

away the powers of self-government from every county in the
state and centralize them in the legislature under a base
counterfeit of the system of government displaced by the
"radicals" in 1868. Under this system—unknown to any other
state—a preponderance of power over elections and election
returns is secured to the majority in the state legislature, so
great that no party retaining it can clear itself of the charge
of corrupt intentions. In South Carolina this same party, now
that rifle clubs and tissue ballots have passed away, confesses,
with the pardonable buoyancy of a relieved conscience, that
those measures were intolerably corrupt. Yet the eight-box system still stands in their stead, raising the same blush of morti-
fication, yet commanding from them the same subjection as
do lynch law and the convict lease system.

Such are the conditions after twelve years of efforts by an
intelligent, accomplished, determined, persistent, heroic people
to hold down free government with one hand till they can set
up pure government with the other. For twelve of our modern
years, each one worth an ancient century, the cry of pure government first has prevailed, not only among themselves but
throughout the nation. For its sake, this nation, almost as universally dazed as they by the bright plausibility of the mistake,
has endured more deadly outrages against its citizens within
its own borders than it would have tamely submitted to from
all the great powers of the earth combined. The mass to be
held in subjection has been the inferior in numbers, prowess,
intelligence, wealth, and every other element of military or political strength; not turbulent and ferocious, but on the Southern white man's testimony tractable, amiable, dependent. The
great national party that, unhindered, might have lifted this
subjection, has for twenty-five years found itself opposed, and
for the last twelve years pinioned, by another party quite or
almost its match in numbers, power, integrity, and skill, ve-
hemently charging it with rushing to the rescue of freedom too
rashly for freedom's good. The class proposing to rule the
South alone, is honest in purpose, still filled with the spirit of

freedom that gave us Washington, and yet as imperial as ancient Rome. It is not they, it is only their policy that is found wanting. If any people on earth could have carried that policy to success they could. They have proved for all time and for all mankind that it can never be done.

The day in which this truth becomes a popular conviction among our white brethren of the South and among millions in the North whose conversion waits only on theirs will be the brightest, gladdest, best day that ever dawned on this continent. I believe that dawn is now breaking.

VII

True, we hear voices through the Southern press crying new schemes for avoiding the simple necessities of free government: the establishment of a Negro territory; a disfranchisement of over half the Negroes by an educational qualification at the polls; their total disfranchisement by the repeal of the Fourteenth Amendment; and in the very Senate a proposition to deport the Negro to Africa at the national expense, although, at the same time and all over the South, men in the same party from which the project comes are stating with new frankness their old doctrine, that though the country shall never belong to the Negro, the Negro simply shall belong to the country. But the very forlornness of these absurd projects, built, themselves, on open confessions that the past is a failure and that something different must be done with all speed, is a final admission that the party pledged to solve the Negro question without consulting the Negro feels that it must change its policy or drop from under the nation's misplaced hopes.

The press of the nation almost with one voice rejects the scheme of a Negro territory. We have more Negro territories now than either white men or Negroes want. Our Indian Territory and Indian deportations and reservations have only wronged the savage, dishonored civilization, complicated the whole Indian question, and still hold it over us in costly and bloody suspense until we shall muster humanity and common sense enough to do unto him as we would that our Southern brother would do unto the Negro—cease condescension, bounty, and fraud, and show mercy, justice, and human fraternity.

The proposition to repeal the Fourteenth Amendment deserves as little respect and attention as it is receiving. It would disfranchise thousands of taxpayers and thousands of men able to read and write, still leaving the franchise with hundreds of thousands of total illiterates paying no direct taxes. It would simply re-establish a system of irrational race discrimination. It is well for the honor of the good state of Mississippi, where the proposition has arisen, that along with it comes word that at last an attempt has been made, with some hope of permanent success, to abolish in that state the convict lease system.

As to the South Carolina scheme to limit the suffrage by an educational qualification, it seems to have died at birth, smothered under the evident fact that a state, nearly half of whose people are illiterate and nearly half of whose population of school age are without public provision against illiteracy, has no reason, as it has no right, to hope for an honest vote to disfranchise the illiterate. Well for it that there is no such hope. For no people ever escapes the incubus of a large illiteracy in its poorer classes except by providing a system of public education ample for the whole people; the demand for ample free education is created not by the contraction, but by the enlargement, of the right of suffrage. The most suicidal thing a party of free education can do is to favor an educational qualification of the suffrage before free education is amply supplied; for whenever the issue is between adequate and inadequate provision the vote that tips the scale aright is just the bugbear itself—the illiterate man's vote.

I hold that to prove the moral wrong of a thing is to prove just so far its practical worthlessness. To disfranchise the illiterate is to make the most defenseless part of a community more defenseless still. There is, I know, an educational qualification in Massachusetts, and there are a few illiterates. But there is no illiterate *class*, and the educational qualification here is not mainly for the protection of the suffrage, but a correctional punishment for inexcusable ignorance. The dangers of illiteracy have been almost as much overstated as its economic loss has been overlooked. Far the greatest danger in a wide illiteracy is to the illiterate themselves, and though there are reciprocal risks, the supreme urgency for its removal is not their dangerousness to the more fortunate and powerful classes, but the dangerousness of those classes to them. As for the Australian ballot system, wherever in this great union of states it goes for the better liberty of every honest voter, learned or ignorant, rich or poor, and for the confusion of bribers and bribe-talkers, learned or ignorant, rich or poor, may God give it good speed. But, alas! for public liberty, purity, or safety, wherever it is put into use to abridge the right of suffrage. No people is justly ready for a system of elections that prevents the voting of the illiterate man until it has first provided full public facility for every such man to learn to read and write, and has then given him fair warning and time to learn.

The last and, it seems to me, the most irrational scheme of all is that embodied in the bill for the deportation of Negroes to Africa. The graceful arguments of its advocates in the Senate have been fully, ably, brilliantly answered in the Senate, and there is no excuse for more than a word to the point here. The early admissions and confessions of Abraham Lincoln have been much used in this debate by excellent men, who still repudiate and antagonize the conclusions of his latest wisdom as they once did his earlier. Let us, in that wonderful spirit of more than Washingtonian generosity which made him impregnable and irresistible in debate, make every supposition of the advocates of deportation that can be supposed. Say the bill is found to be not unconstitutional; that hundreds of thousands of Negroes want to go, and that Southern white men generally will let them go, despite the palpable fact that the men most likely to go will be, to use an old Southern word, the most "likely" men, the men of health, strength, self-reliance, enterprise, and despite, again, the fact that no large emigration can take place without carrying away millions of ready money with it. Every hundred thousand of European emigrants to this country bring about eight million dollars with them. The industrial value of a hundred thousand un-skilled laborers is eighty million dollars. Is a white immigration likely to make up such losses? Let us suppose even this, although no one ever yet heard of one set of emigrants pouring into a country from which a poorer set was pouring out; and although if they will come at all there is abundance of room for them now, without deporting a single Negro.

What shall we say? We say pass your bill; get your ships ready; proclaim free passage to whosoever will accept it. Only let there be no compulsion. As a whole nation we are branded with our fathers' sin of bringing these people here; let us not now add to that our own sin of driving them back. Therefore, no compulsions. But the land is full of compulsions. The main argument for the Negroes going is that we are making their stay here intolerable to them. Before we buy or hire one ship, whether these compulsions are in South Carolina or Mississippi, Illinois, Ohio or Massachusetts, let the compulsions be removed. When state and federal governments have exhausted, as neither has yet done, all their powers of legislation and police to make the Negro in America as free as the white man, then, if the Negro cannot be content, and the people choose to bear the expense of his deportation, let the folly be charged to him, not us, of leaving a free land to which better men were glad to come and fill his voided place. But let this nation never again open the sacred scriptures on Independence Day, or on the birthday of Washington lift up its hands to God, if, as matters now stand, it provides money or ships for the flight back to Africa of the victims of its own tyrannies. This is not the way to settle but only to delay and hinder the settlement of the Negro question. Emigrants have been pouring out of Ireland for forty years, and their government has encouraged their going, and still Ireland is full of Irish and the Irish question is not settled. Pass your deportation bill. Help hundreds of thousands of able-bodied Negroes to sail to Africa. But unless you remove the already existing compulsions upon which you are counting to drive them on shipboard, the white immigrant will not come to take his place, and the Negro and the Negro question will be with us still.

It is true, also, that the infatuation for buying pure government at some other price than the Negro's civil freedom and political co-operation still maintains the iron rule of the one-party idea. It is to this sentiment and policy that we owe the enormities of lynch law, with its record of crimes beyond all cavil darker and fouler than all the robberies of carpetbag governments. For these murderous deeds are committed only because the lovers of order and pure government make no serious effort to prevent them, and these make no serious effort only because to punish these murderers would break the solid square of that one party which makes simple dissent from its doctrines infamous and criminal, the only party that ever has dared to declare openly to this free nation that it must and will rule, whether it represents a majority of the people or not. Is not that the very germinating and perpetuating principle of political corruption? Under what strange skies, on what distant planet, can we believe that such a tree will put forth the flowers and fruit of pure government?

In Nashville lately a gentleman of the Southern political orthodoxy gave me this story as strict fact: A traveler, similarly orthodox, sat down at the large supper table of an Arkansas tavern. The landlord bearing two large steaming covered vessels, identical in size and pattern, one in each hand, passed from guest to guest with always the same hospitable offer of choice: "Tea or coffee?" "Tea or coffee." "Coffee," said one. He poured coffee. "Coffee," said a second. He poured coffee. "Coffee," said a third, fourth, and fifth. Again once, twice, thrice the teapot was deferentially drawn back and the

coffeepot poured forth its strong, black flood. So our traveler
was reached. "Tea or coffee?" "Tea." The landlord drew back,
bristling, but the next instant was gracious again. He brought
the huge teapot nimbly forward and poured from it the same
hot, rank "Rio" that he had been pouring from the other pot,
saying as he poured, "Tea! in Arkansas! No, sir. In Arkansas
you take coffee or you take nothing." Our traveler drank it
without milk. It was, after all, simply his own one-party idea
and he had to swallow it.

VIII

But if the one-party idea still rules in the South, men are
longing and reaching out for deliverance from it now as they
have not done before, since thirty years ago it first laid its
complete bondage upon them. From out the South itself has
lately been heard a strange, new, most worthy, and most welcome sound, the voices of Southern white leaders of thought
and action charging upon the North the duty and necessity
of helping the South to solve the simple question which the
Northern and Southern seekers after pure government through
race rule and postponed rights have snarled into a bewildering
problem. This problem has been drawn into the open field of
literary debate, a field from which, in these enlightened days,
no practical question can escape until it is solved. But the
question is no longer how this problem should be settled; it
is only how to persuade men to settle it.

As to this, let us first of all stop blaming one another; let
us blame things, not men; ill conditions, false theories, bad
schemes. Even among these let us waste no more wrath, no
more grief, no more time, over such as are done and can never
be undone; but give ourselves faithfully, fraternally, unflinch-
ingly to the pursuit and destruction of every living evil in theory or practice.

In the second place, the new material development of the
South must go on. If wealth does not necessarily make a peo-

ple free or virtuous, neither does poverty. But thinking men in
the South must rouse themselves to the economic and political necessity for a wider diffusion of wealth and more prosperous conditions of manual labor. The inattention to the study
of economics in most Southern colleges amounts to a calamity.
To the spirit that prompts this is largely owing a superficial
treatment of commercial and industrial conditions that charac-
terizes the greater part of the Southern press, and misleads a
large class among the Southern capitalists of commerce and
the industries, who count only themselves practical.

And again, the struggle for pure government must be neither abandoned nor abated. Only the effort to procure it at
the expense of free government must be abandoned. Free government, the equal freedom of all in all public relations, must
be recognized as its foremost and supreme necessity. Yet we
do not demand a sudden and complete revolution of Southern
sentiment and policy. All the nation is really impatient for is
to see the South once turn and *start* in the right direction.

To this end let it be understood and declared in Southern
circles, councils, newspapers, that in the Southern states, just
as truly as in Kansas, Ohio, or Massachusetts, a man can favor
the Negro's enjoyment of a white man's public rights without
being either a Republican or a traitor. He can be an Equal-
Rights Democrat. I venture to say that the great bulk of the
Republican party itself will look with more respect and pleasure upon a band of Southern opponents declaring themselves
Equal-Rights Democrats than upon a like re-enforcement to
its own ranks of Alabama protectionists trying to take the piti-
fully impossible pose of color-line Republicans.

If men cannot reconcile it to their self-regard or sense of
expediency to declare for equality in all public rights at once,
let them try a few at a time. Since 1865 the South has found
on experiment, sometimes voluntary, sometimes otherwise, a
great many things consistent with honor, safety, and peace that
they had looked upon with loathing and alarm. Why not try
a few more? Take, at random, any phase of the matter; for

instance, railroad accommodation. If in every Southern town Negroes may ride in streetcars, where people crowd one another and no separate place offers to the ragtag that refuge from the better kept which they always covet, why not try making first-class railway coaches equally free to all kinds of people decent in person and behavior, and require all kinds of ragtag to accept other accommodations? There is no risk in such a step; nobody really believes there is any, it is purely a matter of pride. But be it pride or be it risk, the streetcars offered the extreme case, and in them the question has long been settled.

Or take another case. Probably the most indefensible, wanton, cruel deprivations suffered by Southern colored people on the score of race is their exclusion from the privileges of the public libraries. Let these excommunications from the pure wells of inspiration that are in good books be withdrawn. Let decent white Southerners say to decent colored Southerners, These concessions—or such as these—will we make for you if you will join with us politically for pure men and purifying measures. That were a buying of votes without dishonor to either side; and tens of thousands of colored votes, both of those that money can and that money cannot buy, can be bought at that price. Only let it not be fancied that even Negroes are going to be outwitted more than once or twice by promises that, if they will concede something now, their white fellow citizens will concede something to them by-and-by. Says the Rev. Dr. Thirkield, of Atlanta, in a late allusion to the failure of the Prohibition movement in that city, "The Negro was recognized as a factor in the great civil contest; he was met as a man and a brother; promises were given him as to his civil rights in the conduct of the city government. Through his vote the campaign closed in victory. Then the contact between the two races was broken off; recognition and cooperation in civil, moral and religious work ceased; pledges as to his civil rights were broken. The rum power saw its opportunity, . . . organized for victory, and brought again the reign of rum." So it may always be; there is a vote that divides but not destroys; and there is another that solidifies but does not save.

True, to influence the colored vote men must influence its leaders. But such concessions as we have mentioned are the daily spoken, written, and printed demands of every sort of colored leader, even of those who are accused of being influenced by nothing except the prospect of public office or its equivalent in cash. A full numerical share of public offices, clerkships, and contracts is not, and never was, the ultimatum of the vast colored vote, nor even of its colored leaders. They certainly never got it. No party ever promised them that all or half or one fourth of them should have offices or appointments, or ever gave them all or half, if even a fourth, of the offices or appointments. But for the hostility of the great majority of Southern white men to an equality of public rights, no colored leader need ever have been given an office or appointment which he could not reasonably have been expected to fill with credit and honor. With genuine and coveted concessions offered to them in the matter of civil rights, colored voters will not be long finding leaders to whom it will be enough to concede with sincere and practical intent that merely being a Negro is not an insurmountable bar to the holding of office by one otherwise qualified.

Let the lovers of pure government in the South make such experiments. It can be made in small or large. There are towns, townships, counties, even states, one or two, in the South, where the two national parties are nearly equal in numbers. There, as elsewhere, the Negro cares, as he should, far more about his own civil and political rights than about who gets into the White House. In such a region a party of pure government ought, by reasonable and generous concession to a better and more equal freedom, to gain enough colored votes to enable it advantageously to sacrifice some very bad white ones. Only, these concessions must be made in the spirit and guise, not of condescension and protection, but of civil and

political equality and fellowship, entering frankly and fully
into council with the Negro's recognized leaders, white or colored, appealing to such as are "out of politics" only when those
who are in politics will not listen to reason. Say what you will
of party leaders and managers, the great Republican party itself would rather be hopelessly outnumbered and defeated in
Mississippi or South Carolina by fair means in the interest of
free government than to see a Republican majority tyran-
nously defrauded under the pretense of procuring or uphold-
ing pure government. Nor do I doubt the great Democratic
party also would, in its turn, rather be so outnumbered and
defeated than to see its managers win victory at the price of
honor.

But if Southern white men will not even yet of their own
motion give this method of healing "the nation's running sore"
a fair trial, there are still two ways by which such a trial may
be had. One is a means which no generous mind in this nation would make other than its last choice. I mean, of course,
federal intervention.

I earnestly protest I have learned too much from the teachings of Washington ever to be a partisan. On the race question I am a Republican; on some others I am a Democrat, and
on all questions I know and am ready to avow exactly where
I stand. The Southern party for pure government first has been
given the best twelve years that ever shone on earth in which
to make federal intervention unnecessary, and has so utterly
failed that it is today seen asking in the United States Senate
for a species of federal intervention by no means the safest or
best or most constitutional to help it to remove bodily to Africa the problem whose obvious solution it will not allow even
to be tried. I do not favor federal intervention for the establishment of equal civil and political rights in any state whatever, except as a last resort. As to federal elections, at least,
it is a right placed beyond cavil by the plain letter of the Constitution. But even there the intention that it should be never
other than an unpreferred alternative is plain.

Yet I see today only one alternative intervening. Of it I shall speak in a moment. But for this alternative, it seems to me totally incompatible with the dignity and honor of this nation that, after twelve years of amiable, hopeful waiting, it should let itself be kept indefinitely waiting still for admission to its own simplest rights by the plausible and eloquent doorkeepers of a do-nothing policy. A despair that prompts to action and deliverance is better than any false hope, and if such a despair moves this nation, this year or next, to the action it has borne so much to avoid, it can point to these doorkeepers, whether they be of North or South, and say, The blame of it and the shame of it be on you!

The only alternative I see, a hope of whose adoption can rightly postpone federal intervention any longer, is for the Democratic party of the wide North and West to withdraw its support from the Southern policy now, as it did in 1860. Said one of the national Democratic leaders to me a few years ago, "That is what we have got to do. The votes we lose by it in the South will be more than offset by those we shall gain in the North." But I maintain the case is better for them than this. They will gain votes in the North; but they will no more lose the Southern white vote than they lost it when with cannon, bayonets, and sabers they forced it back into the Union from which it had seceded. Who will say that promptness on this point now may not save them from another such long vacation as procrastination cost them in 1860?

We have yet two years and a half before the next presidential election, in 1892. Let it be hoped and urged that before then the believers in pure government instead of, or before, free government will of their own choice abandon their utterly self-condemned and futile policy and make at least a visible and appreciable beginning upon that experiment of equal rights for all men and all parties, which, in the modern world, at least, has never failed on fair trial. Has never failed; no, and would not fail in Haiti or San Domingo themselves, if they would once give it the supremacy thus far held by the alternating military tyrannies of opposing factions, each delirious with the poison of the one one-party idea.

During these two years and a half let it be made yet plainer than ever before that federal intervention is no willing choice of the Republican, or any, party, and that what it, with the whole nation, most covets for every Southern state is as large, as full, as universal, and as prosperous a self-government as can be found in any part of this Union. And then, in all kindness, for the South's own sake as much as for the sake of any, in the name of the common welfare and the nation's honor, let the word be spoken that if by 1892 any state in this Union has not at least begun, with good show of completing, the establishment of equal American rights for all Americans, the men of this nation who, in whatever party, believe in free government first will strain their every nerve and sinew to give the nation a president and a congress that will establish it peaceably, promptly, and forever.

The day in which that is done, whether by a Southern majority's own motion or by the government's intervention, will be a great birthday. It may date the birth of some momentary and aimless strife, though this I doubt; but it will certainly date the birth of a better peace, a wider, richer prosperity, a happier freedom of every citizen, and a freer, purer government of this Union and of every state in this Union than this continent has ever yet seen. Yea, and complete fraternity between North and South. For it shall not have been long ere the whole South will rejoice in the day of its doing as now it rejoices in the day when Lincoln freed the Negro, and in the day when Washington, by spurning the offer of royal rank and authority, declared that the only road to pure government is free government.

INDEX

Denver, Colo., 252

Deportation of the Negroes,260, 262, 263

Deputies, 19

Developments, industrial, xv, 255; material, 166, 183, 204, 251, 254, 266

Disfranchisement, 260, 261, 262

Distinctions, civil, 14, 34, 112; social, 79, 112, 138–39

Divinity schools, 142

Dr. Sevier, ix, 19, 20, 83

Doctors, 200, 253, 254

"Does the Negro Pay for His Education?" 218

Domination, class, 191; Negro, 248

Donaldsonville, La., 250

Donaldsonville, La., *Chief*, 250

Douglass, Frederick, 193

Drama, 253

Drinking, 22

Dudley, T. U., 107

Durant, Miss., 201

E. T., V. & G. Railway, 72

East, 26, 48, 75, 92, 100, 130, 152, 166

École Polytechnique, Paris, 13

Economics, 231, 251, 266

"Economics of the Southern Question," 201

Economists, 252

Editors, 2, 14, 15, 20, 26, 29, 83, 84, 185, 186, 203, 253, 254; newspaper, xvi, 1, 30, 32, 33, 35, 37, 83, 132

Edmunds, George Franklin, 186, 195

Education, xv, xvi, xix, 43, 44, 78, 129, 144, 159, 165–66, 167–68, 170, 174–75, 213–17, 218, 227–28, 232, 233–34, 243, 250, 255; free, 233, 261; public, 142, 166, 167, 173, 214–15, 218, 231, 232, 261, 262; secular, 228

"Education for the Common

People in the South," 218

Educators, 145

Egypt, 254

Eight-Box voting system, 236, 259

Elections, 206, 210, 261–62; national, 205, 270

Emancipation, xvii, 8, 61, 65, 89, 126, 148, 152–55 *passim*, 157, 162, 171, 176

Enfranchisement, 8, 61, 89, 90, 152–55 *passim*, 157, 216, 246

England, 49, 97, 149, 153, 249

Equality, 9, 30, 64, 104, 188, 267, 268; Christian, 222; civil, xvi, 151, 160, 233; political, 155, 158, 233; public, 146, 151, 161, 166, 168; social, xvi, 10, 29–30, 79, 90, 92–93, 107, 108, 139, 157, 160, 161

Essays, xiv, xv, xix, 2, 20, 21, 26, 27, 55, 83, 84, 85, 185, 202, 218

Ethiopians, 97

Europe, 153, 230, 237, 252

Eustis, J. B., 26, 185–88 *passim*, 203

Examinations, annual school, 28

Expansion, commercial, 165; industrial, 165

Expediency, xix, 70, 125, 164, 267

Experiments, political, 245, 268, 271

Expulsion of Negro pupils, 28, 31, 34

Factories, 128, 134, 150, 230, 231

"Faith of Our Fathers," 25, 133

Farmers, 175

Fayetteville, Tenn., 26, 133

Federal intervention, 127, 236, 269, 270, 271

Federal troops, xi, 91

Fiction, ix, xv, 20, 24, 37, 40, 83